Medical Malpractice

How to Prevent and Survive a Suit

Edited by

Richard J. Nasca
Lee A. Whitehurst
Louise B. Andrew
David E. Attarian

Published by
Data Trace Publishing Company
P.O. Box 1239
Brooklandville, Maryland 21022-9978
410-494-4994   Fax: 410-494-0515

ISBN 1-57400-102-7

Library of Congress Cataloging-in-Publication Data

Medical malpractice : how to prevent and survive a suit / edited by
Richard Nasca ... [et al.]. — 1st ed.

    p.   cm.
    ISBN 1-57400-102-7 (alk. paper)
    1. Physicians — Malpractice — United States — Handbooks,
manuals, etc. 2. Insurance, Physicians' liability — United States —
Handbooks, manuals, etc. [DNLM: 1. Malpractice — legislation &
jurisprudence — United States. 2. Liability, Lega l— United States. 3.
Risk Management — methods — United States.] I. Nasca, Richard.
    RA1056.5.M415   2005
    344.04'121—dc22   2004028809
                                                                CIP

Table of Contents

5719311 2

Preface

For centuries, the medical profession has worked diligently to improve the quality and quantity of human life, thus earning the respect and esteem of society. In modern times, research and resulting advances in diagnostic and therapeutic capabilities have transformed the practice of medicine and surgery from an art with little real influence on the health of mankind into a technology-driven, often very expensive, science. This transformation has brought greater hopes and expectations for consistently improved outcomes, and even "miracles."

At the same time, American society has become far less accepting of error, disappointment, and accidental injury in life. Our evolving legal system has promoted this ethos, fostering the mindset that each and every patient who is dissatisfied with and/or harmed by a healthcare provider has the legal right to seek compensation through the courts. As a result, during the last decade this country and others have experienced an escalating medical malpractice crisis. Doctors are leaving states in which malpractice awards are high and medical liability insurance unaffordable. Many are retiring, some are changing careers, and very few are encouraging their children to enter the profession. Almost all have seen the patient-physician relationship deteriorate as a result of the ever-present specter of malpractice litigation.

The purpose of this book is to provide physicians with a reliable and easily readable source of information on preventing a medical malpractice lawsuit. If one occurs, we hope this book provides information useful to the doctor defendant. Time-proven techniques for managing your practice and handling difficult patients may help the reader avoid entanglement in the legal process. An understanding of the rules and procedures of the courts and insurance and attorney-client roles will provide the reader with useful knowledge in the event of a malpractice claim. Litigation stress management techniques including specific self care recommendations provide a personal, and sometimes vital, cushion of support during this critical time.

This book has been written by experienced medical practitioners as well as individuals with degrees in both medicine and law. We have also obtained valuable input from plaintiff and defense attorneys, as well as individuals with experience in insurance, state medical board regulatory law and advocacy, physician well-being, and financial planning.

The authors and editors believe that the information provided in this book will assist physicians in practicing their profession with more enthusiasm and confidence and with less anxiety, fear, and frustration.

This book is dedicated to all those professionals who have devoted their lives to helping patients deal with the burdens of illness and who have or will experience malpractice litigation, and to our families who have supported all our professional endeavors through the years.

The editors would like to thank the staff at Data Trace for their cooperation and assistance. We are grateful for the time and assistance that retired attorneys Willis Brown, Ed Goldman, and T. J. O'Hagan have given, and to Ann Whitehurst, Edward Nasca, and Howard Koenig for their help.

Richard J. Nasca
Lee A. Whitehurst
Louise B. Andrew
David E. Attarian

Foreword

J. Leonard Goldner, M.D., D.Sc. (hon)[1]

This book includes an array of topics covering all aspects of the medical-legal paradigm. Personal experiences are related by the physician authors. The legal viewpoint is presented by attorneys for the plaintiff and those for the defense. Logistics related to all aspects of preparation for litigation are supplemented by advice to the defendant about how to cope with this adversarial procedure. Preparation and coping are the essence of the defendant's participation.

A physician should be prepared for the unexpected suit long before it occurs. Repetitive conditioning about the possibility of a suit may lessen the effect that an actual suit will bring. This requires familiarity with the legal process and terminology. The immediate response of most of us to an unproven allegation is anger. This occurs because the defendant says, "I did nothing wrong." A suit also increases one's anxiety associated with getting all the proof together. Furthermore, responding to an "expert" who claims negligence does threaten one's ego and confidence.

CLICHÉS AS REMINDERS

Being sued is a serious professional life event. Clichés help illustrate concepts of prevention, prior conversations with the patient, and familiarity with informed consent. Clichés are retained better than formal philosophical statements:

"An ounce of prevention is worth a pound of cure."

"How do I stay out of trouble today?"

"Your expectations are greater than my capabilities."

"There is no guarantee for total success; I will do everything possible to achieve a good result."

1. James B. Duke Professor and Chief Emeritus, Orthopaedics, Duke University Medical Center.

"Informed consent includes the fact that every procedure has documented complications; I will attempt to avoid all of these."

"The standard of care is what is expected of a prudent physician in like and similar circumstances."

"A maloccurrence in spite of every effort to avoid it is not malpractice."

"Maloccurrence must be documented to the patient and the family, and should be revealed contemporaneously."

"The physician's attitude in notifying the family or the patient of the maloccurrence should be one of concern and contrition. An apology does not imply guilt."

POSSIBLE SOLUTIONS

If there is documented negligence and both sides agree, the person undergoing medical treatment should receive a monetary award.

Unfair awards for pain and suffering, outside of economic damages, should be eliminated. The jury, or the arbitration board, should hear scientific data provided by legitimate expert witnesses. An unbiased qualified expert for the plaintiff or the defense should present evidence that encourages the defendant to settle or the plaintiff to withdraw the suit if the expert shows that the standard of care has not been breached. Arbitration would eliminate much of the fear that the defendant has regarding jury bias and going to trial.

The physician should not admit guilt or be penalized for either not recognizing the primary problem or not treating the condition that preexisted the patient's first visit. If the patient's condition is subtle and the physician does not make an immediate primary diagnosis, the unrecognized additional pathology that occurs is not the physician's fault. The defense must then depend on the court to recognize that the true causation was not related to the encounter by the physician being sued even though he or she may have missed the diagnosis.

Hospital and clinic complications conferences provide ongoing education in ways to avoid complications and bad outcomes and techniques to deal with such incidents. These peer review sessions are immune from discovery for purposes of litigation.

Surgical or medical complications, pharmaceutical errors, and systems failure should be documented, defined, and communicated with the help of subspecialty and national organizations. A good example of this is the marking of the "correct site of a surgical procedure" as advocated by the American Academy of Orthopaedic Surgery.

Familiarity with how to avoid complications associated with commonly litigated conditions should reduce their occurrence. Special attention should be given to the prevention and recognition of complications. They should be managed quickly. The patient and family should be informed contemporaneously.

Prevention of "below standard of care" (malpractice) depends on what happens from the initial patient visit until the doctor discharges the patient. All the doctor's education and background are directed toward developing a high level of knowledge and a positive helpful attitude. With an optimistic attitude, with precautions, and with careful communication, malpractice should not occur. However, even with optimism and current medical knowledge, a maloccurrence may result and be interpreted by the patient and the plaintiff's attorney as "malpractice." Unbiased knowledgeable experts, an understanding of the jury system, use of binding arbitration, education of future jurors, and limits on awards for pain and suffering are necessary steps that must be taken to solve the medical malpractice crisis. The patient deserves his or her day in court, but not if the incident is frivolous or a maloccurrence.

Author Affiliation

Louise B. Andrew, M.D., J.D., F.A.C.E.P., Co-editor, Emergency physician and Litigation Stress Management consultant, MDMentor.com, Victoria, British Columbia, Canada; President, Coalition and Center for Ethical Medical Testimony
mail@mdmentor.com

David E. Attarian, M.D., F.A.C.S., Co-editor, Associate Professor, Division of Orthopaedic Surgery, Duke University Medical Center, Durham, NC
attar001@mc.duke.edu

Leonard Berlin, M.D., F.A.C.R., Chairman, Department of Radiology, Rush North Shore Medical Center, Skokie, IL; and Professor of Radiology, Rush Medical College, Chicago, IL
lberlin@rsh.net

Robert M. Clay, A.B., J.D., Patterson, Dilthey, Clay, Bryson & Anderson, Attorneys at Law, Raleigh, NC
RClay@pattersondilthey.com

Stephen H. Johnson, J.D., Law & Advocacy Specialist, medical society counsel, Baltimore, MD
stephen.h.johnson@verizon.net

Thomas R. McLean, M.D., J.D., F.A.C.S., CEO Third Millennium Consultant, LLC; Assistant Professor of Surgery, University of Kansas; Attending Surgeon VAEKHCS, Shawnee, KS
tmclean@dnamail.com

H. Diane Meelheim, B.S.N., M.S.N., J.D., Patterson, Dilthey, Clay, Bryson & Anderson, Attorneys at Law, Raleigh, NC
DMeelheim@pattersondilthey.com

Deborah N. Meyer, B.S.N., J.D., Attorney at Law, Carey, NC
dmeyer@meyermeuser.com

Richard J. Nasca, M.D., Co-Editor, Retired Orthopaedic and Spine Surgeon, Wilmington, NC
rjnasca@aol.com

Theodore L. Passineau, J.D., H.R.M., R.P.L.U., Clinical Risk
Management Consultant, The Medical Protective Company, Fort
Wayne, IN
tpassineau@cablespeed.com

Erle E. Peacock, Jr., M.D., J.D., Health Care Attorney; and
Clinical Professor of Surgery, University of North Carolina
School of Medicine, Chapel Hill, NC
EEPeacockmd@aol.com

John-Henry Pfifferling, Ph.D., Director, Center for Professional
Well-Being, Applied Medical Anthropologist, Durham, NC
CPWB@mindspring.com

Albert E. Sanders, M.D., Orthopaedic surgeon, San Antonio,TX
asanders1@satx.rr.com.

Michael J. Searcy, ChFC, CFP®, Comprehensive Financial &
Strategic Planning, Searcy Financial Services, Inc., Overland
Park, KS
mike@SearcyFinancial.com or www.searcyfinancial.com

Jeffrey J. Segal, M.D., Neurosurgeon and Founder of Medical
Justice Services, Inc., Greensboro, NC
jsegal@medicaljustice.com

David C. Urquia, M.D., Practicing Orthopaedic Surgeon, West
End Orthopaedic Clinic, Richmond, VA; Clinical Assistant Professor, VCU-Medical College of Virginia
UrquiaD@aol.com

Lee A. Whitehurst, M.D., J.D., Co-editor, Retired Orthopedic
and Spine Surgeon; of Counsel Attorney, Becton, Slifkin & Bell,
Raleigh, NC
leealbertwhitehurst@worldnet.att.net

Donald P. Wolfram, M.D., Emergency Medicine/Family Practice/Medical-Legal Consultant, Granger, IN
wolframalliance@sbcglobal.net

Roger L. Young, J.D., Plaintiff's Lawyer, Retired USAF (Lt.
Col.), Judge Advocate General's Department, Wilson, NC
rly@narronholdford.com

1

What Triggers a Patient to Sue His Physician?

David C. Urquia, M.D.

I am a practicing orthopaedic spine surgeon, certainly someone pretty high up on the list for litigation risk, unfortunately. In
the last 15 years of my private practice, I have been sued by patients a number of times. All but one of these suits have been
"nuisance suits" that were dropped shortly after filing. Nonetheless, each experience has been filled with emotion, disappointment, and to a certain extent anger. Defending a suit has always
been a time-consuming and expensive undertaking. Although I
certainly understand how the system works, it never is easy. On
the other hand, I truly will be disappointed with myself as a physician if I ever lose the emotion that comes with complications or
one of my patients not doing well. I never want to become so cal-
lous as to ignore such things, but as a practical matter a practicing
physician has to defend himself, and that is the purpose of this
chapter. We want you to identify "trigger points" when dealing
with patients, so that you can avoid as many of these "triggers" as
possible.

I also can pass on my experience as a physician who has reviewed several hundred medical records sent by plaintiff's attorneys who are considering malpractice suits on behalf of their

patient clients. I should say that I have never advertised or solic-ited for the business of these attorneys. I certainly have learned a lot from these interactions, and have learned from other physi-cian's mistakes. I hope that my experiences as a high-risk spinal surgeon and my experiences dealing directly with the plaintiffs' attorneys will give a unique insight into some of these malpractice questions. I have received records from all over the country. I have appeared as an expert witness in state and federal courts and at arbitrations. I think one of the best ways to defend oneself is to know how this business works, and unfortunately that often comes from personal experience with one's own patients. I can guarantee you that unless there are dramatic changes in tort law and malpractice financial awards, I will continue to see sporadic legal actions taken against me for the remainder of my profes-sional career.

I realize that in today's society malpractice lawsuits are a part of doing business, and make no mistake, medicine is a business. I don't begrudge any patient the right to sue the medical commu-nity. I don't have any fundamental dislike for plaintiffs' attorneys; in fact, most are highly intelligent and reasonable individuals who have worked very hard to become professionals. I just hope that some day we can reform the awards part of the tort system. It also bothers me very much that there is almost no financial disincen-tive for greedy patients to prove lawsuits when attorneys charge nothing unless they win the case. There is just too much financial incentive to go after doctors, and far too many malpractice claims that carry very little merit. Remember, don't blame the plaintiff's attorney for all your problems — it was the *patient* who initiated the legal action, and if there is a backdrop of financial greed this also was driven by the patient. We have a litigious *society*, not too many lawyers. The plaintiff's attorney is not going to do anything the patient doesn't approve.

Now moving to the subject of triggers, I think we can discuss multiple patient factors that set in motion this process of malprac-tice suit.

COMPLICATIONS

Rarely have I reviewed a malpractice case that did not involve a medical or surgical complication as the result of either elective or emergency treatment.

The complication is really what started the ball rolling. The complication was the patient trigger. If a patient believes that he or she has had a "complication," everyone around that patient will immediately begin questioning the aptitude of the physician involved. Since no doctor is good enough never to have a complication of treatment, how you manage the complication is of paramount importance. In many of the records I have reviewed, the complication was almost ignored, as if the effects of the complication would go away if you ignored the problem. I think that is a natural human tendency for physicians, and certainly for surgeons. If you look at a wound long enough, maybe the next time it won't look infected. If you repeat the blood test often enough, maybe it will return to normal. If you don't come clean and explain in detail to the patient the nature of the complication, maybe the patient won't mind, maybe the patient won't figure it out. Again, human nature.

I think the whole key in managing a complication, and preventing that patient from thinking about lawsuit rather than focusing on recovery, is to jump on that complication aggressively. Take action rather than just observing. Again, any medical physician or surgeon is going to have a complication. The complication by itself is not malpractice in the vast majority of cases. I don't know how I could more strongly emphasize the point: The complication by itself may not represent malpractice. It is how one manages the complication that separates the malpractice case from a maloccurrence. You need to get scans, labs, and cultures. You need to make *early* referral to subspecialists. If you do all of this, the patient is more likely to have no permanent harm from the complication. Remember, a complication or even a deviation from standard of care will carry no weight in a malpractice court *if there is no permanent harm.*

BAD OUTCOME OF TREATMENT

Even if there were no formal complications, no errors performed by the physician, and no error or delay in diagnosis, patients can still have a poor outcome of treatment. I tell my patients all of the time that 10% of laminectomy patients will not get satisfying relief of their nerve pain, even if there have been absolutely no technical errors from start to finish. However, the perception by the patient of a bad outcome for treatment certainly can *trigger* lawsuit. I think that is where most of the "nuisance suits" originate. The patient wasn't happy with his treatment and the patient wasn't happy with the outcome, although any physician reviewer would clearly see that all proper steps were taken from start to finish. Nonetheless, the patient feels motivated to sue, because in this day and age good outcomes of treatment are *expected* by most patients, who consider it their natural right. This is the society we live in. I imagine the plastic surgeons see this all of the time in their patients. The patients expect a good cosmetic outcome, but are ultimately displeased with their appearance. They are unhappy, and unhappiness is a key trigger to lawsuit.

ECONOMICS

I think as much as anything, financial loss and economic need are what trigger patients to sue. After all, a malpractice suit is really an economic action in most cases. They may not like the doctor when all is said and done, but the main reason they sue is to gain economic reward or recovery. These are not necessarily greedy people who just want to increase their wealth at the doctor's expense. These are mostly people who truly have financial loss as a result of their illness and are looking for some way to recover. In my business as a spine surgeon, even normal recoveries can be long. Almost all patients are out of work for a considerable period of time. If they happen to have complications or unexpected outcomes, their recovery will be even more prolonged. I truly believe that patients' main motivation, their main trigger for lawsuit, is to recover the economic loss of illness. This is the society we live in. If you have economic loss, somebody has to pay, especially if you are not happy with the outcome of your treatment. This is especially true in several categories of patient, including "self-pay." If you are in private practice, your self-pay patients will be a much higher-risk group for lawsuit. In a similar vein, the workers' compensation patients are much more likely to sue, primarily because of economic issues. That group tends to stay out of work much longer than any other. They tend to be at higher risk of losing their jobs and their benefits, and they frequently will look to you and your insurance company to recover profound financial loss. The workers' comp patients and the self-pay patients tend to be the most economically disadvantaged, and to them you may look like a meal ticket.

FAILURE TO DELIVER PROMISED SERVICES

If a patient perceives that you did not deliver on your verbal contract to treat his or her condition, this can be a significant trigger for lawsuit. This doesn't just apply to medicine. If the contractor building your home fails to provide the construction materials you expected, you are likely to seek renumeration in a court of law. Doctors and patients don't have detailed written contracts, of course, but it is the *verbal* contract that must be upheld. The patient obviously has some idea of what to expect from you, whether you realize it or not. The patient may perceive that the "promised service" was to supply him or her with pain medications on demand, or to answer his or her calls, no matter how numerous they may be. The patient may perceive that you promised some outcome of treatment, and then when the outcome of treatment was not as expected, will blame you. Medical services can be no different than other material goods and services. We are a service industry, we have a product, and the patient expects a certain level of service, expects a certain outcome. It is very important in our communications with patients not to be overly optimistic, not to promise too much. We should become experts at "laying on the crêpe." We should be poster children for disclaimer. Unrealistic expectations by your patient will ultimately lead to unhappiness, and unhappiness is a trigger to legal actions.

PATIENT SENSE OF ABANDONMENT

Much along the lines of the topic of "failure to deliver promised services," patients may be triggered to bring a lawsuit if they perceive that you have abandoned them. I certainly have seen cases and records where the physician actually did abandon the patient, in every legal sense of the word. The patient's insurance ran out and the doctor declined to treat any further. The patient was discharged in the middle of a bad course of treatment, with a bad outcome, with no additional recommendations from the physician. Legally, you cannot unilaterally dismiss your patient until your current treatment course is finished. The treatment course may be finished because the patient is well, or because there is no other reasonable option or service that you can provide despite your best efforts. Of course, you *can* unilaterally discharge a patient for issues of noncompliance, illegal behavior on the part of the patient, or even profane behavior by the patient to your office staff or in your presence. Of course, this all needs to be well documented. Much of the time, the physician himself will not realize that the patient feels betrayed and abandoned. To the physician, it may seem a normal termination in a treatment course. Not all patients do well, not all patients are cured, and certainly a large percentage of my spine patients rapidly exhaust treatment options. However, patients have high expectations. Many believe that there is a treatment and a cure for anything, so when the doctor discharges them it often catches them by surprise. Even my 300-pound, neurologically intact, tobacco-addicted chronic low-back pain patients look surprised and dumbfounded when I tell them I have no cure for their problem.

MISSED OR DELAYED DIAGNOSES

Nothing triggers a more spirited discussion around the family dinner table about your personal competence than a missed or delayed diagnosis. Almost automatically this implies to the patient that you don't know what you are doing. It certainly triggers in the patient's mind a sense that you are guilty of malpractice. I review malpractice charts all of the time where there were perfectly legitimate reasons within the standard of care that a diagnosis was either missed or delayed, but the patient probably won't understand these fine points of medical decision-making. Although failure to diagnose may be a bigger problem for medical physicians dealing with cancer issues on a more frequent basis than I do, I have reviewed many surgical charts as well where delay in diagnosis was the central issue. Most common subjects were things like failure to diagnosis post-op infection, delayed diagnosis of compartment syndrome, failure to recognize spinal or joint instabilities, missed injuries, and post-op epidural hematomas. Other examples I've reviewed include late diagnosis of epidural abscess or other spinal infections, carcinoma of the sacrum in a patient with chronic low-back pain, and a medical physician managing what he thought was a simple ankle sprain, but missing the diagnosis of instability of the syndesmosis.

Delay in diagnosis may mean you were slow to get consults from medical or surgical subspecialists in a patient who clearly is not doing well under your current regimen. Here again, the plaintiff's attorney is looking for proof that the delay in diagnosis caused permanent harm to the patient, and that these delays led to a poorer than expected outcome for a given diagnosis.

UNAUTHORIZED RELEASE OF PERSONAL PATIENT DATA

Obviously in recent times we have become increasingly aware of patient privacy issues, and this has reached the level of federal mandates. You certainly can be fined by the government for violations of patient privacy, but it can also trigger lawsuit. Many of my patients are on short-term or long-term disability because of complex spinal problems, and their continued disability income is dependent upon favorable reports from the physician. I have had any number of unhappy patients who got into trouble with their employer because our medical reports were less than supportive of the patient's disability claim. If the patient loses his or her job as a result of your medical opinions, and those medical opinions have been shared with unauthorized people outside your office, then you will have a very unhappy patient who will be looking for economic recovery from you, and will have the legal teeth to do it. Although to date I personally have never reviewed a case where privacy issues were part of the malpractice claim, these comprehensive federal laws are very new, so it's hard to know what kind of suits we may face in the future. Be aware.

CHRONIC PAIN

Most of my practice in some way involves acute or chronic pain. These are inherently unhappy people, hopefully only on a temporary basis. Unhappy people very easily get mad at you the physician. Unhappiness triggers lawsuit. It is certainly not my goal in life to make every one of my patient clients happy, but I do recognize that factors such as chronic pain are risk factors for lawsuit. Chronic pain patients are more likely to have economic problems. Economic loss triggers lawsuit. When you have patients with chronic pain come into your office for treatment, either surgical or medical, you must choose a careful and conservative path. Don't make lofty promises. Establish rules for medication support, and rules for contact with you. If you withdraw your support, even for legitimate reasons such as patient noncompliance, those patients may feel abandoned. As I just stated, it is very important to establish rules and schedules with these people. Very important to document your expected outcomes of treatment. In this way, it is much easier to document noncompliance. One of the best defenses you will ever have in a potential malpractice claim involves patient *noncompliance* with your treatment. Certainly I have reviewed many malpractice files where the patient believed he or she had chronic pain created by the physician's negligence. This is especially true in the field of spinal surgery. If you have *created* chronic pain as the result of an invasive procedure, then you are certainly at risk of triggering lawsuit. Chronic pain has other potential triggers linked with it, such as unhappiness, economic loss, abandonment, and failure to deliver promised services. Chronic pain is at the core of many suits (the old "pain and suffering" thing).

OVERLY COMPETITIVE MEDICAL COMMUNITY

Yes, we as physicians can be our own worst enemies. Unhappy patients quickly will bolt from your office to seek other physicians, and in this day and age your competition is more than willing to bad-mouth you in front of that patient if it will gain some economic advantage. I practice in a large metropolitan area. The individual surgical groups here are highly competitive with each other, rarely communicate with each other, and are more than happy to take a patient from a competing group if it will gain them a case. A patient seeking a routine second surgical opinion becomes fair game for a surgeon seeking to lure him or her away from the original physician by expounding on his or her own superior skills and outcomes. Thinly veiled criticism of the competition is the norm. Direct advertising to the public raises patient expectations to unrealistic levels, implying perfect outcomes every time!

I think patients are triggered to sue if they get even a sense from the second opinion physician that their original care was flawed in some way. It must be human nature for second opinion MD's to have an inflated sense of their own medical expertise, develop an "ivory tower" mentality, and automatically look for ways to criticize the original treatment plan. Patients pick up on this, and many nuisance lawsuits get started in this way.

As an interesting example of this problem, an orthopaedic surgeon in my state recently lost a defamation lawsuit filed by the original surgeon, who was upset with the comments made in front of a former patient by this defendant second opinion surgeon. According to published reports, the surgeon who lost the lawsuit (to the tune of $425,000, not covered by malpractice insurance, by the way) allegedly criticized the work of the first surgeon but also implied that the first surgeon was in the back pocket of the workers' compensation insurance carrier, and allegedly made these statements in the presence of the patient himself. As I stated, the primary surgeon successfully sued the second opinion surgeon *and* the patient for defamation. The moral of this story is to give fair and honest second opinions, not be economically motivated when you give your opinion, and realize that the patient may misinterpret your comments and criticisms as a personal attack on the character and professionalism of the original physician.

I might also refer you to an article by Heather Crumpton, "Criticizing Prior Care: Are You Chumming the Water in Which You Swim?" (Crumpton 2003). The author concludes that "too often, criticism is written or expressed by physicians who have not reviewed prior records or discussed the case with the previous treating physician, but who instead relied on *patient's* account of what occurred." I can speak from personal experience on this subject. I too had a patient sue me after becoming inflamed by the comments of a second opinion surgeon who relied exclusively on the wildly inaccurate history provided by the patient. I don't believe that his patient was trying intentionally to deceive or distort the medical facts. He just didn't have enough medical sophistication to understand the case and didn't have access to factual clinical data. However, the result was a nuisance lawsuit that was dropped shortly after filing when the plantiff's attorney finally got the real medical data straight. Nonetheless, this inaccurate and inflammatory written report by the second opinion MD (who, by the way, was the same one sued in the above-mentioned defamation case) created the hassle and expense of a nuisance lawsuit. I certainly don't think we as physicians should be covering for each other when patients come to us unhappy about previous treatments. Patients have a right to seek second opinions and to know if their previous treatments were not just marginal but truly substandard. Give these patients an honest answer, but don't be critical of the previous physician unless you truly know and understand all the facts of the case. Your ivory tower academic criticisms may be perceived by the patient as an accusation of malpractice.

I think all of the above-listed triggers are basically ways of identifying potentially litigious patients. You have a limited amount of control over these triggers, unfortunately. You will have patients with complications. You will have patients with bad outcomes. You will have many patients with profound economic loss as a result of their illness or surgeries. You will have many patients with chronic pain. I think why we have so many nuisance suits is because all the above-listed factors happen all of the time to many good physicians. For the purposes of this chapter, it is well enough at least to recognize these triggers so that you will be in a better position to react to them, correct the problem where you can, and defend yourself in any way possible.

REFERENCES

Crumpton, H. 2003. "Criticizing Prior Care: Are You Chumming the Water in Which You Swim?" *Medical Risk Management Advisor* 11(4):1–3.

2

Ways to Avoid Malpractice

David C. Urquia, M.D.

The short answer to the question "How do I avoid malpractice?" is ridiculously simple, but also very impractical: All you have to do is perform no invasive procedures, see no emergency room patients, see no workers' compensation or self-pay patients, inform your patients that you don't diagnose or treat cancer, and spend most of your time reading journals and attending educational conferences. If this is a description of your practice, you do not need to read the rest of this chapter. On the other hand, it goes without saying that if you are poorly educated, don't keep up with CME, and practice poor-quality medicine, there is also no point in your reading the rest of this chapter. You will be sued off the face of the planet. Since there is no way to avoid ever receiving a malpractice suit, you had better focus on how to minimize practice errors, and that is the subject of this chapter. A more appropriate title to this chapter might be "Ways to Defend Yourself Against Malpractice Suit." An appropriate subtitle might be "Communicate and Document."

I can't emphasize enough how important it is for you and your office to *be organized*. Not only does this give you much better malpractice defense, but is clearly in the patient's best interest. You need more than a "catch as catch can" system in place to answer patient phone calls, get test results, and organize medical

13

records. You need excellent and well-documented medical records every step of the way. You need good handwriting. If you are still practicing in the Stone Age by having handwritten office notes, I would stop the practice ASAP. As a physician reviewer of medical records, I can't help but think (maybe incorrectly) that a physician who does all of his office notes by hand must be poorly trained or have inferior diagnostic skills. It seems a natural conclusion to a reviewer. You need to document all "no shows," because patient noncompliance is one of the strongest defenses you will ever have. Document any instance of patient noncompliance with medication or office visits or not showing up for diagnostic testing. I like to put frequent addendums into my office records, dictated and transcribed notes documenting important or unusual patient phone contacts or any relevant clinical information obtained when the patient was not actually in the office. And for God's sake, *don't alter any of your records* after you have gone through the normal proofreading and correction process. You wouldn't believe how many medical records I have seen where the physician actually went back and changed his office notes, after the attorney had already received copies of the original chart. Just as patient noncompliance is your best defense, altering records will sink your boat every time.

I have reviewed several hundred malpractice files, both medical and surgical. It is still unbelievable to me how poorly documented many of these physician records are, especially the records of surgeons. These doctors would have had a much better defense in their malpractice cases if they had documented a thorough neurovascular exam, a thorough physical exam. The basic medical/legal rule still exists: "If you didn't document it, you didn't do it."

Along these same lines, although you want excellent and well-documented medical records, you have to *be careful what you write*. Although I know I am guilty of this at times myself, your office notes should not make insulting, emotional, or personally derogatory statements. I think you can be an accurate observer. You can certainly record what you see, but just be careful not to editorialize after you make these observations. Sometimes the observations themselves in the medical records will speak for themselves and your meaning will be clear without actually insulting the patient. Remember, you must assume that the patient will eventually read everything you write, especially in a malpractice claim. For example, you would *properly* document your observation that there was "a funny sweet smell permeating the exam room and strong on patient's breath; patient demonstrated many bizarre and nonphysiologic movements of right arm; patient gave a dramatic pain-withdrawal response as I palpated his sweater." The *improper* (although accurate) documentation of this same encounter would be "I observed this foul, drunken malingerer."

To avoid malpractice, it almost goes without saying that you establish a meaningful doctor/patient relationship. I suppose that in years past having an excellent relationship was all of the defense you needed against malpractice. Now it is hardly enough. On the other hand, I have seen extremes the other way that just boggle my mind, especially among surgeons who have busy practices. For example, I have reviewed records on some surgeons who have literally all the preoperative and postoperative patient contact performed by their physician extenders such as PA's or nurses. Literally the first time the surgeon ever met the patient was in preoperative holding. I am not talking about academic university practices, where the patients may have been seen by residents. These were private practices. Virtually no doctor/patient relationship existed. I am all for efficiency, but when things went wrong, those surgeons were not going to have much to fall back on. They had essentially decided in advance that they would not utilize a doctor-patient relationship as a defense mechanism against malpractice suit.

I think you can avoid malpractice to a certain extent by having a **generous supply of educational materials** available for the patient. A supply of handouts, booklets, and even websites is clearly a useful defense mechanism for you, and of course will benefit the patient during the course of their treatment. The patient cannot claim that he or she was ill-informed about the nature of treatment. I frequently see in surgical malpractice cases that the patient had a totally confused concept of what the surgery was about, what surgery was to be performed, or the nature of the technology. Patients report on their first postoperative visit being totally surprised that they had a certain implant in their spine. I would say that in most of those cases the patients just didn't pay attention preoperatively, that whatever explanation the surgeon made just went over their heads. Patient retention for these technical aspects of medicine can be very poor. If you ever conducted exit interviews with patients after they left your office, you probably would be shocked how little of your verbal explanation was retained. Nonetheless, it still leaves the physician vulnerable if patients, even through ignorance, claim that they were ill-informed. Many malpractice attorneys don't get very excited about informed consent issues as a basis for malpractice, but why leave yourself vulnerable even to these types of nuisance claims? I get a lot of positive patient feedback from article handouts, CD-ROM educational discs that I have prepared, and references to websites designed for patient education. The patients can never claim that they were ill-informed. You have a much straighter pathway to claiming patient noncompliance if the instructions were spelled out in advance in writing in a handout given to the patient. I think this is a perfect combination of educational efforts that truly benefit your patients, as well as reasonable defensive medicine.

You can minimize the risk of malpractice suit by not making promises you can't keep. This seems an obvious enough statement, but as physicians we are basically programmed to please. We tend to be overly optimistic in our predictions about outcome. We tend to downplay complication risks, especially surgeons in trying to "sell" an operation. Believe it or not, I have reviewed more than one malpractice file where the plaintiff told his attorney, "The doctor told me the procedure was a piece of cake." Clearly, the surgeon left the patient with the impression that the treatment would be simple and uncomplicated.

I think as a way of avoiding malpractice and malpractice suits you have to be able to identify high-risk patients for litigation. I discussed this in the chapter on triggers. To a certain extent this involves street sense on the part of the physician on how to identify these difficult patients. This only comes with experience.

Some patients have dissatisfaction and anger written all over their face from the very first visit. You need to separate these folks right away and put them on the most conservative track of treatment you can think of. These are often patients who have been through two or more physicians before they saw you. You can also identify these high-risk patients as those who decline to answer all of your questions. These may be patients who ask to record your conversations, believe it or not. (Never under *any* circumstances allow a patient to record or photograph anything that happens in your office!) These are patients who won't make eye contact with you even from the very first new patient visit. Somehow figure out right away which patients are in your office primarily for socioeconomic reasons. If they ask about disability on their first visit with you, clearly they are more interested in economics than any disease work-up. These are patients that you need to be that much more careful with about documentation. Treat them conservatively and by the book, and don't embark on high-risk treatment modalities.

Along those same lines, one should avoid recommending elective or even semielective invasive procedures on this group of high-risk patients. I would consider these high-risk patients those with multiple medical risks or the difficult patient with emotional instabilities and a litigious personality, as spelled out in the previous paragraph. Put simply, if you are a surgeon, just don't operate on those people for elective and even semielective situations. On the other hand, "conservative treatment" doesn't mean *no* treatment, or the patient may perceive that you have failed to deliver promised services or have abandoned them. (You can't really abandon a patient if you never actually started a treatment course to begin with.) Nonetheless, a very good way of avoiding malpractice and malpractice suits is to avoid high-risk invasive procedures wherever possible, especially on these difficult patients. Your street sense should be able to weed out this group. Of course, if you are motivated purely on economic grounds for performing procedures, don't really care about a sophisticated screening process, and care more about economic outcomes than clinical outcomes, then all I can say is good luck.

For my money, in this age of poor reimbursement and increasing litigation, when it comes to taking on high-risk treatment situations for elective patients, I say, "Who needs it?" I will tell a 300-pound patient with herniated discs who is neurologically intact that I am simply not going to operate on his spine. I will recommend conservative treatments, and if ultimately they are still unhappy I will recommend second opinions at an academic medical center where they can find three residents to hold retractors during the procedure.

When I say "abandonment," I am not talking about abandoning high-risk patients with life- or limb-threatening conditions. I am talking about situations where you have a choice whether to treat or not. You have a choice how to treat. You present the patient with legitimate treatment options that just happen to be conservative, not the most aggressive option when it comes to surgery. You as a physician are in charge of these elective situations. The way you avoid malpractice is by not getting in over your head. It goes without saying that you should not embark on treatments for which you are not qualified or for which you have marginal experience. However, you can also get in over your head if you perform any invasive procedure on these high-risk patients, who predictably will have some major or minor complication or who will have unhappiness written all over them no matter how skilled your interventions.

We go back to my original, impractical, suggestions, that you perform no invasive procedures, see no ER patients, exclude self-pay or workers' comp patients from your office rolls, and inform patients that you don't diagnose or treat cancer of any kind. (Actually, the more I reread this last suggestion, the more sense it makes!) If your whole goal is to avoid malpractice suits, then you must find a low-risk practice. However, for the rest of us who do have high-risk surgical practices and similar specialties, these suggestions will help you improve your malpractice defense, hopefully reduce your exposure, and in many cases provide better patient care as a nice side-effect of your obsessive-compulsive and defensive nature. They will reduce practice errors and therefore serve in the best interest of patient health.

I have always thought one of the best ways to avoid malpractice was to have regular "complication conferences." We used to do this all the time as part of our surgical division. You are basically learning from other people's mistakes. At the same time, you are getting suggestions from a broader group on how to manage active complications while they are still going on. You are sharing in a *confidential* way your experience managing either complications that could not have been prevented or situations involving human or technical error. Unfortunately, as economics have tightened in medicine and as private medical groups have become increasingly more competitive with each other, these joint conferences have gone by the wayside little by little, except in purely academic medical centers. On the other hand, they are still a goal that can be pursued. Some of the larger medical and surgical groups have the ability to form separate committees by which the internal practices of its members are reviewed in a logical and organized way, without having to expose their dirty laundry to the outside world. You could call it "quality assurance" or "practice review," but if it can be done in an orderly and confidential fashion then future malpractice situations almost certainly will be diminished (and oh, by the way, quality of care improved). I would highly recommend that individual departments or individual groups have a regular mechanism for practice review. As individual practitioners we are not likely to take the time to look at our own data, and certainly not without bias. We really need someone looking over our shoulders at times, sharing opinions, reviewing complications and other patient data. It is better that we do it internally, rather than through the court system or the government. We are bound to lose in those latter two institutions. You always learn more from your mistakes. You seem to learn more by looking at other people's mistakes. It is amazing how much I have learned reviewing malpractice files. I am still going to be sued in the future. I will still make human errors, but I may be able to avoid some of the more obvious pitfalls by educating myself on these issues. On the other hand, I would not recommend that you become a regular expert for plaintiff's attorneys as a source for CME!

The bottom line in this chapter concerning ways to avoid malpractice can be summarized as follows: Communicate, organize, document, identify the high-risk patient, have some form of confidential peer review, and don't make the high-risk treatment alternative your first choice, no matter how well it may reimburse your practice. I think I can accept if a patient comes after me because of a deficiency on my part produced by purely human error. I can accept human error, because I am human. I have a much harder time accepting a situation where I have made poor judgments. Most of the malpractice files I have reviewed resulted from issues of poor judgment on the part of the physician, ignoring or neglecting evolving complications, often in high-risk patients. Remember, "high-risk patients" means multiple *medical* risks, but it also means the patients who are high-risk for *litigation,* with dissatisfaction written all over their faces. In today's world you have to figure out a way to sort out the patients with chronic pain, the patients with psychiatric and emotional problems, the patients who have socioeconomic issues that dominate their presentation, and the patients who abuse the system. Keep them at arm's length from your elective practice wherever you can. There is no law that says you have to operate on chronic pain!

3

Creating Medical Records That Are Suit-Resistant

David E. Attarian, M.D., F.A.C.S.

The medical record is a confidential, formal document that you use in your day-to-day practice to detail and ensure quality patient care, communicate and coordinate services with your fellow healthcare providers and support staff, and facilitate the continuity of future care. Additionally, it fulfills record-keeping requirements of hospitals, the JCAHO, health insurance companies, and the government. In the event of a medical malpractice claim, however, the medical record becomes a legal document that can be your best ally or your worst enemy. When the time comes to defend yourself, you have two basic tools: the spoken word (testimony) and the medical record. As so many attorneys have argued or written in the past, "reality" can only be "proved" in the medical record; if something is not documented in the record, the fact that it happened may not be fully believed by a jury. So the medical record is the foundation upon which your attorney will defend your actions. With these thoughts in mind, how do you create medical records that are suit-resistant? Consider the following five suggestions:

THE MEDICAL RECORD MUST BE ORGANIZED, LEGIBLE, AND PERMANENT

This statement is probably self-explanatory. First and foremost, the medical record (clinic, office, or hospital) must be legible. Write neatly and in black ink so that photocopies can be easily made (in fact, some states have made illegibility a crime based on patient safety issues). For the purpose of suit-resistance, anyone reading the record should have no difficulty interpreting what was written. Every entry should be clearly dated and timed and legibly signed (print if necessary). Avoid the use of abbreviations whenever possible, as they can be confusing and lead to mistakes. Many institutions have lists of acceptable abbreviations. Limit your use of abbreviations to those which are officially endorsed by your major institutions. If your penmanship is terrible, dictate your notes for the record. Also, never write any part of the medical record in pencil or other erasable material.

The medical record should be organized and easily referenced. While the hospital record will usually have a prescribed format and identification system, your office records should also be cataloged and numbered for ease of retrieval. All written records should have a back-up copy, and electronic records must have a hard copy back-up to ensure that some mishap does not result in the complete destruction of a patient's medical record. Ideally, the medical record can be found through multiple sources at different locations. Without an organized, legible, and easily retrieved permanent record, your ability to defend yourself in a medical malpractice suit may be nil.

THE MEDICAL RECORD MUST BE TIMELY AND IN CHRONOLOGICAL ORDER

A timely medical record is one that records the events of a patient's encounter with a healthcare institution or provider shortly after it occurs. Our memory for specific events deteriorates rapidly with time, so the sooner you document an encounter, the more accurate and detailed the record will be. Write hospital rounds/ progress notes immediately after seeing the patient; likewise, dictate or write operative notes at the completion of the procedure.

Dictate discharge summaries on the date of discharge when the facts about a patient are clearest in your mind. Also, the record should reflect real time. The information must be in chronological order for ease of understanding and to assess whether any gaps or omissions exist. Avoid gaps at all times; for instance, in hospital progress notes, if an empty space is noted from the previous note, mark a diagonal line through the space so that it isn't mistakenly seen as a gap and doesn't allow someone else to add information out of chronological order. If a plaintiff's attorney can reveal a significant lag between an encounter and its documentation in the record, its accuracy may be questioned. Also, if the record is not in chronological order, it may be suggested that continuity of care was less than ideal.

THE MEDICAL RECORD MUST BE ACCURATE AND FACTUAL

Every detail in the medical record should be reviewed for accuracy before it becomes the final document (also, new federal law [HIPAA] allows a patient to review and correct factual material in his or her record). Write your notes carefully and completely, and proofread your dictations before you sign them. A factual error may be portrayed as a form of negligence or lack of attention to detail. Also, objectively record only the facts as you observe and interpret them. Do not criticize or ridicule the patient, other physicians, or support staff in the record, and especially avoid written debates in the medical record, as this may only serve to incite further litigation. Acknowledge differences of opinion which appear in the record from nursing notes, and support staff notes, or other physician notes, from your own; and then professionally record your explanation for such discrepancies. In the office setting, attach all received outside documents to the patient's medical record, e.g., other healthcare provider's records, copies of hospital-generated paperwork, laboratory and radiological reports, etc. It is an excellent idea to sign or stamp them with the date received and reviewed and your response.

A medical record that is complete, accurate, and factual is extremely helpful for the defense attorney, especially if the care rendered meets the standard of care. Never record information that is misleading, self-serving, or false.

THE MEDICAL RECORD MUST BE COMPREHENSIVE AND DETAILED

After legibility and permanence, this section may be the next most important aspect of creating a suit-resistant medical record. In spite of the time and expense involved, the record must be comprehensive; that is, it should contain every pertinent detail, observation, and action made by a healthcare provider in dealing with a patient. While preparing a patient's medical record, imagine that it will be reviewed by a medical expert and presented to a jury in the future. You are probably at greater risk for leaving information out of a record, so when in doubt, put it in the record. Examples include the differential diagnoses and thought processes used in managing a patient; pertinent laboratory findings (normal versus abnormal); listed instructions and warnings given to a patient; discussions about alternative treatments and the potential outcome of no treatment; every communication with a patient and/or a family member (e.g., phone calls, prescription refills, etc.), and a patient's failure to keep appointments or follow instructions. Utilization of preprinted forms and orders will help to avoid mistakes and omissions. In additions to improving efficiency, following standard formats for specific events (e.g., SOAP notes, procedure notes, new patient evaluations, and discharge summaries) will also improve record-keeping completeness and accuracy. Finally, be sure to adhere to all confidentiality and HIPAA rules in maintaining the medical record, and keep track of what medical information is released, and to whom.

THE MEDICAL RECORD SHOULD NEVER BE ALTERED, ERASED, OR DESTROYED

The medical record is a legal document, and as such, its original form should never be altered or erased. Always remember that changing the medical record after the fact may be interpreted as fraud and subject to criminal prosecution where billing is concerned. And it is easily and will be used to indicate deception in medical malpractice claims. So if you add something to the medical record at a later time or date, mark the supplement clearly as separate from the original recorded information and indicate why it is being placed in the record out of order. Instead, place a single line through the materials you desire to delete (leaving them legible), and then sign and date your entry and indicate the reason for your action. Even if you think the alteration is minor, don't do it without clearly labeling what you have done. Any unacknowledged or secretive change in the records discovered during the malpractice suit may render your case indefensible. And with electronic files becoming more common, don't believe that alterations in the medical record cannot be detected—they can. So create the medical record correctly one time, and then do not alter or destroy it under any circumstances.

While all healthcare professionals are stressed by the current socioeconomic and medical-legal environment, this is one area in which you can shore up your own defense even before a suit is launched. On the other hand, ignoring or overlooking principles of good medical record documentation will result in dramatically increased personal, professional, and financial suffering when claims of malpractice are brought.

REFERENCES

American Academy of Orthopaedic Surgeons (AAOS). 1993. *A Primer for Orthopaedic Residents and Fellows.* Rosemount, Ill: AAOS, 21–24.

Herbert, D. L. 1990. *Legal Aspects of Sports Medicine.* Canton, Oh.: Professional Reports Corporation, 56–67.

Nora, P. F., ed. 1991. *Professional Liability Risk Management: A Manual for Surgeons.* Chicago: American College of Surgeons, 125–128. (Second edition, 1997.)

4

How to Document Patient Discussions and Operative and Procedure Permits and Properly Dismiss a Patient from Your Practice

David E. Attarian, M.D., F.A.C.S.

Every person has the legal and ethical right to be left alone and to self-determination when it comes to our health; therefore, as physicians and surgeons, we are obligated to disclose and explain fully all pertinent information to our patients so they may accept or refuse our recommended treatments. Complete and accurate documentation of this informed consent process is not only required by such entities as the JCAHO, hospitals, and state governments, but it may prove to be a vitally important tool in defending against a claim of medical malpractice suit. If care is rendered without a patient's permission, the healthcare provider could even be held responsible for battery. If a patient suffers a known complication of a surgical procedure and ultimately a poor outcome, a well-documented informed consent which mentions this complication may result in a successful defense if the patient claims he or she would not have consented to the procedure had he or she known about this complication.

PATIENT DISCUSSIONS

The first guideline in documenting discussions for the purpose of treatment of your patients is that the medical record ideally should reflect an educational process that occurs over a period of time rather than during a single encounter. Informed consent to treat typically begins with the first patient-physician encounter which has been initiated by the patient making an appointment to be seen in the office or by presenting to the hospital emergency room. A complete and accurate medical record will indicate the patient's motive for seeing a physician. As the evaluation proceeds, the record should clearly detail all steps taken by the physician to establish a list of diagnoses and recommended treatments. The record should reflect the patient's implied, verbal, and/or written permission for the physician to obtain medical information, perform a physical examination (chaperoned if necessary), and order basic laboratory or radiological tests. Explain and document each step as you proceed; stop and explain the plan if the patient has any questions. Document the discussions in the medical record as thoroughly as possible, preferably over a period of time, to give the patient ample opportunity to ask questions, consider your recommendations, and make an unhurried, uncoerced decision. Document these discussions in the medical record as thoroughly as possible. Paper-based or electronically accessible educational materials describing the patient's condition and treatment options are also extremely important and useful; the medical record should make reference to these when they are provided to a patient.

The second guideline is to show that your documented discussions meet the legal standard of disclosure. In all states, you must fully explain in understandable language the nature of the condition, illness, or injury that necessitates medical or surgical treatment. The information provided must be accurate, up to date, and unbiased. You must explain and describe the nature and purpose of the recommended treatment or procedure. The risks and complications associated with the treatment or procedure must likewise be listed, described, and explained. The probability of the potential benefit of the treatment or procedure must be defined and explained. It is important, and ideally should be documented, that no guarantee of success is ever implied or stated. All reasonable alternative treatments or procedures, and each of their respective attendant risks and benefits, must be disclosed and documented. Finally, the outcome, risks, and benefits of no treatment must be included in your discussions with the patient.

Adequacy of disclosure has also been established by the courts. The question will be, was enough understandable information made available for the patient to make a valid informed consent? Some states use the professional or reasonable physician standard. In this case, the standard is measured by the customary practice in the local medical community, and is based on the physician's perception of what a patient needs to know. Currently, the patient viewpoint standard is more often required by the courts. Under this standard, any and all information that may have a significant impact on the patient must be disclosed. So even if a reported severe complication (e.g., death or paralysis) is extremely rare for a given treatment or procedure, it should be described, explained, and documented in the informed consent process.

INFORMED CONSENT AND PERMITS

The third and final guideline in the informed consent process is to meet the standard of documentation for your institution. In addition to the items previously presented for inclusion in your discussions with the patient and written in the medical record, you should always use a consent form, signed by the patient and ideally witnessed by yourself and one other person. Hospitals and surgery centers will have their own required consent form or surgical/procedure permit that has been reviewed by legal counsel to ensure adequacy of disclosure according to the law. You should use a similar form for any procedures or surgery performed in the office setting. You must be aware of several special circumstances which may arise in this process. Minors are not able to give consent for themselves except under limited circumstances, typically involving sexual issues, or when they are emancipated. Be sure that you understand the laws in your state when treating minors and obtaining informed consent from a parent or legal guardian. You must also be prepared to deal with a patient's or family's decision to refuse treatment, even if the known outcome is death. In this instance, document your discussions in the record and seek consultations from fellow physicians, an ethics committee, a hospital administrator, or even the courts.

Situations may arise in which a patient is unable to provide consent to treat, and no other relative or legal guardian can be found to give consent. In these circumstances, do what is necessary to save the patient's life or limb, and then clearly document in the record the indications for such action, the inability to obtain informed consent, your efforts to obtain consultation from other physicians to support your treatment of the patient, and the likely outcome if no intervention is attempted. It is a good idea to indicate your intention of obtaining informed consent as soon as it is available. You should also be prepared to deal with a patient's family's decision to refuse treatment, even if the known outcome is death. In this instance, document your discussions in the record and seek consultations from fellow physicians, an ethics committee, or even the courts. Ultimately, the purpose of any patient-physician encounter is to exchange information and provide service that will help to acheive the health goals of the patient under the guidance and treatment of the healthcare professional. Documentation of discussions and obtaining legally sound informed consent for treatment insures that their legal and ethical right of self-determination is protected.

DISMISSING A PATIENT FROM YOUR PRACTICE

Excluding federal/state statutes and hospital bylaws that mandate emergency room call responsibilities, the American Medical Association and all state medical boards recognize the physician's right to choose which patients he or she will or will not evaluate and treat. At the same time, once a physician- patient relationship has started, the physician has an ethical and legal obligation to ensure that appropriate services are rendered until they are no longer necessary so as to avoid being accused of abandonment.

The scenarios leading up to the dismissal of a patient from your practice are myriad; examples include the patient suing you or a member of your group practice; the patient being noncompliant and/or failing to attend appointments; the patient changing managed care plans or moving out of the area; the patient being overly demanding or belligerent to you and/or your staff; the patient failing to pay his or her bills; or you relocating or retiring. No matter what the reason, the physician may not abruptly terminate the relationship with the patient; the patient must be given reasonable notice and explanation, as well as sufficient opportunity and guidance to make alternative arrangements to guarantee continuity of his or her healthcare.

The first step in the dismissal process is to communicate directly with the patient, preferably in person or by telephone (if appropriate for the circumstances), and always in writing. The conversation should be detailed in the medical record; written notice should be by certified mail with return receipt requested. The patient should be given a specific explanation for the dismissal or termination as well as an anticipated date for services to cease. Next, you must agree to continue treatment and/or provide access to services until the patient has enough time to secure care from another physician; most states require minimums of 30 to 60 days, so be sure to know your local legal requirements. Also, you may wish to extend your relationship beyond the minimum time period for the patient's benefit. If necessary or requested, you should provide resources or recommendations to help the patient find another suitable physician. Once the patient has established a new physician-patient relationship, offer to transfer all necessary medical records upon signed authorization of the patient or legal guardian.

By following these guidelines, you should be able to dismiss a patient from your practice within two to three months, maintain the continuity of the patient's healthcare, and avoid being accused of abandonment. If the process seems confusing or too confrontational, you should obtain advice from your attorney.

Ultimately, the purpose of any patient-physician encounter is to exchange information and provide service that will achieve the health goals of the patient under the guidance and treatment of the healthcare professional. Documentation of discussions with your patients and obtaining informed consent for treatment ensures that the legal and ethical right of self-determination is protected. At the same time, fulfillment of this duty will often serve to protect you should litigation occur.

REFERENCES

American Academy of Orthopaedic Surgeons (AAOS). 1993. *Medical Malpractice: A Primer for Orthopaedic Residents and Fellows*. Rosemont, Ill.: AAOS, 25–29.

American Academy of Orthopaedic Surgeons (AAOS). n.d. Code of Ethics

American Medical Association (AMA). n.d. Code of Medical Ethics.

Herbert, D. L. 1990. *Legal Aspects of Sports Medicine*. Canton, Oh.: Professional Reports Corporation, 69–84.

Nora, P. F., ed. 1991. *Professional Liability Risk Management: A Manual for Surgeons*. Chicago: American College of Surgeon, 115–124.

State Medical Boards. n.d. Position statements.

5

Standard of Care

Leonard Berlin, M.D., F.A.C.R.

To hold a physician liable for malpractice, a judge or jury must find that the physician's conduct falls below the standard of medical care. Determining what constitutes that peculiar standard of care against which the physician's actions are measured is not a simple matter, particularly because the legal and medical communities often differ in their perspectives. Nonetheless, the courts are quite consistent in how they define the standard of care. An Ohio appellate decision is typical (*Jewett v. Our Lady of Mercy Hospital of Mariemont*, 612 N.E.2d 724 (Oh. App. 1992)):

> In order to establish medical malpractice, it must be shown by a preponderance of evidence that the injury complained of [by the patient] was caused by the doing of some particular thing that a physician of ordinary skill, care and diligence would not have done under like or similar conditions or circumstances, or by the failure or omission to do some particular thing that such a physician would have done under like or similar conditions or circumstances. . . . The standard of care for the physician in the practice of a board-certified medical specialty should be that of a reasonable specialist practicing medicine in

that same specialty in light of the scientific knowledge in the specialty field.

Such terms as "ordinary" and "reasonable" qualify as determinants of the medical standard of care to judges, but such terms are confusing and perplexing to many physicians. Writing in the *Journal of the American Medical Association*, one physician lamented that "there is no single standard of care." This physician proposed that there are, in fact, seven separate standards of care: the idealized, the academic, the practical, the medical-legal, the economic, the managed care, and the personal (Argy 1996).

Standards of medical care in the medical community do not derive exclusively from external authorities such as government or professional societies, but rather from interaction among leaders of the profession and networks of colleagues, reports in the literature, and educational seminars: it is a decentralized process.

In court proceedings dealing with medical malpractice, proof of recognized medical standards must be provided through testimony of an expert witness. In years past, these experts relied solely on their own knowledge and experience in forming subjective opinions regarding standards of care. In an effort to provide consistency and objectivity to the process of determining the standard of medical care in a given medical situation, government agencies, medical societies, insurance companies, and managed care organizations began more than a decade ago to create practice guidelines known by various names, including "parameters," "algorithms," "clinical indicators," "guidelines," "clinical pathways," caremaps," and "standards." It has been estimated that to date more than 2000 such guidelines have been developed, and the number continues to increase.

The degree to which written guidelines influence a judge or jury in malpractice deliberations depends on both the source from which the guidelines originate and how they are introduced into evidence. Guidelines are generally brought into the litigation process by expert witnesses testifying on behalf of either the plaintiff or the defendant. A number of legislative and regulatory bodies have issued guidelines and continue to do so. These bodies include the United States Congress, the Federal Agency for

Health Care Policy and Research, insurance companies, medical societies, specialty colleges, and virtually all local healthcare facilities in which physicians practice.

The original intent of these bodies was that guidelines would improve patient care and at the same time diminish the incidence of, and the costs related to, malpractice litigation. Some observers expressed doubt early that inserting parameters and standards into the existing litigation process would generate savings and reduce malpractice risks (Garrick et al. 1991). These doubts seem to have been well founded, for they have been confirmed by subsequent events. In a report on practice guidelines and malpractice litigation, researchers at the School of Public Health at Harvard University (Hyams et al. 1994) found that the predominant use of guidelines has been to inculpate rather than exculpate physicians in malpractice cases. Guidelines were used three times more often against physicians than in their defense, and in published judicial decisions, plaintiffs won 17 of 23 cases in which their lawyers cited guidelines. Instead of reducing costs by decreasing the need for expert witnesses, just the opposite effect occurred (Hyams et al. 1994). A *Wall Street Journal* article declared that practice guidelines had become "powerful weapons for plaintiffs in malpractice cases" and quoted a plaintiff's attorney as saying, "Lawyers like me are using them in court all the time to say, 'Gee, your own organization says this is a minimum standard of care, and you didn't follow it'" (Felsenthal 1994).

Various judicial decisions dealing with published guidelines of care in medical specialties have been made. Reviewing some of these decisions should give us an indication as to how courts will likely view standards in the future.

Merely following the practice guidelines of a physician's medical specialty will not necessarily protect the physician in a malpractice lawsuit. In a case in which a neonate died shortly after childbirth as a result of an obstetrician's failure to monitor the mother during labor and subsequent delay in performing an emergency caesarean section, a lower court dismissed a malpractice lawsuit against the obstetrician because he testified that he had followed the standards of care promulgated by the American

College of Obstetricians and Gynecologists. However, ruling that "the standards announced by the American College of Obstetricians and Gynecologists are the minimal accepted standards of his specialty," the appeals court stated that the evidence presented disclosed that the obstetrician had nevertheless "departed from acceptable standards of care in his treatment." The appeals court reversed the lower court dismissal and ordered the obstetrician to stand trial for the alleged malpractice (*Jewett, supra*).

In contrast, a District of Columbia court of appeals found a physician liable for malpractice for not following practice guidelines. In that case, the family of a woman who had suffered cardiac arrest and permanent brain damage during an abortion and tubal ligation filed a malpractice lawsuit against an anesthesiologist. The jury returned a verdict of $4.6 million, but the anesthesiologist appealed. During the original trial, a plaintiff's expert anesthesiologist had testified that the defendant had not followed the standards of the American Association of Anesthesiology. The defendant's attorney argued that these standards were "emerging" and "encouraged" but were not "mandatory." The appeals court upheld the verdict, however, stating that the anesthesiology association's standards "necessarily embody what a reasonably prudent [physician] would do" (*Washington v. Washington Hospital Center*, 579 A.2d 177 (D.C. App. 1990)).

Not all courts have permitted published guidelines to be introduced as evidence. In a case in which a trauma surgeon was accused of malpractice for performing without proper consent a peritoneal lavage on an intoxicated patient injured in an automobile accident, a trial judge in Rhode Island refused to admit the testimony of an expert witness for the defense who had attempted to introduce into evidence standards issued by the American College of Surgeons that expressly obligated a trauma surgeon to perform peritoneal lavage on intoxicated patients who have sustained abdominal trauma. The surgeon was found liable for malpractice and appealed. The state supreme court reversed the verdict against the surgeon and ordered a new trial, indicating that the trial judge should have permitted testimony that the surgeon had adhered to the American College of Surgeons' guidelines (*Miller v. Rhode Island Hospital*, 625 A.2d 778 (R.I. 1993)).

Professional guidelines do influence judicial decisions but are not necessarily compelling. In North Dakota, a malpractice lawsuit was filed against a hospital on behalf of a neonate who had sustained permanent brain damage because the mother had not been promptly transferred to a medical facility that was equipped to perform emergency caesarean deliveries. Noting that the hospital lacked equipment for these procedures, a federal court judge acknowledged that this was "not consistent with the policy of the American College of Obstetricians and Gynecologists which recommends all [required] services be available within 30 minutes in any . . . facility." However, the judge then added *(Anderson v. United States*, 731 F.Supp. 391 (U.S. Dist. N.D. 1990)):

> The American College of Obstetricians and Gynecologists guidelines in and of themselves are fine, presenting a thoughtful and reasoned approach to the perils of childbirth. The [hospital], however, is faced with the reality that human and economic resources are limited.

Guidelines promulgated by a private insurance carrier do not carry the same legal weight as those issued by established government agencies or professional societies. In a case in which a physician was accused of malpractice because he did not adhere to risk-management guidelines recommended by his malpractice carrier that called for physicians to perform follow-up examinations to detect breast cancer "within 6 weeks after discovery of a palpable lump," a Colorado appeals court upheld a lower court decision that ruled that these guidelines had no legal validity, stating (*Quigley v. Jobe*, 851 P.2d 236 (Colo. App. 1992)):

> The trial court determined that the guidelines are not relevant because they were promulgated by a private insurance company as part of an insurance contract and did not reflect a generally recognized standard of care within the medical profession. We agree with that analysis. . . . The insurance contract was intended to provide liability protection to the defendant, and . . . the express purpose of the

risk management guidelines was to attempt to "decrease the possibility of a malpractice case, increase the possibility of prevailing or decrease the eventual loss."

Occasionally, courts must grapple with guidelines that are not in accord with each other. A case decided by the Supreme Court of Pennsylvania dealt with conflicting standards issued by two different prestigious professional organizations. In that case, a woman who developed breast cancer sued her physician because he had not ordered a routine mammogram. The plaintiff asserted that her physician violated the recommendations of the American Cancer Society, which that held that physicians should order "a mammogram every year" after a patient reaches her 50th birthday. The defendant replied that according to the American College of Obstetricians and Gynecologists, only "regular," as opposed to "yearly," mammograms were required, which to him meant that the decision to order them was within the physician's discretion. The jury found the doctor not negligent, and the patient appealed, arguing that the obstetrician-gynecologist should have followed guidelines of the American Cancer Society rather than those of the American College of Obstetricians and Gynecologists. In determining whether the defendant physician's conduct fell below the proper standard of care, the appeals court discussed the "two schools of thought doctrine." The court explained that the doctrine provides a complete defense to a malpractice claim when the prescribed medical practice or procedure has been approved by one group of medical experts, even though an alternate group recommends another approach. The doctrine is applicable, stated the court, only when more than one accepted method of treatment or procedure exists and each method must be recognized or advocated by a "considerable number of respect, reputable and reasonable" medical experts. The court stated (*Levine v. Rosen*, 616 A.2d 623 (Pa. 1992)):

> With respect to whether the doctor should have ordered a yearly mammogram, [the patient] introduced evidence that the American Cancer Society recommended a yearly test for women over fifty years of age. The defendant

introduced evidence that the American College of Obstetricians and Gynecologists recommended that mammography be performed "regularly" for that same group of women. Unquestionably the evidence established that there were a considerable number of respected physicians who subscribe to each school of thought—regular versus yearly mammograms. . . . A physician may rightfully choose to practice his profession in accordance with a school of thought which differs in its concept and procedures from another school of thought. Even though the school that he follows is a minority one, he will not be deemed to be negligent of practicing properly, so long as it is reputable and respected by reasonable medical experts.

The court admonished, however, that the two schools of thought doctrine does not relieve a doctor from liability for failure to recognize symptoms of an illness (*Levine, supra*).

It should be emphasized that standards of care are not absolute, and ultimately the standard of care becomes whatever a contest of experts can persuade a jury is the most appropriate standard for the case at hand. As most attorneys and courtroom observers will attest, it is difficult, if not impossible, to predict how a jury will rule after a trial is completed. No matter how a jury rules, however, another jury hearing the same evidence and confronted with the same facts could well reach an opposite verdict.

REFERENCES

Argy, O. 1996. "Standards of Care." *JAMA* 275:1296.

Felsenthal, E. 1994. "Doctors' Own Guidelines Hurt Them in Court." *The Wall Street Journal,* 19 October, B1, B12.

Garrick, D. W., A. M. Hendricks, and T. A. Brennan. 1991. "Can Practice Guidelines Reduce the Number and Costs of Malpractice Claims?" *JAMA* 266:2856–2860.

Hyams, A. L., J. A. Brandenburg, S. R. Lipsitz, and T. A. Brennan. 1994. *Report to Physician Payment Review Commision: Practice Guidelines and Malpractice Litigation.* Boston:

Harvard School of Public Health, Department of Health Policy and Management.

6

Proximate Cause

Leonard Berlin, M.D., F.A.C.R.

To be successful in a medical malpractice lawsuit, the plaintiff must prove four elements: the defendant owed a duty to the plaintiff, there was a breach of that duty, the plaintiff sustained damages, and there was a causal connection between the breach and the damages (Flamm 1998). The legal concept of causation, referred to as *proximate cause,* is quite different from the medical concept of causation, referred to as *etiology.* Etiology is usually considered to be the major cause, or even the most immediate cause, of an injury, whereas proximate cause need not be the only cause, nor even the last or nearest cause, and in fact may concur with some other cause acting at the same time (*Sinclair v. Berlin,* 758 N.E.2d 442 (Ill. App. 2001)).

Of the four *sine qua non* allegations that must be proven in order for a plaintiff to succeed in a malpractice lawsuit, the one claiming that the defendant has breached the standard of care, in other words has acted negligently, is the most frequently contested (Berlin 2001). The question of whether the defendant owes a duty to the plaintiff is less frequently disputed, but the question is raised if there is doubt that a legal physician-patient relationship exists (Berlin 2002). Whether the patient has sustained an injury is usually not a contentious issue, although the issue does occasionally arise in cases in which patients claim they have sustained emotional damage in the absence of physical injury, such as being afflicted with fear of a decreased life expectancy if a diagnosis of cancer has been delayed (*Boryla v. Pash,* 960 P.2d 123 (Colo. 1998)).

Challenging whether the last of these four elements—proximate cause—has occurred is not a frequent occurrence. Nevertheless, proximate cause is an important legal concept that in certain situations can provide an effective affirmative defense in malpractice lawsuits (Flamm 1998). This point is illustrated by reviewing three cases in which proximate cause—or the absence of it—directly impacted the outcome of malpractice litigation.

In Illinois, a 60-year old man with sudden onset of weakness and numbness of his left side was brought by his family to a hospital emergency department at 2 a.m. A CT was not obtained until 9:30 a.m., at which time a massive cerebral hemorrhage was diagnosed. The patient lapsed into coma and died three days later. The family filed a medical malpractice lawsuit against the emergency physician, alleging that the patient would have survived had a stat CT been ordered at the time of admission. At a jury trial, two expert medical witnesses retained by the plaintiff testified that the failure of the emergency room physician to order an earlier CT while the patient was undergoing observation in the emergency department was a breach of the standard of care, and that an immediate diagnosis would have permitted surgical intervention that would have saved the patient's life. On cross-examination, however, the two experts, a neurologist and an emergency department physician, acknowledged that the only benefit that would have been gained by an earlier diagnosis would have been referral to a neurosurgeon, and they did not know what a neurosurgeon would have done at the time. At the conclusion of the trial, the jury found in favor of the plaintiff and awarded substantial damages. The trial judge, however, reversed the jury verdict, finding that "no reasonable fact finder could conclude that the death of the decedent was proximately caused by the failure to conduct a CT scan" in a more timely manner. The plaintiff appealed, but the appellate court sustained the trial judge's reversal

(*Aguilera v. Mount Sinai Hospital Medical Center*, 691 N.E.2d (Ill. App. 1997)):

> The trial court reasoned that even if defendants deviated from the standard of care in failing to order an earlier CT scan, plaintiff failed to offer evidence that this negligence was the proximate cause of plaintiff's injury. . . . Plaintiff must establish that it is more probably true than not true that the negligence was a proximate cause of the injury. Plaintiff must prove not only that an earlier CT scan would have revealed the condition, but, under the appropriate standard of care, the diagnosis would have triggered medical or surgical intervention to prevent the decedent's death. . . . Defendants argue that a CT scan is a diagnostic tool that cannot alleviate a condition.
>
> To the extent a plaintiff's chance of recovery or survival is lessened by the malpractice, he or she should be able to present evidence to a jury that the defendant's malpractice proximately caused the increased risk of harm or lost chance of recovery. . . . Here . . . the evidence reveals that no medical treatment was available for decedent's fatal illness. . . . The record before us contains no evidence to support the opinion of plaintiff's experts that the negligent delay in administering a CT scan lessened the effectiveness of treatment. . . . On cross-examination, defendants elicited testimony from plaintiff's experts showing that their conclusion that a delay in ordering a CT scan was a proximate cause of decedent's death was not supported by the facts. The experts testified that they did not know if surgical intervention should have been ordered if a prompt CT scan had been administered, [and] that the decision of whether neurosurgery should be performed would not have been made without input from a neurosurgeon. . . . The absence of expert testimony that . . . an earlier CT scan would have led to surgical intervention or other treatment that may have contributed to the decedent's recovery creates a gap in the evidence of proximate cause fatal to plaintiffs' case.

In another Illinois case, a 37-year-old woman complaining of high fever, diffuse back pain, and foul-smelling cloudy urine was admitted to a hospital emergency department. Concluding that the patient had a urinary tract infection, the emergency department physician ordered blood tests and a urine culture, placed the patient on intravenous antibiotics, and had the patient admitted to the medical floor. The following day the patient became hypotensive, went into respiratory arrest, and died. An autopsy revealed that the patient had an obstructing renal calculus that had led to a severe infection, septic shock, and ultimately death. A medical malpractice lawsuit was filed against the emergency department physician and the hospital, alleging that the emergency physician was negligent by failing to order abdominal radiographic and CT studies that would have disclosed the presence of a kidney stone, thereby permitting immediate diagnosis and avoidance of the fatal septic shock. The case was tried, and at its conclusion the jury returned an $850,000 verdict in the patient's favor. The defendants appealed the verdict, arguing that the plaintiff had failed to prove proximate cause.

The majority of the three-member Illinois appellate court agreed with the defendants and reversed the verdict. The Court focused on testimony of the plaintiff's expert witnesses, who admitted that it was not they, but rather a urologist or an interventional radiologist, who would have performed the procedure to remove the renal calculus had it been diagnosed immediately. The Court pointed out that there was no evidence in the record indicating what a urologist or an interventional radiologist would have done to relieve the obstruction. The decision to overturn the jury verdict was not unanimous, however, for one appellate judge submitted a dissenting opinion (*Townsend v. University of Chicago Hospitals,* 741 N.E.2d 1055 (Ill. App. 2000)):

> The evidence is that the plaintiff's decedent died as a result of an undiagnosed urinary tract obstruction. [Plaintiff's experts] testified that without the obstruction being relieved, the decedent had a zero chance of survival. Had the obstruction been relieved, the plaintiff's decedent had a 40 to 60 percent chance of survival. The defendant did

not remove the obstruction. The plaintiff's decedent died. The plaintiff is critical of the [defendant's] failure to call in a urologist or an interventional radiologist [and] to order abdominal tests . . . all of which were deviations from the standard of care.

I do not believe that evidence as to the specific type of treatment which would have been used to relieve the obstruction is necessary to allow a jury to determine that a failure to render any treatment to relieve the obstruction is a proximate cause of the injury and subsequent death of the plaintiff's decedent. . . . The jury is charged to determine, from the facts, proximate cause based on the expert evidence. The jury in this case met its responsibility. We should not abrogate its verdict by requiring a multicolored roadmap when a simple black line will do.

As can be seen by the split decision rendered by the appellate court in this case, the determination of whether proximate cause has been proven is frequently far from clear-cut. Individual juries or appeals court judges can be presented with the same set of facts, deliberate over the same evidence, and yet reach diametrically opposite conclusions.

The question of whether proximate cause has been proven becomes even cloudier, however, when a defendant-physician is charged with malpractice because of injury sustained by a patient who already has a preexisting illness, perhaps one that is chronic yet nonfatal, or one that is fatal and involves a patient who may be in a preterminal stage. A recent case decided by the Illinois Supreme Court illustrates this point quite well. A 55-year-old woman visited her family physician because of severe back pain that had begun one month earlier. The physician ordered radiographs and a radionuclide bone scan that disclosed a compression fracture in the mid-thoracic spine. Several days later, upon developing numbness and tingling in her legs, the patient went to a hospital emergency department. Finding that the patient's temperature and white blood count were elevated and suspecting that the patient had either an infection or a malignancy, her physicians ordered a CT. The CT was interpreted as disclosing a compression fracture most likely related to a carcinoma, and the patient was hospitalized. Over the next several days the patient experienced increasing difficulty in moving her legs and controlling her bowel and urinary bladder function. Then the patient became paraplegic. However, hospital nurses failed to apprise the treating physicians that the patient was experiencing a gradual loss of sensory and motor functions, and thus the physicians later claimed they assumed that the loss of function occurred suddenly. This misled the physicians into believing that the patient was suffering from a malignancy rather than a treatable inflammatory process. Eventually, a diagnosis of osteomyelitis of the thoracic spine was established, and the patient was left with permanent paraplegia and loss of bowel and urinary bladder control.

The patient filed a medical malpractice lawsuit against the radiologist, her attending physician, and hospital nurses. The lawsuit alleged that both physicians had been negligent, the radiologist for failing to diagnose osteomyelitis on her radiologic studies and the attending physician for failing to appreciate the gravity of the patient's physical findings and call for immediate neurosurgical consultation. Just before trial was to begin, the radiologist and the attending physician settled the lawsuit for $2,950,000. The case against the hospital proceeded to a jury trial, at the conclusion of which the jury awarded the patient $8.7 million. The hospital appealed the verdict first to the appellate court, which upheld the verdict, and then to the Illinois Supreme Court.

In the appeal, the attorney for the hospital argued that the verdict should be reversed because proximate cause had not been established. The hospital's defense attorney claimed that the plaintiff presented no evidence to indicate that even if the nurses had in more timely fashion informed the patient's attending physicians of the gradually appearing motor and sensory problems that the patient was experiencing, prompt surgical intervention would have prevented the permanent neurologic deficits that ensued. In addition, the hospital's attorney argued that the trial judge had committed errors by allowing into the record certain testimony and comments made by witnesses and attorneys that were prejudicial to the hospital and unfairly influenced the jury into returning a verdict in favor of the plaintiff. Although the Supreme Court did reverse the jury verdict because it agreed that the hospital had not been given a fair trial, the Court rejected the hospital's argument that proximate cause had not been established. The Court's comments regarding proximate cause are quite germane (*Holton v. Memorial Hospital*, 679 N.E.2d 1202 (Ill. 1997)):

> When a plaintiff comes to a hospital already injured, or has an existing undiagnosed medical condition, as in the case at bar, and while in the care of the hospital is negligently treated, the question of whether the defendant's negligent treatment is a proximate cause of the plaintiff's ultimate injury is ordinarily one of fact for the jury. In the case at bar, defendant asserts that it was entitled to [reversal of the verdict] for the failure of plaintiffs to present expert testimony that an earlier call to [the patient's] physicians would have prevented her paralysis. . . .

> [The plaintiff] was not required to prove that an earlier call to her physicians would have resulted in a more favorable outcome. [She] did not base her case solely on defendant's delay in the reporting of her condition. Instead, she contended that the failure of defendant's nursing staff to accurately report the progression of her decline was a proximate cause of her paralysis. The record contains evidentiary support for plaintiff's theory. [The doctors] explained that they based their erroneous diagnosis and treatment decisions upon incorrect and incomplete information regarding [the patient's] condition in the hours preceding her total loss of motor control. . . . Had the doctors been given the opportunity to properly diagnose the patient's condition based on accurate and complete information, they would have had the opportunity to treat her condition by ordering the appropriate treatment. Because of the hospital's negligent failure to accurately and timely report [the patient's] symptomatology, the appropriate treatment was not even considered. . . .

Although it may appear more difficult to assess exactly what harm negligent medical treatment may have caused when the patient has a pre-existing illness or injury, juries routinely are asked to determine whether, and to what extent, a defendant's negligent treatment proximately caused the injury upon which the patient's lawsuit is based. [The jury was instructed by the judge that] the defendant's negligence need only be a cause of the harm, or any cause which, in the natural or probable sequence, produced the injury of the plaintiff, not the only cause, nor the last or nearest cause. It is sufficient if it concurs with some other cause acting at the same time, which in combination with it, causes the injury.

The Court then went on to discuss the question of whether it is necessary for a plaintiff to prove that there would have been at least a 50% chance of surviving or recovering from an existing illness or injury had the negligence not occurred:

Where there is evidence that a plaintiff's estimated chance of surviving or recovering from an existing illness or injury, absent the malpractice, is 50% or less, some courts have concluded that proximate cause under the traditional definition is lacking. [In other words], plaintiff must show better than even chance of survival absent alleged malpractice to sustain burden of proof on proximate cause. Other courts have recognized that victims of medical malpractice should be able to seek damages arising from their doctors' or hospitals' negligent treatment, notwithstanding that the patients' chance of recovering from existing illnesses or injuries may be less than 50%. . . . The better rule is that evidence which shows to a reasonable certainty that negligent delay in diagnosis or treatment lessened the effectiveness of treatment is sufficient to establish proximate cause. . . . To the extent a plaintiff's chance of recovery or survival is lessened by the malpractice, he or she should be able to present evidence to a jury that the defendant's malpractice, to a reasonable degree of medical certainty, proximately caused the increased risk of harm or lost chance of recovery. We therefore reject the reasoning of cases which hold, as a matter of law, that plaintiffs may not recover for medical malpractice injuries if they are unable to prove that they would have enjoyed a greater than 50% chance of survival or recovery absent the alleged malpractice of the defendant. . . . To hold otherwise would free healthcare providers from legal responsibility for even the grossest acts of negligence, as long as the patient upon whom the malpractice was performed already suffered an illness or injury.

The Court concluded:

Disallowing tort recovery in medical malpractice actions on the theory that the patient was already too ill to survive or recover may operate as a disincentive on the part of healthcare providers to administer quality medical care to critically ill or injured patients.

In a concurring written opinion, one of the Supreme Court justices emphasized that each codefendant may be found liable for malpractice if his or her negligent conduct proximately caused patient injury, even though other codefendants may have contributed to the patient's injury. The Justice focused on and stressed the importance of one jury instruction that contained the following words:

More than one person may be to blame for causing an injury. If you decide that the defendant was negligent and that its negligence was a proximate cause of injury to the plaintiff, it is not a defense that some third person who is not a party to this suit may also have been to blame.

The concept that each defendant is liable for his or her own negligent acts even if others also are negligent deserves further attention. Radiologists whose only involvement in the medical care of a given patient is interpretation of a radiologic study upon which the attending physician may or may not have substantially depended may well be included as a codefendant in a medical malpractice lawsuit filed because of alleged negligent treatment given by that attending physician. Under such circumstances the co-defendant-radiologist may feel that the fault lay not with him or her, even if the radiologic interpretation was inaccurate, but rather with the attending physician who had at his disposal far more clinical and laboratory information than a single, albeit less than totally accurate, radiologic report. Shouldn't, may ask the radiologist, the negligence committed by another physician subsequent to a defendant radiologist's negligence absolve the radiologist of liability or, to state it another way, shouldn't an intervening act of negligence break any causal connection that may exist between the initial act of negligence and patient injury? The answer to this question has been given directly and succinctly in an Ohio Supreme Court decision (*Strother v. Hutchinson*, 423 N.E.2d 815 (Ohio 1981)):

> The fact that some other intervening act contributes to the original act to cause injury does not relieve the initial offender from liability.

The law thus recognizes that more than one co-defendant physician may contribute to an injury incurred by a patient, and in that situation the law will therefore hold each codefendant participating in the injured patient's medical care similarly liable.

REFERENCES

Berlin, L. 2001. "Defending the "Missed" Radiographic Diagnosis." *AJR* 176:317–322.

———. 2002. "Communicating Findings of Radiologic Examinations: Whither Goest the Radiologist's Duty?" *AJR* 178:809-815.

Flamm, M. B. 1998. "Medical Malpractice and the Physician Defendant." In *Legal Medicine,* 4th ed., ed. S.S. Sanbar, A. Gibofsky, M. H. Firestone, and T. R. Leblong. St. Louis: Mosby, 123-131.

7

What You Should Know about HIPAA

Stephen H. Johnson, J.D.

The receipt of a subpoena can be a disturbing event for a physician. If the subpoena requests medical records or other information about the health care provided to a patient, the physician will want to be sure to comply with the applicable provisions of federal and state law protecting health information.

The federal rules regarding confidentiality of medical records are generally found in the regulation implementing the privacy mandates of the federal Health Insurance Portability and Accountability Act of 1996, known as the "Privacy Rule" or "HIPAA." The latter designation will be used here.

The Maryland law regarding medical records confidentiality is found in the Medical Records Act, located in the Health-General Article of the Maryland Annotated Code.

The general rule, in both federal and state law, is that medical records (or "protected health information" as HIPAA designates the object of protection) must be kept confidential.[1] The Maryland requirement is found at the Medical Records Act at § 4-302(a) and states that a healthcare provider must

---

1. The HIPAA requirement of confidentiality is found at 42 CFR 164.502(a): "a covered entity may not use or disclose protected health information except as permitted or required by [this regulation]."

keep patient records confidential and only disclose it to the extent permitted either by the Medical Records Act itself or other law.[2]

The HIPAA regulation defines the protected object as "protected health information." To be protected health information, the information in question must relate to the healthcare and be identifiable with an individual. Identifiable is not the same as identified with. HIPAA lists a number of ways in which information could be identifiable, even without use of traditional identifies such as name, address, and social security number.

However, certain individually identifiable health information is explicitly excluded from the definition of protected health information.[3]

Maryland state law defines the protected object as a "medical record," which is "any oral, written, or other transmission in any form or medium of information that . . . is entered in the record of a patient or recipient; . . . identifies or can readily be associated with the identity of a patient or recipient; and . . . relates to the health care of the patient or recipient."[4] The following are explicitly included in the definition of "medical record":

- Documentation of disclosures of a medical record to any person who is not an employee, agent, or consultant of the health care provider;
- File or record maintained by a pharmacy of a prescription order for drugs, medicines, or devices that identifies or may be readily associated with the identity of a patient;
- Documentation of an examination of a patient regardless of who requested the examination or is making payment for the examination;
- File or record received from another healthcare provider that relates to the healthcare of a patient or recipient received from that healthcare provider; and identifies or

---

2. Maryland Annotated Code, Health-General Article, § 4-302(a).
3. Specifically, certain education records and employment records held by a covered entity in its role as employer. See 42 CFR § 164.501.
4. Maryland Annotated Code, Health-General Article, § 4-301(g).

can readily be associated with the identity of the patient or recipient.

HIPAA preempts "contrary" state law unless it is "more stringent" than the HIPAA provision covering the same issue. "Contrary" means that "a covered entity would find it impossible to comply with both the State and federal requirements; or the provision of State law stands as an obstacle to the accomplishment and execution of the full purposes and objectives [of HIPAA]."[5]

For a state law to be considered "more stringent" than HIPAA with respect to a disclosure of information to a third party, such as occurs with subpoenas, "the [state] law [must] prohibit or restricts a use or disclosure in circumstances under which such use or disclosure otherwise would be permitted under [HIPAA]."[6]

Physicians and other custodians of medical records need to be aware of both the state and federal restrictions on disclosure. Since HIPAA controls except where state law is more restrictive, the easiest approach may be to determine if a disclosure is permitted under state law—if is not, then there is no need to go on, and if it is, then determine if that disclosure is also permitted by HIPAA.

A good general rule to follow is to contact the patient or the patient's attorney whenever there is a subpoena or other demand for patient information. Notifying the patient will enable the patient to protect his or her rights and could assure the physician that there is no objection to the release.

As stated above, the general rule is that protected health information must be kept confidential and cannot be disclosed except by a specific exception. That being said, certain types of records receive special treatment under Maryland law, including the following:

Drug and alcohol treatment records: State law states that if any individual seeks counseling, treatment, or therapy,

---

5. 42 CFR 160.202.
6. *Id.*

for any form of drug or alcohol abuse, from a health professional licensed under the Health Occupations Article treating patients within the scope of the professional's practice, or hospital, or a person who is certified by the Administration for counseling or treating drug or alcohol abuse, the oral or written statements that the individual makes and the observations and conclusions that the health professional, hospital, or other person derives or the results of an examination to determine the existence of an illegal or prohibited drug in the body of an individual are not admissible in any proceeding against the individual, other than and subject to the federal regulations concerning the confidentiality of alcohol and drug abuse patient records.

The federal regulations referenced are those found at 42 CFR Pt. 2. These regulations protect "any information, whether recorded or not, relating to a patient received or acquired by a federally assisted alcohol or drug program" by providing strict limitations on how it may be disclosed. "Program" refers to "an individual or entity who holds itself out as providing, and provides, alcohol or drug abuse diagnosis, treatment or referral for treatment." "Federally assisted" includes programs with federal tax exemptions.

The Medical Records Act provides that records falling within the scope of the state and federal regulations applying to drug and alcohol abuse treatment are outside the scope of the Medical Records Act and disclosure under state law is entirely governed by those rules. HIPAA, however, will also apply, meaning the custodian of substance abuse treatment records must also consider whether the records are covered by HIPAA. Physicians who deal with substance abuse records should study the federal regulations carefully.

Mental health records: A medical record "developed primarily in connection with the provision of mental health services" is subject to special rules for disclosure under Maryland law. "Mental health services" means "health care rendered to a recipient primarily in connection with the diagnosis, evaluation, treatment, case management, or rehabilitation of any mental disorder."

Physicians who have received records falling within the above definition must comply with both the rules covering all medical records and the rules specifically governing mental health records.

PERSONAL NOTES

A mental healthcare provider may maintain "personal notes" regarding a recipient of mental health services. To be considered a personal note, the material in question must be the work product and personal property of a mental health provider and kept in the provider's sole possession. According to the statutory language, it "does not include information concerning the patient's diagnosis, treatment plan, symptoms, prognosis, or progress notes." It must be maintained separately from the recipient's medical records and loses its status as a personal note if it is disclosed to anyone other than the mental health provider's supervising health care provider, a consulting healthcare provider, or an attorney of the healthcare provider that maintains the confidentiality of the personal note, all of whom must maintain its confidentiality.

A personal note is protected from disclosure in many situations, but disclosure can be made or required if the patient has initiated an action for malpractice, an intentional tort, or professional negligence against the health care provider.

HIPAA has a similar concept of "psychotherapy notes," which are defined by the Privacy Rule as in the following manner:

1. notes recorded (in any medium) by a health care provider who is a mental health professional

2. documenting or analyzing the contents of conversation during a private counseling session or a group, joint, or family counseling session and that are separated from the rest of the individual's medical record. Psychotherapy notes excludes medication prescription and monitoring,

counseling session start and stop times, the modalities and frequencies of treatment furnished,

3. results of clinical tests, and any summary of the following items: diagnosis, functional status, the treatment plan, symptoms, prognosis, and progress to date.

PSYCHOLOGICAL TESTS

Maryland law provides that a provider may not disclose a portion of a medical record relating to a psychological test to any person, including a subject of the test, if the disclosure would compromise the objectivity or fairness of the test or the testing process.

Before the raw test data relating to a psychological test can be discovered or admitted as evidence in a criminal, civil, or administrative action, a court must determine that the expert witness for the party seeking the raw test data is qualified by the appropriate training, education, or experience to interpret the results of that portion of the raw test data relating to the psychological test.

RULES APPLICABLE TO SUBPOENAS FOR ANY MEDICAL RECORDS

The main question to be asked is who is seeking information and for what purpose are they seeking it? The following are useful classifications of potential requestors which parallel the Maryland statute:

Criminal investigation agencies
Health licensing boards
Civil case litigants

CRIMINAL INVESTIGATION AGENCIES

If the information is being sought for use in a criminal case by a grand jury, a prosecutor, or a law enforcement agency, then the information may be released if it is sought for the sole purpose of investigating or prosecuting criminal activity and the entity seeking the information proves that it "has in place procedures for ensuring the confidentiality of the records."[7]

HIPAA allows this under 42 CFR 164.512(f)(1)(ii)(b) under the following conditions:

1. The information is requested by means of a judicially issued subpoena, warrant, or order; or

2. Pursuant to an administrative request (i.e, one coming out of the investigating agency and not endorsed by a court) which is part of an investigative process authorized by law if

   a) "the information sought is relevant and material to a legitimate law enforcement inquiry."

   b) The request is specific and limited in scope to the extent reasonably practicable in light of the purpose for which the information is sought; and

   c) Deidentified information could not reasonably be used.

HEALTH LICENSING BOARDS

A health occupation licensing or disciplinary board may subpoena records without providing the certificate described above to the patient and the physician if the records are subpoenaed for the sole purpose of an investigation regarding licensure, certification, or discipline or improper performance of a health profession.[8]

This would be permissible under HIPAA, as HIPAA permits disclosures to a health oversight agency for oversight activities authorized by law and necessary for appropriate oversight of the healthcare system. The investigation should be aimed at the healthcare entity and not the patient to meet the requirements of this exception.

However, if the records requested are mental health records, the subpoena must name specific patients (for example, the li-

---

7. See *Shady Grove Psychiatric Group v. State*, 736 A.2d 1168 (Md. 1999) ("the subpoena in this case was issued pursuant to an investigation of criminal activity. H.G. § 4-306(b)(7) requires a health care provider to disclose medical records in such instances, provided that the State proves that it has 'written procedures to protect the confidentiality of the records'").
8. Maryland Annotated Code, Health-General 4-306(b)(2).

censing board may not obtain a sample of records without knowing in advance the names of patients).[9]

CIVIL CASE LITIGANTS

In general, a person or other entity subpoenaing a medical record in a civil case is required by Maryland law to include with the subpoena a certificate stating that a copy of the subpoena has been served on the person whose records are being sought or that service has been waived by a court for good cause.[10] For mental health records, the requirement is more specific, in that the patient must receive notification specifically stating that his or her records are being sought, identifying the provision of law justifying the request, and providing information about how the subpoena can be challenged.[11]

HIPAA imposes a somewhat stricter requirement for responding to subpoenas. A covered entity under HIPAA may release protected health information in response to a subpoena only in accordance with state law and only if the party seeking the information provides "satisfactory assurance."

The necessary assurance can be either

1. That the party requesting the information has given appropriate notice to the individual whose records are sought and that the time in which that individual could raise objections has elapsed with either no objections being raised or that all objections have been resolved and the subpoena demand is in accordance with that request;

2. That attempts have been made to secure a qualified protective order, which means a court order that prohibits the parties from using or disclosing the PHI for any purpose other than the litigation or proceeding for which the information was requested and which requires the destruction of the PHI at the end of the proceeding. The parties must either have agreed to a qualified protective order or the party

---

9. *Id.*, 4-307(k)(1)(vi).
10. *Id.*, 4-306(b)(6).
11. *Id.*, 4-307(k)(1)(v).

seeking the information must have requested one from the court or tribunal involved.

Some Maryland lawyers studying the interaction of HIPAA and state law have noted that condition # 1 cannot be fully satisfied in Maryland since there is no time requirement in which objections to a subpoena must be raised. This issue was brought to the attention of the Maryland General Assembly but no action was taken in the 2004 session. This means that to be certain that they are in absolute compliance with the requirements of HIPAA, medical record custodians must insist that condition # 2 be satisfied. Alternatively, HIPAA allows the physician or other provider still to release the information if they provide the necessary notice or seek a qualified protective order themselves, where the requestor of the information has not provided the above described assurances.

PURSUANT TO A STIPULATION BY THE PATIENT OR A PERSON-IN-INTEREST

If the individual or entity making the request for information establishes that it is doing so pursuant to a formal legal stipulation by the patient or a person in interest, the information may be provided in accordance with the terms of the stipulation. To comply with HIPAA, this stipulation should include the assurances described above.

IN ACCORDANCE WITH A DISCOVERY REQUEST PERMITTED BY LAW

If the patient is involved in litigation, the physician may receive a request for patient medical records as part of pretrial discovery proceedings. Again, the key to providing the requested records is whether or not "satisfactory assurance" has been provided. It may be prudent to advise the patient or the patient's attorney after receiving a request in which it is unclear whether the requirements have been met. This will help ensure that the request is compliant with the law and give the patient the opportunity to object if it is not.

IF THE REQUESTOR IS ANOTHER HEALTHCARE PROVIDER AND THE INFORMATION IN THE REQUESTED RECORD RELATES TO A CLAIM IN A CIVIL ACTION THE PATIENT HAS FILED

The Maryland Medical Records Act provides that a healthcare provider shall disclose "to a health care provider or the provider's insurer or legal counsel, all information in a medical record relating to a patient or recipient's health, health care or treatment which forms the basis for the issues of a claim in a civil action initiated by the patient, recipient, or person in interest."[12] This provision was a less formal alternative to the civil discovery process. However, a federal court decision in *Law v. Zuckerman*[13] held that this provision was preempted by HIPAA to the extent that it would allow releases of information beyond what is allowed under HIPAA, specifically the rules discussed above governing the release of information in judicial proceedings,[14] and therefore this provision should not be relied on to authorize a disclosure not falling within those rules, at least without further judicial action.

As a general rule, the physician's office should not release any records without a signed release from the patient unless the request is supported by a judicially issued subpoena, warrant, order or pursuant to an administrative request from a investigating agency which is part of an investigative process authorized by law. The information sought must be relevant, specific, and limited in scope to the extent reasonably practicable.

---

12. Health-General 14-306(b)(3).
13. Memorandum Opinion, Civil Action No. CBD-01-1429, 2/27/04.
14. 42 CFR 164.512(e).

8

Personality Characteristics of the Litigant Patient

Richard J. Nasca, M.D.

Malpractice insurance carriers stress prevention as a way to avoid malpractice suits. Physicians are taught to diagnose and treat in medical school. The personality of the patient is mostly ignored during the training process. A few residency programs spend time in discussing patient personality types and how these characteristics have an impact upon treatment results.

Most physicians accept patients at face value. Rarely do they question the patient regarding their relationship and interactions with previous physicians and other caregivers. Physicians want grateful patients who respond to their recommended treatment. Surgeons want to perform a successful operation without complications and return the patient to normal activity as soon as possible. The results in most elective procedures are directly related to choosing the "right patient," namely, picking a winner.

So, as physicians, what can we do to avoid placing ourselves in jeopardy with those patients who are potential litigants? Certain red flags are out there if we look for them. The following personality traits may signal potential problems in the physician-patient relationship.

61

HARD-TO-PLEASE PEOPLE

Since our earliest days, we have all had contact with people who were extremely hard to please. It seems that nothing can be done to satisfy them. These people have unrealistic expectations and expect miracles from their physicians. An unexpected complication, even though explained to the patient prior to treatment, can often fuel their anger and precipitate a malpractice action. A bad result will have similar consequences. These people seem to thrive on poor outcomes. Only the most predictable and necessary treatment modalities should be offered to these people. Consultation with other caregivers and referral to tertiary care facilities are often prudent. A multispecialty team approach to treatment is also beneficial in managing these patient.

THE DEMANDING PATIENT

Those patients who want concessions and additional physician time and who call frequently after hours can be characterized as overdemanding. These people want complete control over their medical care without regard for the physician's time and schedule. They want to be seen at their convenience. They often pressure the caregiver to provide medications and treatment which may be inappropriate and unnecessary. When these patients fail to get their way, they retaliate by failing to keep their appointments or leaving the practice. A poor treatment result may provide the stimulus for these patients to file a malpractice complaint. It is probably wise for the physician to discharge these patients early in the relationship rather than risk future potential liability.

SUBSTANCE ABUSE PATIENTS

Patients addicted to alcohol and narcotics are some of the most difficult people to treat. These patients are more likely to suffer traumatic injuries and other life-threatening illnesses because of their lifestyles. When these people present for treatment, they are often in the worst physical and mental condition to undergo invasive and reconstructive procedures. Complications are common and are expected. Failure to follow instructions often results in poor outcomes and further need for treatment. The subsequent treatment may be more complicated and require more risk then the initial treatment.

A case in point is that of a 55-year-old male who was admitted to a medical center with a comminuted fracture of the distal femur involving the knee joint as a result of a motor vehicle accident. The patient, who was under the influence of alcohol, was responsible for the accident. He was managed in skeletal traction since he was considered a poor operative candidate. He was not cooperative and removed his traction on several occasions. This resulted in loss of position of the reduced fractures. After much discussion, the patient was taken to the operating room for an open reduction and internal fixation. A vascular complication occurred, which was not recognized for several hours after the operation. This complication required a vein graft to the femoral artery and fasciotomies to save the extremity. Needless to say, a suit was filed against the surgeon for the complication, delay in diagnosis, and poor outcome. A modest settlement resulted. Treatment in this case was markedly compromised by the alcohol addiction and the uncooperative patient.

THE MALCONTENT PATIENT

Unhappy people make poor patients. These people have a poor self-image and blame others for their shortcomings. They find fault with most recommendations and are usually not compliant. They fail to keep appointments and to follow instructions regarding care of their medical problem. These patients usually experience more complications as well as social and mental problems during their illnesses. Some type of mental illness usually coexists in these patients. Communication with the caregiver may be difficult and their understanding of complex procedures may be lacking. All but the simplest treatment regimens should be utilized in managing these patients. Since many procedures require long periods of rehabilitation and recovery, these individuals can be expected to experience difficulties. These patients often target the doctor as the cause for their poor results following treatment.

PATIENTS CRITICAL OF OTHER CAREGIVERS

Not infrequently, patients seek you out for another opinion because of their dissatisfaction with a colleague. They will usually voice their displeasure with the previous physician almost in the same breath as they relate how many good things they have heard about you. As we all know, this is a cardinal red flag for future trouble. These patients will sing your praises one day and the next file a complaint against you for the slightest provocation.

A case in point: a young government worker is referred for a minor surgical procedure by her family physician. During the history-taking, she indicates her marked dissatisfaction with a fellow colleague who is known to be competent and caring. She expresses anger toward the previous surgeon. She is on medication for anxiety and depression. After a thorough evaluation and much discussion, she schedules the proposed procedure. She then cancels the procedure and states her fear of having an anesthetic because of a family history of problems during anesthesia. She then returns and, after much discussion, decides to reschedule the procedure. Just prior to the procedure, she cancels again. During this period she misses a great deal of time from work. The workers' compensation carrier requests information regarding her ability to return to work. She signs the release forms and the information is sent.

She subsequently returns to work after several months of absence. She passes out in the lobby of her office and is taken to a local hospital, where there are no significant findings or injuries found. She subsequently files a malpractice suit against the surgeon, who released the requested information to her carrier that she could return to work with proper accommodations. The workplace provided all of the requested accommodations to her. She claimed that because she was forced to return to work, this caused her subsequent "injury," further mental anguish, suffering, and inability to work.

The lesson to be learned here is that the surgeon should have provided only a second opinion and referred the patient back to the primary care physician to deal with the emotional and workers' compensation issues. Furthermore, the surgeon should have heeded the patient's warning when she expressed anger and hostility toward the previous surgeon.

PATIENTS WITH COMORBIDITIES

Patients who have one or more medical comorbidities must be carefully evaluated before recommending elective and reconstructive surgical procedures. When complications occur in these patients, they are often serious and life-threatening. Infection in diabetics is common with or without surgery. The infection rate for clean major surgery should be 1/2 to 1% for most procedures. The infection rate for diabetics undergoing major clean surgery may run 7 to 8% in spite of prophylactic antibiotics.

Patients with hypertension, even though controlled, present an increased risk of untoward cardiovascular events during anesthesia and surgery. Patients on anticoagulants can present with treacherous, life-threatening coagulopathies and embolization after surgery, often requiring heroic measures to manage successfully.

For example, a 50-year-old poorly controlled diabetic presented with unremitting back and leg pain due to degenerative spondylolisthesis at L4-L5. Various types of medication provided no relief. She noted little improvement after several months of physical therapy. Multiple epidural injections with corticosteroids provided only temporary relief. Bracing and bed rest were beneficial but prevented the patient from full employment. After much discussion, including warning her of the high probability of infection, the patient requested decompression and fusion with instrumentation. The procedure was done without difficulty. Postoperatively the patient's incision healed without difficulty. At three and one half weeks postop she developed increasing pain. Office evaluation was quite unremarkable, except for a superficial scab on her incision under which a scant amount of pus was found and sent for culture. The incision was healed and was not tender, inflamed, or indurated. She was given a prescription for Keflex, which she failed to have filled. Forty-eight hours later, the culture report indicated a staph aureus sensitive to all antibiotics. The patient was readmitted to the hospital a few hours after the surgeon received the culture report. She was alert and her neurological examination was normal. However, the midline incision appeared to be breaking down, and there was drainage. Her white count was elevated, as was the sedimentation rate. The patient could not tolerate a MRI, but a CAT scan was interpreted by the radiologist and by two surgeons as showing no evidence of an abscess. She was placed on triple antibiotic therapy after being seen by the infectious disease consultant. This consultant and the primary care physician did not indicate any urgency for surgery at the time of readmission. The day after admission the patient developed seizures and profound hypotension due to septicemia. She died 60 hours after admission. An autopsy revealed extensive infection, extending from the right iliac bone graft donor site down to the laminectomy and around the instrumentation at L4-L5. Septic emboli were found in the cerebral menengies.

A wrongful death suit was filed. The plaintiff's expert opined that prompt surgery would have saved the patient's life. The defense experts indicated that there was no urgency for surgery until there was definite evidence of an abscess. They further indicated a reluctance to operate on the patient without a firm diagnosis and during her premorbid condition shortly after admission. The case was settled prior to trial for $700,000.

The lesson to be learned from this case is that a commonly done procedure with low morbidity becomes very risky in a patient with poorly controlled diabetes. When the infection occurred is debatable but appeared to be of late onset and probably was not amenable to surgical intervention.

COMMUNICATION PROBLEMS

Patients who are difficult to communicate with are difficult to treat. Simple instructions are often ignored or forgotten. Understanding the nuances of various treatment options presents a major stumbling block. The assistance of a third party is often helpful. A spouse or close relative can be invaluable in dealing with these patients. Simple written information about the proposed treatment, given to the patient and his or her family, is beneficial. Many patients are in a high state of anxiety during their office visit. They probably retain very little of what is said to them.

Trying to explain a complicated procedure and have them understand it may be next to impossible without assistance from a third
party. It is wise to document in detail what is discussed with the
patient and his or her family prior to embarking on any procedure.
It has been documented in several studies that very little of what
is said during a preoperative conference is retained by even the
most astute patient. It is helpful to use teaching aids, such as anatomical models, when discussing complex surgical procedures.

A case in point is that of a 52-year-old used-car salesman
who presented with intermittent severe back and leg pain. He had
undergone two previous laminectomies for herniated discs. His
family physician had treated him with narcotics, muscle relaxants,
and antiinflammatories without much improvement. He was hospitalized on several occasions and placed in traction and given
physical therapy. He was referred for surgery by his family physician. His preoperative studies indicated a recurrent herniated
disc at L4-L5, arthritic facet joints and degenerative disc disease
at both L4-L5 and L5-S1. The patient was a heavy smoker and
agreed to stop smoking.

The patient was scheduled for a decompression at L4-L5 as
well as a fusion with instrumentation to be done at L4, L5, and S1.
The patient was told that smoking inhibited surgical fusion. He
was also told that he would need a brace following surgery and
that this would have to be worn until the fusion was solidified.
The details of the surgical procedure were discussed with the patient, as well as the potential complications, including the possibility that the fusion might not heal and additional surgery might
be required to augment the fusion. The patient underwent the procedure without difficulty. However, he was reluctant to get out of
bed following surgery. Prior to being discharged from the hospital, he did walk with his brace on. When he returned home, he
commenced smoking and, against the surgeon's recommendations, did not get out of bed for a period of about six weeks. During his follow-up visits he was told to stop smoking and was
instructed to wear his brace. He indicated that he was doing well
and did not need the brace. He promised to stop smoking. At
about six months following surgery, he underwent a disability

evaluation. He was told by the examining disability doctor that his surgery had not been done properly. This caused the patient to become angry. He called the surgeon's office and demanded his records and X-rays.

As predicted, he failed to return to the surgeon. At eight months after his first surgery, he underwent another surgery, at which time the fusion was augmented with bone graft and the instrumentation was removed. He was relieved of his back and leg pain but did not return to work. He filed a malpractice case against the first surgeon, claiming that the improper installation of the instrumentation had caused his delayed fusion. During trial, the patient denied ever been told to stop smoking or to wear his brace. The medical records indicated that on several occasions he was told to stop smoking and to wear his brace. The jury found in favor of the surgeon after a three-day trial. Good record-keeping and documentation of the patient-doctor discussions were key points in defense of the physician in this case.

REDUCED COMFORT LEVEL

There are some patients in whom the physician has a reduced comfort level. These patients are usually cynical and may be distrustful. They are not open or friendly. They rarely express positive thoughts. Occasionally they will try to tape-record your consultation or have their spouse take copious notes during your consultation. Some of these patients are doctor-shoppers. These people keep you guessing as to their motives and intentions. It is probably best to have a frank discussion with them about your comfort level with them before you undertake any significant course of treatment.

If they do not come around and express trust and confidence in you, it is best to discharge them from your care. It is prudent to provide them with the names of other physicians and surgeons who might offer similar services prior to terminating your professional relationship with them.

CAVEATS

The physician and surgeon should pay close attention to the patient's personality characteristics and factor them into the decision-making process when complex treatment is required. One should avoid making exceptions and bending the rules in any doctor-patient relationship. These courtesies can often comeback a haunt the caregiver. People who are chance-takers frequently sustain injuries due to their own neglect. This type of personality is well known to orthopedic and trauma surgeons. These patients may try to profit from their injuries. Establishing a meaningful doctor-patient relationship at midnight in an emergency room with a patient with multiple injuries under the influence of drugs and alcohol is next to impossible. In most cases we proceed with treatment and the patient gets better and goes on his way. However, we are all too familiar with the patient who retains a lawyer to help with dealing with his or her medical bills and subsequently files suit against everyone involved in his or her care. Although we all like to avoid these patients, they are a reality of our professional existence. Legislation could be mandated to deal with this problem on a national level.

SUMMARY

During the day-to-day contacts with patients in the controlled setting of the office, it is wise to have an established protocol to deal with hard-to-please people, patients who criticize other physicians, and patients who expect too much from their caregiver. It is wise to discharge those people with whom you cannot establish a good comfort level and transfer those patients with comorbidities that present challenges that are above the capabilities of your practice environment. The patient's personality must be evaluated and factored into the treatment decision-making process. Many cases are filed because of a bad result with no fault, except the litigant's belief that someone is always to blame. Hopefully, the physician will reduce his or her liability by being more sensitive to the patient's personality characteristics. Identifying and dealing with the potential litigant patient in an effective manner may be helpful in preventing malpractice litigation.

SUGGESTED READINGS

Bovberg, R., and K. Petronis. 1994. "The Relationship between Physicians' Malpractice Claims History and Later Claims: Does the Past Predict the Future?" *JAMA* 272:1421–1426.

Hickson, G. B., C. F. Federspiel, J. W. Pichert, C. S. Miller, J. Gauld-Jaeger, and P. Bost. 2002. "Patient Complaints and Malpractice Risks." *JAMA* 287:2951–2957.

Levinson, W., D. L. Roter, J. P. Mullooly, V. T. Dull, and R. M. Frankel. 1997. "Physician-Patient Communication: The Relationship with Malpractice Claims among Primary Care Physicians and Surgeons." *JAMA* 277:553–559.

Sloan, F., E. M. Mergenhagen, and B. Burfield. 1989. "Medical Malpractice Experience of Physicians: Predictable or Haphazard?" *JAMA* 262:3291-3297.

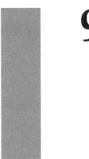

9

How to Structure Your Office to Avoid Malpractice

Deborah N. Meyer, B.S.N., J.D.

INTRODUCTION

The attitude of patients and their view of the healthcare delivery system has evolved over the last century, from a reverential view of the long-suffering family physician to an expectation that the system deliver quality services in an efficient, timely, and no-nonsense manner. Today's patients view themselves as a consumer of the healthcare system and evaluate care provided by your practice with an intelligent, savvy eye, utilizing the same criteria they would employ evaluating any service they purchase. Patients are active participants in their healthcare decision-making and demand a high-quality product, prompt response to their questions, and physician accountability.

The increase in patient participation can often have a positive influence on patient outcomes. However, the rapid pace, growing regulatory demands, and escalating issue of medical malpractice leave the physician somewhat bewildered about how to best manage his practice, provide high-quality care, and avoid problems with the legal system. The specter of the plaintiff's malpractice attorney and the slam of the gavel inside a courtroom are enough to send shivers down the spine of most physicians. The purpose of this chapter is to provide guidance to the physician on the day-to-day operation of a medical practice in a manner which will decrease the physician's risk of becoming the target of the plaintiff's attorney.

STAFFING

Maintaining a well-trained, competent staff is essential to your ability to provide the highest possible level of care. Your staff is frequently the first point of contact with your patients, and patients consider the entire office visit from the moment they make an appointment until concluding the billing transaction when evaluating their experience with the healthcare services your practice provides. You should carefully select your staff based upon their communication skills as well as their technical qualifications.

The physician is responsible for the care his staff provides to his patients. When hiring new employees, check their references and call their state licensing agency to see if the individual has been subject to disciplinary action or restrictions on his or her ability to practice. Disciplinary actions are frequently a result of providing care below the minimum acceptable standard of care. Under the doctrine of *respondeat superior,* a master is responsible for the actions of his servant. The physician directs the work of his or her staff and is vicariously liable for torts committed by his or her employees within the scope of their employment.[1] Thus, it is essential that your staff maintain the highest level of professionalism and competency. It is important to determine that a prospective employee has not been disqualified from participating in Medicare and Medicaid. If your practice employs a physician, physician extender, or nurse excluded from participation, you may not bill for the services they provide. The Office of Inspector General maintains a website which includes the names of individuals which have been excluded from participation. Exclusion

---

1.   *Gammons v. North Carolina Dep't of Human Resources*, 344 N.C. 51 (N.C., 1996).

from Medicare and Medicaid often results from fraud and abuse or delivery of substandard care.

When working closely with staff, a physician often develops a close rapport with staff members. While this is healthy and can have an overall positive impact on patient outcomes, it is important to maintain an appropriate professional relationship with staff members. Develop and implement an employee handbook to inform your staff of your expectations while giving them a guide to what they can expect from the practice. Establish disciplinary guidelines and stress the importance of their patient interactions in your overall evaluation of their job performance.

Use extreme caution in providing medical care to your staff. In the easy, familiar relationship that often develops between a physician and his staff, it is easy for the physician to provide undocumented and often substandard care. Avoid the casual distribution of prescriptions and sample drugs for your nurse's or secretary's cold or coughs. If you are going to treat your staff, ask them to make an appointment, open a chart, and document the care you provide in the same manner you would for any patient.

Also be aware that once you treat a member of your staff, even providing the casual prescription, you have formed a physician-patient relationship. Consequently, you are subject to the same standards to which you will be held for any patient, including sexual misconduct. This has created a real quagmire for many physicians, who suddenly find themselves facing a malpractice claim which is often excluded from their policy coverage because of the "intentional" nature of a sexual misconduct malpractice claim.[2] A physician will also be forced to defend himself or herself in front of the state licensing agency for sexual misconduct with a patient, even when the charge is made by a disgruntled employee and is totally without merit.[3]

---

2. For an additional, nominal amount some malpractice insurance companies provide additional coverage for intentional torts.

3. Most state licensing agencies publish advisory opinions or position statements describing its position on a number of issues. These advisory opinions contain a wealth of information on how to avoid potentially troublesome situations.

PATIENT INTERACTION

COMMUNICATION

There is an undeniable link between patient satisfaction and the communication style of physicians. Patients rate a higher level of overall satisfaction and quality of care when the physician uses a person-focused approach to communicating with patients (Focke et al. 2002). Active listening is critical, whether during an office visit or when communicating by telephone. I recently attended the deposition of a plaintiff bringing a malpractice claim against a nursing home. She testified that she thought about suing the doctor too, but decided against it because the doctor "always listened and seemed to care about my family and problems." You are your own best advocate when communicating with your patients.

AVAILABILITY

The physician is responsible for providing on-call coverage for his practice, and most state medical boards provide guidelines on patient coverage. If your practice does not provide after hours or weekend coverage, you should notify patients in writing at the first office visit that such coverage is not available and instruct them to use either urgent care or emergency room services for matters arising after your office hours and on weekends.

TELEPHONE CALLS

Document your communications with patients after hours and on weekends. It is easy to forget the 3:00 a.m. call. Without documentation there is no way to verify the care or instructions you provided over the telephone. The use of handwritten notes or a Dictaphone to document the call for later transfer to the medical record is essential. You do not want to be caught in a situation in which a patient is making allegations about your recommendations and you have no way of verifying the conversation.

Follow up on calls that you take during the evenings and on weekends. Ask your office nurse to follow up on the patient's condition and to schedule new appointments where appropriate with the patients you speak with after hours. Be sure to document the patient's response to those inquiries and your recommendations.

ONLINE PRACTICE

Today's technology makes it possible to respond quickly to patients' concerns by e-mail. Surveys indicate that the majority of patients want to consult their physician via e-mail, particularly when they request information and there is no urgent health issue involved (Carns 2002). While some malpractice defense lawyers object to the use of "e-visits," if you develop and implement an appropriate policy for the use of e-mail, its use can enhance your patient's experience with the practice.[4] Furthermore, there is no reason to assume that there will be greater liability for e-mail than for telephone calls or faxes to your patients. So long as you take the necessary precautions, e-mails provide an excellent source of documentation, and e-mails to and from patients should be saved and become part of the permanent medical record.

Develop a policy for the use of e-mail. Your policy should consider a number of factors beginning with the security of your transmissions. If you are using e-mail to communicate with your patients, you must use encryption to prevent a breach of security of your communication. There are multiple encryption programs which can be downloaded from the Web, as well as commercial programs which provide an encrypted, password-protected message.[5]

The physician is expected to make an informed judgment in treating patients and should consider the scope of the questions and the advice he is willing to address via e-mail. Limit the communications to routine types of information and avoid addressing urgent or new concerns. Avoid communicating abnormal laboratory or test results over e-mail. Such communication should oc-

---

4.   The Federation of State Medical Boards and eRisk Working Group for Healthcare published guidelines for the use of email consultations in 2001. They can be accessed at www.medem.com/corporate/corporate-erisk.cfm.

5.   A description of the various encryption programs and providers can be found in Terry (2001).

cur in an environment in which the patient can engage in a meaningful exchange of questions and answers. While e-mail can be an excellent vehicle for making appointments, renewing long-standing prescriptions, or handling insurance and billing matters, it can never replace a physical examination and eye-to-eye contact with the patient.

Provide your patients with a copy of the practice's e-mail policy and ask them to sign a verification that they have been provided a copy and consent to the use of e-mail in office communication. Allow them to limit the scope of information they wish to have conveyed by e-mail. Make certain that your policy reserves the right to discontinue e-mail communication with patients who abuse the system or with whom you have communication difficulties.

Final words of caution: before you click "send," consider what you have written. Individuals communicate in a multitude of ways. When you have an individual encounter with a patient, both of you enhance communication with the inflection or tone of your voice and with facial expression and body language, all of which are as critical to an understanding of the interaction as the spoken words. When communicating by e-mail, you lose the context of the words and misunderstanding can arise. Never shoot off an e-mail when you are upset or frustrated with a patient. Ironically, individuals will put things into e-mails which they would never consider saying. The lack of formality in e-mails as opposed to letters also increases the tendency to be flippant. Once you transmit the message, the words cannot be taken back, and an inflammatory e-mail written in the heat of the moment can come back to haunt you. It is common for a malpractice attorney to request all the e-mails saved on your back-up tapes or hard drives in order to look for damaging communications. Read your e-mails carefully. If in doubt about the appropriateness of the message, consider revising the contents or not sending them.

PHYSICAL EXAMINATION

Physicians may view the actual physical examination of their patient as a routine part of their workday. However, to many patients it is a physically awkward if not actually painful ordeal. Our societal ideals of human dignity dictate a certain level of individual control. It is often an assault on the patient's sense of dignity and control to be placed in a cold examination room, made to disrobe, and contorted into unnatural positions. Anything you can do to protect patient dignity and prevent misunderstanding about the care you are providing is invaluable to the patient experience. Your staff should routinely explain to patients when you are running behind in your schedule and delay asking the patient to disrobe until shortly before you will see the patient.

Privacy is a pivotal concern to most patients.[6] Make certain your exam rooms provide an adequate level of privacy. It is extremely awkward when the patient can hear an encounter between you and another patient in the examination room next door. Provide appropriate drapes for the patient and never require the patient to disrobe in front of the staff or the physician. Explain to the patient the purpose of the examination and what the physician is doing at each stage of the examination. Knowledge is a powerful tool. If the patient understands why a certain procedure or part of the examination is necessary, it decreases embarrassment and allows the patient to maintain a sense of dignity and control.

A physician is responsible for controlling the emotional climate of the examination room. It is his responsibility to keep the interaction in the examination room on a professional level while maintaining appropriate communication with his patient. The physician should be alert to inappropriate patient behavior, control the situation and not allow an examination to escalate into a situation in which the physician can be charged with inappropriate conduct toward the patient.

The physician should never examine a patient without an attendant present, regardless of the sex of the patient. This is critical to provide both a sense of privacy and to have a third party who can assist in dissipating any uneasiness in the course of the examination.

---

6.   The HIPAA privacy regulations are addressed elsewhere in this book.

Some physicians, in an effort to make it more convenient or less costly for their patient, will agree to meet a patient at the office after hours or on weekends. This is a mistake, unless you have staff on call to accompany you when you see the patient. Without an attendant, you are at risk for charges of misconduct, in which it is only your word against that of the patient. Granted, the majority of your patients will not make a claim or charge of misconduct. However, it only takes one charge before the physician is facing claims which can jeopardize his or her practice and personal life.

Be cautious about conversations held just outside the door to the examination room. One patient recently complained about the protracted argument between two physicians outside the door to her examination room. They could not agree over a diagnosis or the course of treatment indicated for her. She left the office confused, agitated, and angry at what she viewed as "incompetent physicians." There are legitimate differences related to differential diagnosis and the best course of treatment for a patient. However, legitimate, professional debate and decision-making should be made well outside of the hearing range of patients.[7]

SEXUAL EXPLOITATION

It is the responsibility of the physician to provide patients with a safe, comfortable environment, free from intimidation or coercion. The unique relationship between a physician and his or her patient is such that a fiduciary duty arises which requires the physician to consider foremost the need of the patient to develop a therapeutic relationship based upon mutual trust. The detailed physical examination, together with providing a history of often personal and intimate details of one's life, can make a patient feel anxious and vulnerable (Puglise 1999/2000). As a physician you have a fiduciary duty to act in good faith while considering the best interests and well-being of your patient (Hall 2001). The inequitable feeling of vulnerability and dependence upon the

---

7.   Any decision-making is subject to informed consent of the patient, which is addressed elsewhere in the chapter.

physician makes it imperative that physicians avoid any sexual impropriety and some commentators believe the inequity in relationships makes it doubtful that a patient can truly provide an informed consent to the relationship (Hall 2001). Physicians have recognized the potential for exploitation since the time of the Hippocratic Oath, which states, "Whatever houses I may visit, I will come for the benefit of the sick, remaining free of all intentional injustice, of all mischief, and, in particular, sexual relations with both female and male persons, be they free or slaves" (Puglise 1999/2000).

When considering the nature of the relationship between patient and physician, the American Medical Association has determined that it is unethical to initiate or be involved in a sexual relationship with a patient, regardless of whether such relationship is consensual ("Sexual Misconduct" 1991), and in most states even a consensual relationship is grounds for suspension or termination of licenses (Johnson 1993). The AMA recommends that at a minimum, the physician-patient relationship should be terminated prior to initiating a sexual relationship with the patient (Johnson 1993).

Not only does a sexual relationship with a patient jeopardize the physician's license, under some circumstances it can expose him or her to potential malpractice claims. Some courts have taken a broader view than the AMA, and consensual sexual contact between the patient and physician historically has not given rise to a medical malpractice action unless the physician is a psychiatrist mishandling the "transference phenomenon"[8] or a physician's sexual contact is purporting to be part of the treatment regime.[9] The courts based their opinions on the premise that any sexual act or conduct by the physician is not a form of rendering a professional service for which liability will attach,[10] and only

---

8. For a discussion of transference see Puglise (1999/2000).

9. *Korper v. Weinstein*, 57 Mass. App. Ct. 433, 435 (Mass. App., 2003).

10. *South Carolina Med. Malpractice Liab. Ins. Joint Underwriting Ass'n v. Ferry*, 354 S.E.2d 378, 380 (1987), quoting *Marx v. Hartford Accident & Indem. Co.*, 157 N.W.2d 870, 872 (1968).

when the conduct is in the guise of "therapeutic" intervention will the courts impose liability.[11]

Other courts have broadened the concept of rendering professional services to include situations in which a non-mental health physician was providing "counseling" services to the patient. The courts looking at the fiduciary relationship, the trust and confidence the patient places in the physician, and the personal nature of the counseling and have held that when the physician is treating the patient's psychological needs, a claim for professional malpractice can arise from the consensual sexual relationship between the patient and the physician.[12]

Regardless of how the courts in your state handle sexual relationships with patients, it is important to establish boundaries with your patients. Do not accept costly gifts from your patients. Avoid meeting patients after hours. Tactfully change the subject when they begin to ask personal questions about your life, shifting the focus back to them and their healthcare issues. The parameters of the relationship should remain focused on the patient's health and well-being.

PRESCRIPTIONS

Only in rare circumstances should a physician write prescriptions for a patient he has not examined. Physicians are charged with prescribing drugs based upon their training and experience and using their best medical judgment. While a new history and physical examination might not be necessary for established patients, prescribing for patients with whom you have not established a relationship can place you in an awkward position.

Develop a policy outlining the circumstances under which you will renew a prescription or prescribe a new medication without an office visit. Do not prescribe medication in the absence of a documented physician-patient relationship. If a new patient has been on long-term medication, it may be reasonable to write the prescription for enough medication to last a day or two while

---

11. *Korper, supra,* note 9.
12. *McCracken, et al. v. Walls-Kaufman,* 717 A.2d 346, 352 (D.C. App. 1998); *Hoopes v. Hammargren,* 102 Nev. 425, 431–432, 725 P.2d 238 (1986).

scheduling an office visit, but this should occur only rarely. When prescribing for established patients over the telephone, document the basis of your decision in the same manner you would document an office visit, noting the patient's objective concerns, any relevant information about the patient's history, and your assessment.

Check with your state medical board for its guidelines on the writing of prescriptions, and become familiar with the state and federal regulations related to the use of controlled substances. Do not use presigned prescription pads. When writing prescriptions, print legibly using ink or typed or electronically printed prescription pads. Do not put multiple prescriptions on the same prescription form. You will find that these simple precautions can prevent you from getting into difficulty with your patients or with state and federal regulatory agencies.

BILLING

There are few topics that can raise ire more than that of an individual's finances. Enter any public forum and you will eventually hear the conversation turn to the rising cost of healthcare. Physicians are feeling the pinch as well, and the costs associated with running a medical practice are escalating. The convergence of individual concerns and the physicians' need to remain fiscally responsible creates a highly charged situation which can quickly lead to dissension between the physician and patient. Such dissension can leave you with a disgruntled patient, unhappy with his care and prone to seeking the advice of a plaintiff's attorney.

Your billing person is also essential to the maintenance of a good working relationship between your practice and your patients. Not only should your billing clerk be well versed in all insurance matters, it is critical that they have communication skills which foster an atmosphere of cooperation between the practice, the patient, and third-party payers. If your billing person develops an open line of communication with your patients, they will be more likely to pay your fees promptly and cheerfully. To avoid problems with billing, develop a billing policy and procedure and provide a copy to your patient at the time of the first office visit.

The policy should explain your position on copays, filing for insurance, payment responsibilities, and the consequences of the patient's failure to be financially responsible. Provide a mechanism for patients to make inquires about the cost of their care, without fear of recrimination.

CONCLUSION

Involvement in medical malpractice litigation is costly, both financially and in terms of the time and energy diverted from your practice and patients. Structure your office in such a way as to avoid the upheaval. The information provided above is only a beginning point. Correct problems as they arise, and initiate frequent reviews of your office policies and procedures.

REFERENCES

Carns, A. 2002. "Doctors Advised on E-Mail Visits." *The Wall Street Journal*.

Focke, S. A., W. L. Miller, and B. Crabtree. 2002. "Relationship between Physician Practice Style, Patient Satisfaction, and Attributes of Primary care." *Journal of Family Practice* (October).

Hall, K. H. 2001. "Sexualization of the Doctor-Patient Relationship: Is It Ever Ethically Permissible?" *Family Practice* 18:511–515.

Johnson, S. H. 1993. "Judicial Review of Disciplinary Action for Sexual Misconduct in the Practice of Medicine." *JAMA* 270:1596–1600.

Puglise, S. M. 1999/2000. "'Calling Dr. Love': The Physician-Patient Sexual Relationship as Grounds for Medical Malpractice—Society Pays while the Doctor and Patient Play." *J. L. & Health* 321.

"Sexual Misconduct in the Practice of Medicine." 1991. *JAMA* 266:2741–2745.

Terry, K. 2001. "E-Mail Patients? Don't Be Nervous. Do Be Careful." *Medical Economics* (3 September)

10

Avoiding Complications and Managing Risk

David E. Attarian, M.D., F.A.C.S.

The current social, medicolegal, and economic climate creates a stressful environment for every practicing physician and surgeon. Each and every doctor can now expect at least one medical malpractice lawsuit during a 20- to 30-year career. So how do you cope and continue to practice when any given patient encounter can result in a malpractice claim with potentially devastating professional and financial consequences?

This specific question was posed to the members of the Piedmont Orthopaedic Society (graduates of the Duke University Division of Orthopaedic Surgery training programs). Questionnaires were mailed requesting information on type of practice, years in practice, techniques developed for avoiding complications, and managing malpractice risk. Approximately 100 responses were received. The average time in practice was 22 years per surgeon; two-thirds of the respondents were in private practice and half described themselves as subspecialists. This compiled information represents over 2000 years of experience, and it summarizes practical approaches to achieving the standard of care, avoiding complications, maintaining patient safety, and managing the risk of medical malpractice claims.

AVOIDING COMPLICATIONS

Clearly, complications and poor outcomes are a primary source of patient dissatisfaction that may result in a claim of malpractice. If these problems can be avoided, the chance of a lawsuit becomes more remote. The most common method garnered from the survey responses for avoiding complications was *to practice evidence-based medicine.* Of the respondents, 88% recommended use of specific protocols documented in the scientific literature, such as prophylactic antibiotics before surgery to decrease infections and anticoagulants for prevention of deep venous thrombosis/pulmonary embolus after surgery. Two-thirds of the respondents believed that *careful preoperative planning and preparation* were another way to obtain good outcomes and avoid complications. Two-thirds also suggested that *following a routine in the operating room, following clinical pathways in the outpatient/inpatient settings, or using preprinted orders* helped to reduce errors. Half the group emphasized *compulsiveness and attention to detail* in their management of patients; they recommended that you should never cut corners or act in haste in managing a patient. Twenty-five percent described a *protocol to avoid wrong-site surgery* (which is considered inexcusable and indefensible). Interestingly, about a third recommended *referring complex or difficult cases away from their practices,* and 20% advised *obtaining consultations* whenever the patient had problems beyond their capability or outside of their specialty. Twenty-three percent suggested *avoiding fatigue and stress.* They emphasized the need for a physician to maintain a healthy lifestyle for his or her own benefit as well as their patient's, fully realizing that a tired or impaired physician will not provide optimal patient care. Finally, 13% *acknowledged their limitations* through practice audits, and only performed procedures they did well.

MANAGING RISKS

But the reality of the practice of medicine is that even if you do everything humanly possible, some of your patients will nonetheless suffer complications or poor outcomes. And others will either be unhappy with your patient care, or just not like you, your colleagues, or support staff. Therefore, minimizing the risk of a medical malpractice lawsuit in each of these situations is critical. The most common response of the Piedmont Orthopaedic Society survey for managing or limiting risk was the *need for developing and maintaining honest, ethical, and caring interpersonal relationships with patients;* 75% of respondents believed that patients rarely sue physicians they like and respect even when the outcomes are poor and/or the standard of care is in question. Thus, excellent communication skills by a physician and his/her colleagues and support staff are crucial. Sixty-eight percent stressed the importance of *a detailed, legible, and permanent medical record for each and every patient encounter;* this also included documentation of the informed consent process. The complete, unaltered medical record was described as the best (factual) "expert witness" in the event of a medical malpractice claim.

OTHER SPECIFIC RECOMMENDATIONS FOR REDUCING RISK

1. *Acknowledging and rapidly addressing complications*—denial can be your worst enemy, so don't neglect a complication thinking it will go away or take care of itself;

2. *Maintaining continuity of care by communicating sufficiently with physicians providing practice coverage*—sign out your practice in detail when others are covering in your absence. Failure to maintain appropriate continuity of care is indefensible in a court of law;

3. *Emphasizing conservative over surgical care whenever possible*—if conservative care will provide an equivalent or superior result for a patient, avoid the temptation of generating more revenue by performing surgery;

4. *Disengaging from problem patients when ethical*—if a patient is a behavior problem or repeatedly fails to follow your medical advice, remove them from your practice (see chapter on patient dismissal);

5. *Avoiding association with substandard physicians*—if you recognize another physician as substandard or impaired, avoid direct professional contact or association. On the other hand,

social, legal, and ethical mandates may require that you report such a physician to appropriate credentialing bodies or State Licensure Boards for peer review;

6. *Avoiding criticism of colleagues in writing or speech*—this behavior is essentially inviting a lawsuit from a patient. If you have a disagreement with a colleague or peer, resolve it in a private conversation;

7. *Relocating a practice to a more favorable medicolegal environment*—the demographics of medical malpractice lawsuits are well known and easily obtained. Choosing to practice in a low-risk area is a technique utilized by many physicians and surgeons to maintain their professional viability;

8. *Supporting tort reform at the state and federal levels*—successful tort reform, especially in the form of caps on non-economic damages (such as in California) has proven to diminish frivolous lawsuits and lower medical malpractice insurance premiums;

9. *Carrying medical malpractice insurance*—when available and affordable, this insurance is mandatory in the event of a medical malpractice lawsuit. Without it, there are techniques for "going bare," but this approach may increase your risk of professional and personal financial ruin; and even

10. *Retiring*—many physicians who can afford to retire are doing so earlier than planned in an effort to avoid the hassles and risks of continued practice altogether.

While following the recommendations listed above provides no guarantee that you won't be sued for medical malpractice, the Piedmont Orthopaedic Society survey confirms that experienced, well-trained orthopaedic surgeons have developed a variety of mechanisms to insure the highest-quality healthcare for their patients through medical knowledge and preparation, implementation of evidence-based medical practices, adherence to patient safety initiatives, and, so far as possible, avoidance of complications and/or poor outcomes. Furthermore, they aggressively pursue risk management beyond patient care, given the reality of their profession and its sometimes overwhelming demands. In particular, these physicians are cultivating their communication skills and interpersonal relationships with patients, attending to self-care, creating and following protocols, and maintaining a detailed medical record for protection in the event of a medical malpractice claim. Regrettably, some physicians have found the current situation to be unacceptably risky. They are limiting their practices, relocating, or even retiring to reduce or eliminate the chance of being sued for medical malpractice.

11

Anatomy of a Lawsuit

Robert M. Clay, A.B., J.D.

FIRST CONTACT

A physician's first contact with possible litigation generally takes one of three forms: a request for a copy of the medical record from the patient or a lawyer; receipt of a demand letter from a lawyer; or a request for a meeting with the patient or the patient's family and possibly with their attorney. It is important that you know how to respond.

It is not generally an unusual event for a patient to request a copy of the medical record. However, if the patient had a bad result from the medical care provided, then it would behoove you to be suspicious. You must nevertheless provide a copy of the medical record if you are presented with an appropriate authorization. Often, patients will not know what form of authorization is appropriate. Authorization must conform with the specific requirements set out in the HIPAA form. A sample copy is attached at the end of the chapter. If the patient is deceased or incompetent and the request comes from a family member, then it will be necessary that an appropriate authorization be executed by a person authorized to do so either as administrator or executor of the estate, or the guardian of an incompetent or a person with a power of attorney for the incompetent. HIPAA has a requirement that the information to be released be described. Most release forms will specify the entire record, which means everything contained in the doctor's file jacket. If there are parts that are not readily copied, then the patient must be advised that those parts exist but were not copied.

In the event the request comes from an attorney, it also must be accompanied by an appropriate authorization form signed by the patient, a duly appointed representative of the estate, a person with power of attorney (a copy of which must be attached), or a guardian. In each instance, a copy of the document giving that party the authority to request the records should be furnished to you.

If the request for records comes in a case that had a bad result, or if it comes from a lawyer, it is a good idea to notify your insurance carrier and allow them to arrange for you to be advised. This is especially true if the request is for a meeting with family members, the patient, or a lawyer in a case with a bad result. You should be advised by a lawyer representing you before consenting to such a meeting. If a lawyer is going to be there representing the patient's interest, you will need an attorney there to represent your interest. You must not go unprotected and unprepared into such a meeting.

If you receive a demand letter, it is urgent that you send it to your insurance carrier immediately and get them involved in a response. A demand letter is any letter from a lawyer for a patient in which you are notified that a possible claim may be made. You must not contact the lawyer or the patient or family yourself.

If you receive a subpoena to produce medical records, it will be important to determine where they are to be produced. If they are to be produced in court for a case, then there is a procedure where you can certify the records to the court and mail them to the court or have them delivered to the courtroom clerk. The judge will then decide whether any of the lawyers gets to look at the records. However, if the subpoena directs you to send or bring records to a lawyer, you must be very cautious. You will need to know whether the lawyer represents the patient. If the lawyer does not, then the records can only be produced if the patient's lawyer is aware and has the opportunity to object to the records being produced. If records are produced, everything contained in the patient's chart must be produced. You must not make any alteration in the chart of any kind.

THE SUIT STARTS

In most jurisdictions, a medical malpractice lawsuit is commenced by the filing of a summons and complaint with the court. The summons is really an order from a court official to commence the suit by serving the defendant. The complaint is a series of numbered paragraphs in which the attorney filing the suit describes the parties and makes a formal claim against the defendant. They can be served in a variety of ways: by personal service, by a law enforcement official, or by a process server, in which a copy is delivered to you. However, the copy can be left at your office or home. You can also be served by certified or registered form of mail. Written discovery may also be served with the summons and complaint.

When you receive these documents, it is *urgent* that you *immediately* send everything that is served on you to your insurance carrier, and that you make sure that they receive it. You will only have 30 days to answer the complaint in state courts, and 20 days in federal courts.

You should expect to have the attorney appointed by your insurance carrier to contact you in less than the period set out in the summons. If that does not occur, you must follow up and contact the insurance carrier. At the first meeting with your attorney, it is reasonable for you to ask for information concerning the lawyer's experience in handling cases of this sort. However, your insurance carrier will be very familiar with the lawyer's experience and ability. The lawyer will take the responsibility for gathering the information necessary to answer the complaint, and will prepare and file the answer for you. It is important that you review the answer in detail yourself and notify your lawyer if it contains any factual misstatement.

Cases must be filed in a proper *venue,* that is, they must be filed in a court where one or more of the parties reside. If they are filed in an improper place, your lawyer can file a motion to have the case transferred to a proper venue.

After studying the medical record, your lawyer will meet with you, and possibly your insurance representative as well, in order to discuss the facts of the case and plan your defense. It is important that you make yourself available and participate in your own defense, but you must not undertake investigations on your own or contact experts yourself, unless your lawyer requests that you do so. Your interest is best served by being completely honest with your lawyer. Your lawyer has an ethical obligation not to disclose the information that you share with the lawyer in any way that is against your interest. There is no one else involved in this whole process who has that same duty.

Your lawyer will arrange for a review of the case by expert witnesses. You can make suggestions about the identity of the experts, but you should let your lawyer make the actual contact, so as to avoid the appearance of someone doing you a personal favor. Selection of the experts is a shared obligation between your lawyer and you. If you have never actually seen an acquaintance testify, it would probably be a good idea to defer to your attorney's judgment about the experts. At some point in the proceedings, your lawyer will share the results of the reviews as well as the identity of the reviewers with you. Your lawyer may want to wait until after your deposition is taken in order to limit the discoverability of expert identities.

In most jurisdictions, a discovery scheduling order will be entered by the court, or possibly by consent, that will set out a date by which plaintiff (the party suing you) must designate their experts, and how long they will have to make their experts available for deposition. It will also provide a date by which defendants (you and anyone else sued) must designate their experts and provide how long you will have to make them available for deposition. The order may also provide for a date for dispositive motions, which means motions that would dismiss all or part of the lawsuit. Finally, the order will likely provide a date after which the case can be set for trial. Medical malpractice actions are complicated litigation and take longer to prepare than you might think. It is not unusual for such cases not to come to trial until anywhere from one to one and a half years have elapsed from the filing.

In most states, such suits must be filed within the applicable statute of limitations, which is frequently three years or less, except in the case of minors or incompetents, who have special rules.

WRITTEN DISCOVERY

The term *discovery,* in a legal context, refers to a set of rules that specify the means the parties to a suit have to obtain information from the other side. One of these ways is by sending written requests to the other side demanding the information sought. There is a time limitation within which a response must be served on the party promulgating the requests, and a failure to make a timely response can result in severe penalties, even dismissal of the case if a plaintiff is the offender, and striking the answer and entering judgment against a defendant.

Interrogatories are simply written questions. The rules in many states provide for a limitation on the number of interrogatories that may be submitted. You will need to assist your attorney to prepare answers to the interrogatories you receive. You must sign the interrogatories in many states.

Requests for production of documents are requests that you produce copies of particular classes of documents, such as medical records, your CV, lists of CME courses taken, etc. Most frequently, copies of the documents are provided with the responses. Your lawyer signs that response.

Requests for admission are written requests that you admit the truth of statements, or the authenticity of documents. There is a time limitation for your response, and if you do not respond in a timely fashion, the request will be deemed admitted, frequently with disastrous consequences. Your attorney will be responsible for filing your response

All the above written discovery types can be used by either side. There are a couple of additional types that are only used by defendants. In states that forbid plaintiffs from specifying the amount of money they are asking for in the complaint, there is a pleading that allows a private inquiry about how much is sought. Also, in states where plaintiff must allege that the case has been reviewed by an expert who has approved it, there can be special interrogatories to inquire about that expert.

FACT DEPOSITIONS

A deposition is another means of discovery. When your deposition is going to be taken, your attorney will meet with you in order to prepare you. Then your attorney will sit with you during the deposition. You will go to a conference room, where there will be a court reporter and possibly a videographer. The lawyer on the other side will be there to ask you questions. The court reporter will take down the questions and answers verbatim. If there is more than one defendant, the attorney for the other defendant will also be there and may ask questions. Even though your lawyer will be present, your lawyer cannot answer the questions for you and is not permitted to suggest answers to you during the deposition. The parties to the suit have the right to be present if they wish. The witness is under oath, just as though testifying in court. At the conclusion of the deposition, the witness is offered the option to read and sign the deposition before it becomes final.

Typically, the depositions of the plaintiffs, the defendants, family members, or others who have knowledge of the facts are taken, as well as non-party treating physicians and experts.

EXPERT DISCOVERY

In the most frequent situation, plaintiff files and serves a document in which they disclose their experts and provide a CV and a summary of what they will testify about. Then, within 60 days, they must make their experts available for deposition. Defense counsel take the depositions of those experts either by going to where they are and doing the same sort of deposition that we did with fact witnesses, or by video-teleconferencing or telephone.

After the depositions of plaintiff's experts are obtained, defendant must name experts in the same fashion and provide their experts for deposition. After the depositions of defense experts are obtained, in many cases plaintiffs are allowed to designate re-buttal experts to testify in areas that were addressed by defense experts, but not by plaintiff's experts. These experts are also made available for deposition.

MEDIATION

In many jurisdictions there will be court-ordered mediation. This is a process in which the parties (both plaintiff and defend-ants) and their lawyers and a representative of any insurer in-volved all gather in a conference room with a mediator. The mediator has no power to judge the case, or to compel anyone to settle. The only power the mediator has is to compel everyone to go through the process. The mediator will make some introduc-tory remarks, and then one lawyer for each side will make a brief presentation about his or her respective case. The parties then separate into separate rooms, and the mediator goes back and forth and tries to facilitate a settlement.

Before the mediation takes place, you should meet with your lawyer and hopefully with the representative of your insurance carrier. You should receive information from the lawyer about the strengths and weaknesses of your case as well as your opponent's case. This is the point at which you need to express your opinion about whether you want the case settled or not. Many insurance policies provide that the insurance carrier cannot settle the case unless the doctor consents. However, if the doctor wants the case settled and the insurance carrier does not want to settle, then the lawyer who represents the doctor, but is paid by the insurer, has a conflict, and it will be necessary for the doctor to obtain his own counsel, who can demand that the company settle within policy limits.

In some states, including North Carolina, the state bars have issued ethics opinions addressing this issue. They generally hold that when a lawyer is employed by an insurer to defend an in-sured, such as a doctor, the lawyer has two clients: both the doc-tor, and the insurance company. The lawyer may not take a position contrary to either of them. In the event the doctor wants the case settled and the insurer does not, or when the possibility of judgment in excess of the policy limits becomes apparent to the attorney, the attorney must notify both the doctor and the insurer that a conflict exists and that they should settle their differences independent of the lawyer. At the premediation meeting, you should be given a clear understanding of the plans of the insurance carrier relative to settlement. You then can determine if you are in agreement.

You must weigh the risk of an adverse verdict in excess of your insurance limits against the consequences of a settlement. In the present market, each settlement on a physician's record makes the physician more and more difficult to insure and to credential. The decision can be very difficult. It is not unreasonable to seek a second opinion from an experienced trial lawyer who has nothing to do with your case. You will have to pay for the opinion, but it will be money well spent.

MOTION PRACTICE

At every stage of the litigation process, both your attorney and the other attorney will likely have recourse to motion practice. A motion is a document addressed to the court, requesting that the court grant a specific relief to the moving party. It may be for extensions of time, or for an order compelling discovery which the opponent has failed to furnish all the way up to dispositive motions, such as a motion for summary judgment, in which the court is asked to enter judgment against the opposing party. Some motions can be ruled on without a formal hearing, but most will require notice and a hearing before a judge.

TRIAL

If the case does not settle, and if motions to dismiss the claim are not successful, then the only remaining alternative is to go through the trial. It will be in a public courthouse and will be open to the public, and there quite likely will be some publicity in local newspapers.

Jury selection—In many state courts, jury selection can be very lengthy, as each attorney questions each juror. In some federal courts, the judge does all the questioning and selection is brief. Federal courts and some state courts have reduced the number of jurors from 12 to 6.

Opening statements—One attorney for each side is allowed to make a factual statement to the jury in order to forecast for the jury what that side contends the evidence will show.

Plaintiff's case—In states that impose no limits on the number of experts who can testify about issues such as standard of care or causation, it is not unusual for the plaintiff's presentation of evidence to consume more than a week. The family, standard of care experts, causation experts, life care planners, and economists will testify. All of them must also be cross-examined.

Defendant's case—Defendants frequently call a greater number of experts than plaintiffs, and they typically address the same issues.

Plaintiff's rebuttal—In order to have the last word, many plaintiffs save back some experts or some emotionally charged evidence having to do with damages.

Closing arguments—The attorneys for each side are allowed to make a presentation in which they can marshal the evidence in the light most favorable to their side. In recent years, presentations have become more sophisticated, with computer technology being widely utilized.

Charge of the court—The judge reads instructions describing the law to the jury, which is taken from pattern jury instructions, which the judge has on his laptop. The jury must apply the law, as instructed, to the facts it determines.

Jury deliberation—The jury goes to a private jury room and deliberates and agrees upon a verdict. The jury verdict must be unanimous, unless the parties agree otherwise. Typically, the jury will have to decide if the defendant was negligent, causing harm to plaintiff, and if so, how much is awarded in damages.

Post-trial motions—After the verdict is in, any side can make a motion that the Court set aside the jury verdict.

Appeal—The losing party has an automatic right of appeal to whatever first-level appellate court there is in your jurisdiction. In most jurisdictions, the appeal does not stay enforcement of the verdict, so that a losing defendant may have to post a bond in the amount of the verdict in order not to have execution made against the defendant. In many jurisdictions, an appeal will take up to one and a half years to reach final resolution.

The appeals process itself is limited to things that are done by the lawyers and judges. No additional evidence is taken on appeal. Appeals are judged on the law. A transcript of the trial and copies of the pleadings and documents introduced as evidence are prepared and comprise the case on appeal. If there is disagreement about what should be included, then the trial judge must decide. The case on appeal is filed in the appropriate appellate court, with the notice of appeal, and the exceptions noted by the appealing party. A briefing schedule is made, and the appealing party must prepare and serve its brief, which is a legal argument with citations to the record, as well as pertinent legal authorities. The other party must respond with a similar brief within a fixed period of time. Then the matter will be scheduled for oral argument, at which time the attorneys for each side will appear and argue their side of the case before a panel of judges. Some weeks or months later, an opinion will be issued by the court, either affirming, reversing or modifying the judgment of the trial court. In jurisdictions with more than one appellate level, it may then be possible for there to be an appeal to a higher level. If the case is affirmed, it is over. If it is reversed or modified, then it might have to be tried again in whole or in part.

HIPAA FORM

AUTHORIZATION FOR RELEASE OF INFORMATION

Section A: Must be completed for all authorizations

I hereby authorize the use or disclosure of my individually identifiable health information as described below. I understand that this authorization is voluntary. I understand that if the organization authorized to receive the information is not a health plan or health care provider, the released information may no longer be protected by federal privacy regulations.

Patient name: _____ ID Number: _____

Persons/organizations providing the information:

Persons/organizations receiving the information:

Specific description of information (including dates):

Section B: Must be completed only if a health plan or a health care provider has requested the authorization

1. The health plan or health care provider must complete the following:

   a. What is the purpose of the use or disclosure?:

   b. Will the health plan or health care provider requesting the authorization receive financial or in-kind compensation in exchange for using or disclosing the health information described above? Yes _____ No _____

2. The patient or the patient's representative must read and initial the following statements:

   a. I understand that my health care and the payment for my health care will not be affected if I do not sign this form. Initials:

   b. I understand that I may see and copy the information described on this form, with the experience of, if I ask for it, and that I get a copy of this form after I sign it. Initials:

Section C: Must be completed for all authorizations

The patient or the patient's representative must read and initial the following statements:

1. I understand that this authorization will expire on 01/15/2004 (DD/MM/YR). Initials:

2. I understand that I may revoke this authorization at any time by notifying the providing organization in writing, but if I do it won't have any affect on any actions they took before they received the revocation. Initials:

Signature of patient or patient's representative

Date *(Form MUST be completed before signing.)*

Printed name of patient's representative: Relationship to the patient:

* YOU MAY REFUSE TO SIGN THIS AUTHORIZATION* You may not use this form to release information for treatment or payment except when the information to be released is psychotherapy notes or certain research information.

12

What a Plaintiff's Attorney Looks for in a Malpractice Case

Lee A. Whitehurst, M.D., J.D.
Roger L. Young, J.D.

The patient had been prescribed medications for back pain by a physician's assistant. Subsequently, a MRI showed a lumbar epidural abscess. The patient was admitted through the emergency room, where a physician's assistant documented hyperreflexia in the lower extremities and a normal rectal examination.

Before surgery, the operating surgeon's partner did an incomplete physical exam, including not checking the patient's reflexes and referencing the physician's assistants finding of normal rectal tone. The operating surgeon did not do a physical exam. Several hours after the lumbar abscess evacuation, the patient developed paraplegia. An MRI showed a thoracic epidural abscess. Did the physicians carelessly do anything that would attract the attention of a plaintiff's attorney? Were there red flags in the medical records?

Will your patient's complaints about you or the outcome of your patient's treatment entice a plaintiff's attorney to file a malpractice suit against you? Hopefully, this is not the case. This chapter is written to help you understand what you can do to prevent this scenario. It explains what an attorney looks for when determining the viability of a potential malpractice suit.

Most competent physicians are sued because the patient experiences a bad or unexpected outcome from treatment. The patient or patient's family believes that it has grounds for winning a lawsuit against you. The plaintiff will choose a medical malpractice attorney, make an appointment, and then tell the attorney why you were negligent. The plaintiff's attorney will listen, ask questions, and then perform due diligence. The due diligence includes reviewing the medical records. The plaintiff's attorney knows that medical malpractice suits are difficult to win and costly to prosecute. Once a plaintiff's lawyer agrees to prosecute a medical lawsuit, the attorney knows that he or she may lose a substantial amount of money, which the client cannot pay, and may expend hundreds of hours of time. Expert witnesses commonly charge $250 to $500 dollars per hour to review records and even more to testify. Deposition expenses can amount to over $1000 per deposition, not counting what is paid to the person who is deposed. Due to the high cost of prosecuting a medical malpractice case, many medical malpractice lawyers will not consider taking a case with damages estimated to be less than $250,000. Will your patient's situation entice the attorney to gamble on a win at your expense? As a rule of thumb, there are probably 10 complaints of medical negligence for every complaint that attorneys choose to support with their time and money. You, the physician, and the medical records will be the prime determinants in whether you will be sued.

INITIAL ASSESMENT OF A POTENTIAL CASE

Since malpractice attorneys usually work on contingency and are paid only if they win a case, they must be selective in choosing cases. They will assess the potential client to determine how the client will appear before a jury. For example, will the jurors be sympathetic to or turned off by the litigant? You, as a historian, have an opportunity to let the potential plaintiff's attorney know what kind of person the plaintiff really is. Did the plaintiff say that he or she was angry at the last treating physician? Did she say that she wanted to have money to buy a second home? Did she say that that she did not like her job? Negative personality traits or characteristics cause a plaintiff's lawyer to pause when considering whether he or she wants to present the person to a jury. Remember to document comments or statements carefully that reveal the mindset of your patient.

Many cases are turned down because the doctor carefully documented indicators of personality traits, mindset, and thought process deviations through the use of self-assessment forms. Self-assessment forms that document pain patterns and pain complaints may persuade a plaintiff's attorney that the patient exaggerates or embellishes pain. Did the patient draw a pain figure with horns and nonphysiologic pain patterns or score high enough on an Oswestry test that anyone can see that the patient is a malinger or hysterical? Usually, the more self-assessment forms that your patient completes, the more likely there will be something in them that will discourage the plaintiff's attorney. Did the potential client document in her own handwriting, before you treated her, that preoperatively she was so painful that she could not sit for more than five minutes? If she is now telling the plaintiff's attorney that she cannot sit for more than five minutes, then where are the damages? Without high damages, the plaintiff's attorney cannot afford to take the case. The self-assessment form documents that her complaints are not significantly changed from the preoperative state. Without the self-assessment forms in your medical records, the plaintiff's attorney would conclude that you indeed damaged your patient. Remember to document as much as possible by self-assessment forms and by your own dictation or writing.

WAS MEDICAL NEGLIGENCE COMMITTED?

The most common description of medical malpractice is a failure to meet the standard of care. This implies that the physician has the requisite knowledge, exercises reasonable care and diligence, and uses good judgment. These standards of practice are defined by doctors, based on medical literature and experience. Some would say that the standard of care amounts to a definition of what is minimally acceptable under the facts of a given case. In most instances, there is no rigid definition of the standard of care, since there are often several equally acceptable approaches to a medical problem. A river coursing between two banks is a useful analogy. The boundaries to the definition of the standard of care allow for movement within the recognized banks of the river, but will not include care that is beyond what is recognized as appropriate care under the circumstances.

Some states further define the standard of care in terms of the community in which the care is delivered. Other states apply what is loosely called a national standard of care. In the former situation, medical experts must be able to testify that they are familiar with the standards of practice that apply in the community where the care was delivered—or in a community that is substantially similar. The relevant factors in determining whether two communities are similar include the nature of the care being rendered; the size of the community; and the availability of necessary support services, equipment, trained support personnel, and consulting medical specialists for the procedure in question. The goal is not to hold a community physician to the same standards that would apply to an academic physician working in a teaching hospital, where the level of care would be markedly different. Most physicians seem to feel that there is a national standard of care for most situations. They find the idea of a community standard of care somewhat anachronistic, but the law is often behind the times in terms of the reality of the present situation.

Medical negligence is not intentional misconduct or wrongdoing. The law does not require gross negligence or egregious misconduct or malfeasance to hold a physician liable for medical errors. A surgeon need not be intoxicated in the operating room to be negligent. Rather, the standard is simple negligence—a failure to do what a reasonably prudent physician would do under the same or similar circumstances. It is the same basic concept that applies to motor vehicle negligence. It does not require that the malfeasance be habitual or even characteristic, but rather only that with regard to one patient on one day, the physician failed to possess the requisite knowledge to give appropriate care; to use reasonable care and diligence while providing care; to use sound judgment; or to meet the applicable standard of practice.

THE MEDICAL RECORDS

Most plaintiffs' attorneys will carefully review the facts of the case as reported by the potential client. Just as you take a history prior to treatment, the attorney spends time talking to your patient about what you did, why you did it, and why he or she wants to bring a claim against you. The plaintiff's attorney will review the medical records with a fine-tooth comb looking for information to verify the client's story and to evaluate the way you diagnosed and managed your patient's problem. The plaintiff's attorney will form an opinion regarding how careful you were in your documentation? For example, did you do a careful neurological examination, or did you fail to check sensation in each dermatome by light touch and pin-prick? Did you respond to changes in vital signs? Did you note tachycardia? Did you give a differential diagnosis? Did you document discussing your patient's condition with physicians covering for you in your absence? Did you order certain tests on an emergency basis? Did you return pages from nurses in a timely manner? Did you adequately document an informed consent? Did you timely document lab and test results? Did you carefully document your monitoring of a patient's condition? Does your examination portray you as being careless and sloppy or professional and meticulous? If your notes were not dictated, was your handwriting illegible or neatly written? Did you try to alter the record? Impressions do make a difference. Strive to present yourself in the medical record as a careful professional who leaves no questions about your patient unanswered. Formulate your medical record in anticipation that it will be reviewed by a plaintiff's attorney who is trying to decide whether or not he or she wants to be a party to a suit against you. Remember the old adage: If it's not documented, it didn't happen. Whether it's absolutely true or not is not the point—if you follow this principle, you'll avoid having to answer a lot of questions that could be asked years later in the legal arena.

NEGLIGENCE ON THE PART OF THE PATIENT

Did you document how well the patient followed your orders or recommendations? Did the patient contribute to his or her bad outcome? Many patients do not follow their doctor's orders. In North Carolina, for example, if the plaintiff's attorney sees that it is well documented that the patient negligently failed to follow orders, more likely than not the doctor will probably not be sued. In North Carolina contributory negligence by the plaintiff, which is coincident in time to the negligence of a physician, precludes an award to a plaintiff. Even though it is rare to establish that a patient was contributorily negligent in a technical sense, if the record demonstrates that the patient failed to take apppropriate responsibility for his own care, it will make it harder for the plaintiff to convince a jury that the physician should be held liable for his or her injury, even if the injury could and should have been avoided. Most states utilize comparative negligence law by which an award to a plaintiff is reduced by the extent to which the plaintiff's own negligence contributed to his or her own injury or death. Remember to document each time your patient does something that threatens your treatment outcome. Such documentation may dissuade the plaintiff's attorney because the client contributed to his or her injury or demise.

EXPERT REVIEWS

The attorney will often consult with other physicians in your specialty to get an assessment of management of the potential litigant's case. Often there are red flags raised by these reviewers about things you did or failed to document that you did. Often the reviewer will be misled because the physician did not present his or her treatment plan logically in the chart. In one interesting incident, a neurosurgeon had a case filed against him based on the medical record. During the discovery stage of the case, a letter was obtained which had been written by the neurosurgeon in response to his patient's complaint to the state medical board. The letter explained his treatment rationale to the patient, which resulted in the expert changing his assessment of the case. As a result, the suit was dismissed. Do you present your treatment plans so that a reviewer will conclude that you considered alternatives and that you had valid reasons for treating as you did? Is your operative note sufficiently clear to explain what you found and why you did what you did at surgery? Did you freely consult before you treated? Did you document informal consultations? A reviewing expert will carefully evaluate your records. Will he or she see you as a careful physician or one who is sloppy and cavalier? Will the reviewer be inclined to encourage the plaintiff's attorney to take the case or to turn it down? An experienced plaintiff's lawyer will carefully evaluate all of the potential medical issues raised by the client's history. The medical records will be carefully analyzed, and discussions with one or more reviewing physicians will take place prior to filing a claim. A poor result is not necessarily due to negligence and a breach of the standard of care. Your documentation will help tremendously in determining whether your care met the applicable standard or not.

You, the physician, are the captain of your ship and often the master of your fate. Your medical records may steer you away from a lawsuit suit. By careful documentation and by facilitating patient self-documentation, you can present yourself to an inquiring plaintiff attorney as too formidable a target, too well documented and too big a financial risk. As the old adage goes, "An ounce of prevention is worth a pound of cure."

13

Players in the Malpractice Arena

Richard J. Nasca, M.D.

As in most activities in life, in medical malpractice litigation there are many participants with varied agendas, goals, and ambitions. The plaintiffs, defendants, codefendants, attorneys, experts, insurance carriers, and adjusters are all players with varied interests and alliances. The mediation and arbitration boards, judges, and juries are the referees.

As a defendant, you must keep in mind that there will be significant interaction between all the parties with a vested interest in the claim, much of which will take place outside of your awareness. Peripheral individuals will also weigh in with various opinions and recommendations. As a physician defendant, you must understand that you will stand or fall on the merits of your medical decisions and treatment. However, at times other factors out of your control may affect the final outcome and settlement of the claim. For example, your malpractice insurance carrier may recommend that you agree to settlement if the payment demanded by the plaintiff is less than the anticipated cost of going to trial. Another reason to offer settlement is that the case will be tried in a hostile venue with a history of excessive jury awards which may exceed the limits of the physician's malpractice policy coverage. A very common reason to settle is the effect a "sympathetic plaintiff" such as a brain-damaged child has on a jury.

Often it is difficult to predict in the early period of the claim what roles and relationships these players will have, when they will appear, and what effect they will have on the eventual outcome.

The purpose of this chapter is to discus the characteristics and biases of the various participants as well their common behavior patterns.

PLAINTIFFS

Most patients who sue their doctor are upset and angry with their care, or the results of their treatment, or the way the doctor interacted with them on a personal or professional level. Whatever their reasons for filing a claim, they want vindication and recompense for their suffering or that of a loved one. In most cases, under the contingency system there is little if any financial risk to the plaintiff. The possibility of a good payoff at the end of the process provides further incentive to go forward with a claim. Several of these individuals are quick to blame and find fault. They desire retribution for all wrongs. Some plaintiffs are of the mindset that the doctor defendant has deep pockets and, being well-insured, takes a claim not as a personal affront but merely as a business expense. Although considerable stress is imposed upon the patient plaintiff during the entire litigation process, it does not compare to the burden carried by the defendant doctor.

DEFENDANTS

Most physicians who have a claim filed against them are emotionally distraught, hurt, frustrated, and fearful. With rare exceptions, they consider the claim an attack on their person, competence, and profession. Because of this conviction, the physician's impulse is to fight back and not concede or consider settlement until all other avenues and approaches have been exhausted. A good deal of this mentality is fostered by the need to report most all settlements on behalf of an individual practitioner to the National Practitioner Data Bank, State Licensing Boards, hospital credentialing committees, insurance companies, HMO's, as well as other third parties. Certain payments made in the name of clinics, hospitals, and professional associations are not required to be reported, as are some types of high-low settlements and agreements to the National Practitioner Data Bank (NPDB 2001).

CODEFENDANTS

These individuals are usually included in a lawsuit by the plaintiff in order to cover all the possible torts and claims in the case and prosecute all the healthcare providers who *may have* rendered negligent treatment or contributed to the ultimate result.

A 15-year-old male was transferred from a small rural hospital to a medical center with a complex spinal fracture and a profound neurologic deficit after a high-speed auto accident. Multiple physicians and surgeons who cared for this boy were named by the plaintiff and his father in the suit. They alleged that delay in treatment, rather than the accident, resulted in the young patient's neurologic deterioration. The boy was not wearing a seatbelt and was thrown out of the car and found outside the car in a roadside ditch. His definitive treatment was somewhat delayed by his short stay overnight in the rural hospital. His care at the medical center was carried out in a timely fashion and resulted in his walking out of the hospital six weeks later. He eventually regained nearly normal neurologic function following decompression, reduction, and stabilization of his T7 fracture dislocation. Just prior to trial, the plaintiff's attorney called the offices of several of the codefendant doctors and offered to "let them out" for $5000. The case was subsequently thrown out of court by the judge when he received notification that the plaintiff's expert, a former professor, had been dismissed from his university teaching position many years before, did not have a valid license to practice in the United States, and had not performed surgery for several years.

Codefendants may be insured by a multitude of carriers and represented by attorneys with various concerns and agendas regarding the suit. Many times these entities are at variance with the doctor's defense team's strategies and goals. Some of these codefendants would rather settle than go to trial. This may leave one or more physicians eventually out there alone in the suit. Sometimes the settlement will fall on the defendant with the highest liability coverage (deepest pockets). This scenario should not discourage one from proceeding to defend one's interest vigorously against the claim. It is also wise not to discuss your case with your codefendants and those people who work with them, such as the risk-management people at your hospital, administrators, and your colleagues who hold appointed or elected positions on hospital committees and boards.

PLAINTIFF'S ATTORNEYS

Attorneys are similar to physicians in that they are service providers. They are involved in getting a settlement (money) for the plaintiff or getting the defendants dismissed. Although attorneys practice law by a set of rules or principles of law, each case demands personal intellectual input and creative approaches to result in a successful outcome, not unlike the way medicine is practiced. The plaintiff's attorney contracts to represent the plaintiff for a percentage of the settlement. In order to fund the expenses of the case, the attorney must be convinced that the case has merit and that the plaintiff has suffered harm and injury as result of the treatment or lack of it for which compensation is sought. There are some plaintiff's attorneys who file frivolous suits. However, the *majority do not,* since the cost and time spent in pursuing these cases are not financially rewarding. It is estimated that less than 1 in 10 cases brought to a plaintiff's attorney are filed. A number of claims may be dropped during discovery when it becomes evident that there is insufficient evidence to proceed further.

EXPERTS

The majority of experts are well-educated and very knowledgeable about their area of expertise. However, these folks come with a lot of surprises and their own hidden agendas. These individuals are the real unknowns in the legal process. Most experts are good talkers and make good appearances at depositions and in the court room. Although some defense attorneys want to pick the doctor experts without much input from the doctor defendant, I think the physician should have a major say in the choice of the defense expert(s). It is wise for the defendant to think long and hard about his or her recommendations in this matter. It is a good idea to visualize what type of appearance your expert will make in the courtroom. Will he or she come across as arrogant, defensive, and overbearing, or caring, fair, and informative? The professorial type with outstanding credentials but no bedside manner may be a poor choice as a defense expert, in contrast to a respected community practitioner with good people skills and controlled demeanor. As you are gathering your thoughts about who to recommend as your expert(s), you might discuss with your attorney and adjuster what sort of track record these potential experts have with giving depositions and court room testimony. A seasoned individual who has a similar type of practice mix to yours and is in your geographic area is usually a good choice as an expert.

INSURANCE CARRIERS

These people hold you in the palm of their hand. They will pick your attorney and make the final determination on whether or not to settle and for what amount. After the settlement, they may continue you on as an insured, add a surcharge to your premium or a deductible to your policy, or drop you from their coverage. Most mutual insurance companies are required to set aside an amount of money to cover claims that are filed or likely to be filed. This money is placed in investment accounts (stocks and bonds). There is no great hurry for your insurance carrier to rush your case to settlement, especially when their investments of your set-aside money are generating a tidy return.

Most medical mutual insurance companies have a board of medical specialists who meet on a regular basis to review claims and make recommendations regarding how to defend or settle these claims. The insured should be aware that oftentimes the board may be lacking a medical person with expertise or qualifications in the physician's specialty, yet recommendations may be made without recourse to further consultation. Most of the presentations are made by the adjusters, who are responsible for summarizing the medical records and providing the pertinent facts of the claim. The recommendations of the insurance advisory board are rarely made known to the doctor defendant. The insurance adjuster can be a help to the defendant as a sounding board on how the case is proceeding or a roadblock to information and communication. A good, well-balanced, and fair-minded adjuster can be an invaluable ally.

ARBITRATION AND MEDIATION

Individuals involved in lawsuits will often participate in mediation and arbitration in an attempt to reach a settlement and avoid a costly legal battle in court. In arbitration each side is represented by an arbitrator of his or her choice. A third arbitrator is chosen by mutual consent of both parties. After each side presents evidence regarding the claim, the arbitrators render a final judgment based on the majority vote. Mediation is another alternative dispute resolution process that is used preliminary to trial (Mitchell and Walker 1997). The trial court judge refers the case for mediation. A mediator is chosen from a list by the parties involved in the litigation (Brown n.d.). If they cannot agree on a mediator, the court will appoint one from a list of available mediators kept by the clerk of the court. After hearing both sides of the case, the mediator meets with each party in an attempt to resolve the matter. If an agreement is reached, a memo of settlement is reported to the court for final disposition. If no agreement is reached, the court will proceed to schedule a trial. Both of these types of pretrial resolution require each party to share equally in the costs. Remember that in arbitration the three arbitrators act as "judges" and there is usually no appeal process provided. In the mediation process, one individual functions as the negotiator and the facilitator. However, if one or both parties do not agree on settlement, the court will schedule a jury trial.

JURIES

Most of us will be called upon at one time or another to serve on a civil, criminal, or grand jury. Often, most professionals are rejected from serving because of their status in the community, education, association with attorneys and judges, and numerous other factors. This is unfortunate since these people could be useful contributors to the courts and legal process.

I was recently called for jury duty. The plaintiff's attorney inquired as to my stand on reimbursement for pain and suffering since his client, a teenager, had been injured in a low-speed motor vehicle accident by a young adult woman. I was promptly dismissed after I indicated I was not a proponent of compensation for pain and suffering.

Most of the people picked for juries are asked if they can serve without prejudice or if they have a bias that might influence them in rendering a fair and impartial verdict. The juror takes an oath to decide the case "upon the law and the evidence." The judge will state and clarify the law related to the facts presented to the jury (*Handbook for Trial Jurors* n.d.). Remember that the judge determines the law to be applied in the case, while the jury is charged with deciding the facts of the case. The jury's duty is to reach its own conclusions based on the evidence presented. The fundamental obligation of the jury is to maintain objectivity and base its verdict on the testimony and exhibits presented as evidence in the trial. A juror should disregard any statement or argument put forth unless it is supported by the evidence presented during the trial. The verdict is reached without regard to the opinion of the judge as to the facts. However, the judge may explain what facts are in dispute, summarize the evidence bearing on the questions of fact, and direct the jury's attention to the real merits and issues of the case.

JUDGES

Judges may be appointed or elected (Brannon 1998; Brown n.d.). They are forbidden to practice law privately. There is a chief judge for each district, who is responsible for assigning all the judges and magistrates to court sessions and scheduling all matters related to the district court under his or her jurisdiction. During a trial, the judge may be asked to decide on a question of law with the jury present. On occasion the judge may dismiss the jury and hear the arguments of the opposing attorneys for or against an objection. The law requires that a judge decide such questions A ruling by the judge does not indicate that the judge is taking sides. The judge is responsible for clarifying the law and ensuring a fair trial. It is up to the jury to maintain objectivity and base their verdict on the testimony and exhibits presented as evidence during the trial. Remember: the law is what the judge declares it to be.

In summary, try to keep your perspective and concentration during the litigation process despite all the ongoing players and their game plans. Most physicians want to get suits behind them as fast as possible. This may not be in your best interests. Just as in an athletic contest, there will be highs and lows. Keep track of the various players. Know what to expect and anticipate strategies that might derail your defense. Don't be blind to a change in direction and new tactics as the process plays out.

REFERENCES

Brannon, J. G., ed. 1998. *The Judicial System in North Carolina.* Raleigh, N.C.: Administrative Office of the Courts.

Brown, W. n.d. Personal communication.

Handbook for Trial Jurors Serving in the United States District-Courts. n.d. Washington, D.C.: Administrative Office of the United States Courts.

Mitchell, B. B., and R. A. Walker. 1997. *Mediated Settlement Conferences in Superior Court Civil Actions* (February).

National Practitioners Data Bank (NPDB). 2001. *NPDB Guidebook.* Fairfax, Va: NPDB (September).

14

Evaluating Your Assigned Attorney

David E. Attarian, M.D., F.A.C.S.

You've been named in a medical malpractice lawsuit. You are mad, sad, frightened, and in disbelief. You don't particularly like or trust attorneys, but one has been assigned to your case by the insurance company or your employing institution. You are going in to an important legal battle with the help and guidance of a strange ally; so, how do you evaluate your attorney? This will ultimately be a personal decision, but you will utilize the same thought processes you have employed for important decisions in the past, such as postgraduate education, career choice, marriage, etc.

Your first and most urgent action should be to meet face to face with the attorney. Schedule a time and place that is convenient for both of you, although most attorneys will accommodate your schedule and even come to your office or place of work. Plan on meeting for at least one hour without interruptions. Have as much of the medical file as possible available for the encounter, and take notes summarizing every detail of the conversation. Get to know each other and become comfortable communicating openly.

Tell the attorney about your personal and professional background; then ask the attorney about her or himself. Briefly review the facts of the case, and ask the attorney for an initial opinion. If you feel comfortable at the end of the first meeting, you are on your way to a positive working relationship. Remember that the legal system works slowly and deliberately, so it may require several meetings over weeks or months to fully evaluate your attorney.

The next step is to become confident with your attorney and his or her abilities. It is prudent to acquire as much information about your attorney as you need to satisfy yourquestions. You should consider inquiring about the following:

1. Does the attorney understand and agree with your goals, i.e., defending or settling the lawsuit?

If you perceive the lawsuit to be frivolous, your attorney must agree to defend the case to the very end. Also, there should be no controversy between you and the attorney as to whether or not the lawsuit can be successfully defended. If your attorney is wavering, make it clear that your goal is nothing less than victory, given that the repercussions of a loss may significantly affect your reputation, professional standing, licensure, insurability, and perhaps even your ability to make a living. On the other hand, if you have made an honest mistake or briefly wandered below the standard of care and this has resulted in a injury or poor outcome for a patient, you must have an honest discussion with your attorney about the benefits of a settlement, e.g., less expense and fewer hassles for everyone involved. If you both agree on a settlement, proceed accordingly but keep in contact with your attorney so that you understand the details, monetary payments, and how it will affect your relationship with the insurance carrier in the future. It may take several weeks or months to decide on your ultimate goal, namely to defend or settle. You and your attorney may need to wait on several expert reviews before making a final decision. If you and your assigned attorney cannot agree on the ultimate goal of defense or settlement, ask the insurance company for another attorney as soon as possible and start the process over.

2. Does the attorney provide you undivided attention and behave in a professional manner during meetings or phone calls?

Like you, a good attorney has many clients and different cases to manage at any one time, so you need to be considerate when requesting times to meet or speak by phone. That said, the attorney should be prepared, professional, and courteous, as you would be for your patients. The attorney should be interested and sound knowledgeable about the case, and as the case proceeds, the attorney should know the pertinent medical details and events as well as you do. The attorney should not appear or sound distracted during communication sessions, taking other phone calls during a meeting or allowing interruptions from staff about unrelated issues. In other words, you should expect the same level of attention and courtesy to you and your malpractice case as you should give to each and every one of your patients.

3. Is the attorney easily accessible to you when you have questions or concerns?

The attorney should provide an agreed-upon method for communication, such as a private phone line or e-mail, so that, when necessary, you can receive a response the same or next business day. It is important not to abuse this privilege as a client, but the attorney must make the option available. Nonurgent questions should be addressed in a timely fashion by the attorney, and the definition of "timely" must be clear at the beginning to avoid misunderstandings. A timely response often depends on the legal process, and it may take weeks or months to gather discovery responses and obtain rulings on legal motions. Your attorney should keep you updated on these matters. Your questions should never be ignored or criticized.

4. Does the attorney clearly explain the process and legal terms so you understand them?

The legal system is foreign and intimidating to the vast majority of physicians and healthcare providers. Your attorney should assist you in understanding the new vocabulary, e.g., causation, civil action, negligence, deposition, discovery, hearsay, interrogatories, etc. The attorney should outline the general process and timetable from start to finish, and then explain the legal events and repercussions as they occur. When the lawsuit is initially filed, the complaint may read in such a way that you interpret the statements as demonization or criminalization of your actions. Before you go into complete despair or become uncontrollably angry, ask your attorney for an explanation of why the legal documents describe your interactions with the plaintiff/patient in such negative terms.

5. Does the attorney explore all of the legal options with you?

Just as you may discuss alternative treatments with your patients, your attorney should discuss the various legal avenues available to deal with your malpractice suit. This may include a motion to dismiss the case, a settlement, or an all-out defense with a jury trial. The key points for each option should be outlined by the attorney, including the potential for success or failure, the time and cost involved, and the possible personal, professional, and financial risks. While your attorney may suggest one approach over another, you should ultimately decide on which option is best for you. Remember, your attorney is far more experienced in these matters and will recommend the most appropriate, pragmatic, and cost-efficient solution compatible with the law.

6. Whom does the attorney represent in the case, e.g., the insurance company, the hospital, other healthcare providers; and are your interests the prime allegiance?

This issue should be discussed very early in the process, and the answer from the attorney must be complete and transparent. Your attorney's ethical obligation is first and foremost to you, the client. Who is paying the attorney for the services rendered in defense of your malpractice suit? Is the attorney a subcontractor, or an employee of the insurance carrier or self-insured institution? Is the attorney defending just you, or multiple defendants, e.g., the hospital, other physicians, etc.? Is the attorney's prime directive to serve your legal needs, or others at your expense? Will the attorney follow your instructions, when appropriate, or will he or she just act to limit the insurance company's or institution's financial losses? Will the attorney take legal action without your knowledge for the benefit of others? But be aware of the conditions of legal defense defined in your legal contract with your insurance carrier; it is possible that you and your attorney have some limitations. For example, the attorney may be required to settle a case as opposed to going to trial. In any event, you must be comfortable and feel secure with your assigned attorney's answers to these questions as you move through the process.

7. Will the attorney handle your case personally, or will junior attorneys be involved, and to what degree?

Most attorneys practice in groups, and senior attorneys will often rely on junior associates or aides to assist with the mundane issues of collecting records, filing motions, etc. It is important to know that the assigned attorney will personally oversee all aspects of your malpractice suit, and ultimately perform the key items for your defense, such as a court trial. On the other hand, your assigned attorney may admit to being a junior partner in a firm; if this is acceptable to you, you must also ask how and when the attorney will seek out or employ more senior, experienced assistance to ensure the best chance for a successful outcome.

8. How long has the attorney been in practice and in what geographic areas?

Your assigned attorney should be able to provide you with documentation of his or her professional experience, as well as some references of other medical malpractice clients he or she has represented in the past. You can also contact your state's bar association by phone, mail, or the Internet to determine your attorney's biographical information and area of practice expertise.

9. How much experience or training has the attorney had in medical malpractice, especially for the defense?

This is a critical question to ask. Most plaintiff's attorneys never do defense work, and defense attorneys rarely do plaintiff's cases. The majority of attorneys do plaintiff's work. There are fewer defense counsel with specific training to defend medical malpractice suits. This type of training may be lacking in some in some law schools. It is imperative that your attorney be able to document substantial additional training or experience in this subspecialty.

10. How successful has the attorney been in defending medical malpractice cases, and can she or he provide documentation to confirm their claims?

There is no substitute for hard evidence of successful outcomes in the attorney's previous defense of malpractice suits. Your attorney should be able to provide you data on the number of cases managed, number of cases defended, number of cases settled, and number of cases won.

11. How much experience and success does the attorney have in the courtroom?

This is particularly important if the lawsuit comes to a jury trial. Many busy, successful attorneys have rarely or never been in a courtroom in front of a jury. Trial in a courtroom is an art, and previous experience in this setting is extremely important for the attorney defending your lawsuit. It is also good to know how successful your attorney has been in winning cases in the jurisdiction where your case is pending.

12. Is the attorney willing to become intimately familiar with all of the medical facts of the case and provide guidance for your preparation?

Your assigned attorney must understand every detail of your case, including, but not limited to, the medical record, the standard of care, and any pertinent literature for or against your actions. The attorney may solicit your assistance in identifying unbiased expert witnesses to review your case and potentially testify in your favor. The attorney may request your personal teaching in order to understand complex concepts relevant to the suit; at the same time, the attorney should give you step-by-step guidance in preparing for each and every aspect of the case, e.g., preparing for the deposition, rehearsing truthful testimony, studying supporting literature, etc. You should feel confident that your assigned attorney knows the facts of the case as well as you do.

13. Does the attorney carry malpractice insurance?

This is a question that your assigned attorney should be willing to answer one way or the other, although the majority of attorneys do carry such coverage. You should at least explore your options and recourse in the rare event that your legal representation does not meet appropriate legal standards.

Evaluation of your assigned attorney may not be easy, but if you are diligent, your careful assessment of your legal representation's capabilities and potential will allow you to make an educated decision as to whether or not you are satisfied with the services offered and provided. If it becomes obvious that a good working relationship cannot be achieved with your assigned attorney, you may want to employ a personal attorney. This subject is discussed in another chapter.

REFERENCES

Nora, P. F., ed. 1991. *Professional Liability Risk Management: A Manual for Surgeons.* Chicago: American College of Surgeons. (Second edition, 1997.)

15

Personal Legal Representation during Medical Malpractice Defense

Erle E. Peacock, Jr., M.D., J.D.

A North Carolina State Superior Court judge with a long and distinguished tenure on the Bench called the main office of the firm I was an associate in and asked to speak to one of the senior attorneys on our staff. He had recently learned that his son, a prominent orthopedic surgeon in the western part of the state, had been charged with medical malpractice and was faced with defending what both father and son considered to be a frivolous lawsuit. The purpose of the judge's call was to obtain the services of one of our attorneys as personal counsel for his son. Several of us told the judge that we were acquainted with the lawyer his son had been assigned by his insurance company and could assure him that his son would be provided a good defense without the need of a personal attorney. The judge listened patiently to what we had to say and then replied in a tone which left no doubt about his conviction, "I said I want my son to have a personal attorney and my decision is in no way affected by your confidence in the insurance company or their assigned lawyer. Do you want to personally represent him or not?" We did accept the judge's request. The reasons we accepted an experienced trial judge's request when his own son's welfare was at stake comprise the substance of this chapter. The subject is a very difficult one to write about since it may appear to be drumming up business for lawyers. Nothing could be further from the truth. To justify the need for a personal medical malpractice defense attorney, it is necessary to review the duty of the insurance company and its lawyer to the insured physician and the role of a personal attorney in representing the interests of the doctor served with a medical malpractice suit.

DUTY OF THE INSURANCE COMPANY

It usually comes as a severe disappointment to physicians to learn that the duty of their insurance company under the law is *not* to defend them against medical malpractice allegations (Syverud 1990). A search of practically any medical malpractice insurance policy will fail to find the word "defense" anywhere or in any context. It simply isn't there. It comes as an even greater disappointment to discover that common law precedent clearly establishes that the primary duty of an insurance company is *not* to its insureds (doctors) but to its stockholders (Thomas 1995). Case law states unequivocally that the primary duty of an insurance company when faced with a medical malpractice suit against one of its insureds is "to investigate and settle expeditiously."[1] Moreover, there is little or no solace to be garnered from that word "expeditiously," for the following reason. Upon learning of a medical malpractice action against one of their insureds, an insurance company will seek a lawyer whom it knows from previous experience will give the company the highest settlement value that is possible with a straight face and with practice. The insurance company also wants to know the lowest settlement value of the case, even if settlement is a remote possibility. Insurance company business is very much sought by trial attorneys, so it is not difficult to get the two values being sought at both ends of the scale. The first or high value is the most important because the company is then entitled to place that amount of money in an escrow account that collects interest tax-free for as long as the suit remains

---

1.   *Shuster v. South Broward Hospital District Physicians' Professional Liability Ins. Trust*, 591 So.2d 174,177 (Fla. 1992).

open. There is no financial incentive to close the case rapidly. It is actually possible in a high-value lawsuit that remains open for a considerable period of time and ultimately settles for one reason or another at a much lower value for an insurance company to make money on a lawsuit. It is very important to remember that neither the plaintiff nor the defendant insurance company expects or wants to proceed to trial on a medical malpractice lawsuit. The suit is always filed with the hope and expectation of settlement. The defendant's insurance company will usually oblige if a reasonable amount can be agreed upon. It is possible, for an increased premium, to obtain medical malpractice insurance that does not permit settlement without the insured's permission. This is a real two-edged sword, however. If the physician refuses to settle and the ultimate award exceeds the agreed-upon settlement, the physician may be responsible for some of the additional expense.

DUTY OF AN APPOINTED INSURANCE COMPANY LAWYER

The primary duty of any lawyer is to carry out the wishes, within the law, of the entity who hired him. Such an entity, of course, is the insurance carrier. Fortunately, in most cases the duty of the lawyer to his or her employer does not conflict with his or her duty to the insured. However, at times there may be some significant disagreements. Insurance companies can and frequently do put very rigid controls on lawyers, including how many expert witnesses they can enroll, how much an expert witness can be paid, how many lawyers can work on the case, how many depositions can be taken, how much can be spent on all phases of discovery, etc. These are all important factors in the ultimate outcome of a lawsuit. For instance, if an insurance company decides that a lawsuit is only likely to cost them $25,000 to lose, they will not authorize their lawyer to spend $50,000 lining up distant and expensive expert witnesses to ensure winning at trial. Thus, an attorney who knows he can win with a generous discovery allowance and realizes the case may be headed for a modest loss or small settlement with a restricted discovery budget may have an ethical dilemma. If the defense attorney cares about the defendant doctor's overwhelming goal to clear his name and avoid being reported to the National Practitioner Data Bank, a further conflict of interest arises. Some lawyers find clever ways to resolve such matters, while others simply ignore them and follow the dictates of the insurance company. Insurance company-appointed lawyers desiring to continue working for the same insurance carrier must never forget that success in the view of an insurance company *is measured by keeping expenses and settlements as low as possible.* Litigation is to be avoided at any reasonable cost. An outstanding example is the recent case of a CRNA anesthetist who was being unfairly sued for malpractice and wrongful death. Because the victim was relatively young and the mother of small children, the insurance company was afraid of trial, even though every bit of evidence strongly pointed toward culpability of the supervising anesthesiologist and internist—not the anesthetist, who only followed the directions she was given. The plaintiff would not settle for less than several million dollars, so the insurance company felt they had to proceed to trial. The trial went smoothly and there was every indication to most observers, including the judge, that the defense was going to prevail. In other words, the system appeared to be working. After the jury had been out for about two hours, however, an insurance company claims agent monitoring the trial lost confidence in the jury, contacted the home office in another state, and instructed my colleague and me to make a $300,000 settlement offer before the jury returned. I stalled as long as I could and, to my delight, the jury returned their verdict before the settlement offer could be made. The verdict was complete exoneration of the defendant nurse anesthetist. This would never have happened if the insurance company orders had been followed quickly.

FACTORS TO BE CONSIDERED BEFORE RETAINING A PERSONAL ATTORNEY

When considering the possible need for a personal attorney, defendant doctors should pay particular attention to:

1. Evaluation of the appointed lawyer during deposition of expert witnesses. It is at this time that the personal skills and experience of an assigned lawyer should manifest themselves. It should be apparent what skills will be needed if the case proceeds to trial. If the plaintiff has obtained the services of professional witnesses who are going to have to be impeached in order to present a strong defense, a defense attorney with aggressive attack skills is needed. If reliable, unattackable experts have been recruited, a more patient, informed approach will be needed. An assigned lawyer without natural skills and proven experience of either type must be replaced or assisted by retaining personal counsel.

2. It is usually apparent after a few sessions with the claims representative and the assigned attorney how the insurance company views the case. They may consider it a minor nuisance to be dispensed with as rapidly as possible, or there may be genuine concern on the part of the carrier to win rather than just resolve the case. If it is clear that settlement is imminent and the appointed lawyer is not willing to consider alternative ways in which a settlement can be structured in the best interest of the physician, it may be prudent for the defendant to obtain personal counsel. Such is particularly true in constructing a strong defendant's statement to the National Practitioner Data Bank. For example, the Data Bank report might read as follows: "It was the opinion of the defense attorneys that this case was medically defensible on all counts. It was settled for economic feasability or because the trial had to be conducted in a hostile jurisdiction in which excessive awards have been the rule rather than the exception."

3. How much time is the assigned lawyer prepared or allowed to spend in the background check of potential jurors, preparation of expert witnesses and assisting the defendant during preparation for and during trial? A trial is very much like a rollercoaster and the defendant and his or her family may go from the height of anticipation to the depth of despair several times a day. A compassionate attorney can do much to alleviate anxiety and prepare people going through the ordeal for the first time. Staying power is crucial, and no one is more important than the defendant's

attorney in achieving that objective. Personal counsel often can be extremely helpful when such is the case.

4. Is the attorney familiar with the venue in which the trial will be held, and what has been his or her track record in trials there? Local legal representation can be a significant factor in selection and appeal to a jury as well as in some instances, to the judge. If assigned counsel demonstrates speech and manner characteristics of an outsider, strong consideration should be given to retaining local personal counsel.

5. Finally, and perhaps most importantly, does the defendant feel comfortable with the assigned attorney and have confidence that he or she will defend him or her in a competent manner? No matter how good a reputation an attorney has, an individual client has to feel that he or she is being represented by the best that is available. If there is a perception that the attorney assigned is not working in the defendant's best interests, regardless of the reason, corrective measures should be taken, including requesting the insurance carrier to assign other representation and/or employing personal counsel to help fill any voids that may exist.

How do the duties of an insurance company-assigned lawyer differ from the duties of personal counsel ?

Theoretically their duties are the same. A common finding in many medical malpractice actions is that, although the insurance company employs the lawyer, the real client is the insured and the assigned lawyer's duty to the insured is genuine. If there is genuine difference in the goals of an assigned lawyer and those of personal counsel, one or the other has an ethical responsibility to resign. A defendant simply cannot be represented simultaneously by lawyers with different goals in defending the same client. Thus, if the problem, as perceived by the client, is one of inadequate legal defense, the solution is to insist that the insurance company correct the situation, even to the extent of replacing assigned counsel. If there is any reasonable justification, insurance companies usually will reassign counsel, at least once. Frivolous complaints, however, obviously cannot be entertained. There must be a substantial basis for such requests. Retaining personal counsel, therefore, should not be done to overrule or try to replace assigned counsel; it should be to add support and reinforce the defense, not fight or replace it. Although the addition of a personal attorney should be made with the concurrence of the insurance company and the assigned attorney, such approval is not mandatory. The addition of a personal attorney is usually welcomed by an assigned attorney if done properly. The choice of a personal attorney should be someone the assigned attorney can work with smoothly, at least as far as can be determined at the time personal counsel is retained.

There is one major practical difference between the duties of personal counsel and the duties of assigned counsel. That is the fiduciary duty owed the defendant client by personal counsel. Even though there is theoretical similarity between the duty assigned counsel owes his client (the insurance company) and duty personal counsel owes his client (defendant physician) there can be a perceived difference. Differences do arise, and the most compelling one is the matter of whether to settle or go to trial. A typical example follows.

An orthopedic surgeon developed a method for handling extruded lumbar discs that pretty much eliminated spinal fusion. The majority of orthopedic surgeons in the state were fusing the spine after excision of the herniated disc, in spite of a variety of recognized complications. As is inevitable in lower-back surgical patients, regardless or what is done, a few poor results occurred from the new procedure in the form of recurrent pain. An aggressive plaintiff's attorney found out that a different procedure was being performed in his area and that there were some patients with less than ideal results. By a number of less than noble methods, he identified most of the patients who had been operated upon and, contacted them in a variety of ways, including advertising, and in a short period of time filed approximately 17 lawsuits alleging medical malpractice because a procedure was performed which he and his advisors did not believe met the standard of care in that community at that time. Because there were a number of unusually complicated technical aspects to be considered, the defendant surgeon retained me as personal counsel. Before agreeing to serve in that capacity, I met with the assigned lawyer and found him to be one of the finest medical malpractice attorneys I had ever encountered. He was a brilliant lawyer, an experienced trial attorney, and a genuinely compassionate and humanistic person. In my opinion, the defendant had been assigned the very finest lawyer that was available. He recognized clearly the need for all the help he could get and seemed particularly appreciative of my services, ostensibly because of my orthopedic surgical background and experience. In his words, we could be a stellar team. He felt so strongly about what I could contribute that he went to his client (insurance company) and sought their permission to retain me as part of their team. The answer was No. In their opinion, the cases were not worth two lawyers, and although I was welcome if the insured wanted to pay me, the insurance company clearly saw the defendant as indefensible and felt that a single lawyer was all that was needed to work out multiple settlements. Moreover, they felt certain that the plaintiff's lawyer did not want to try any of the cases and, of course, neither did they. Several nationally recognized specialists in orthopedic surgery, who were also pioneers in modern lumbar spine surgery, reviewed all of the cases and agreed to testify that the defendant had not deviated from the standard of care. The plaintiff's expert, a local economic competitor, was not impressive. Both lawyers for the defense (assigned and personal) agreed that the cases, particularly the first case, could be defended successfully and strongly recommended proceeding to trial.

The cases were filed in districts that required an attempt to mediate before going to trial. The insurance company communicated through their lawyer a strong desire to settle during mediation. The assigned lawyer was forced, therefore, to attempt mediated settlement. I, as personal attorney, had no such responsibility and was perfectly free (and with the agreement of the assigned lawyer) to do anything I could to keep mediation from succeeding. I was successful in doing so but the insurance company was still too afraid of going to trial and losing the first case. Lack of confidence in the defendant as a witness was the reason given. Personal counsel argued as strongly as possible not to settle, but the insurance company ordered their attorney to settle and ended up, as predicted, settling all of the remaining cases— every one of which might have been voluntarily dismissed if a strong win could have been achieved in the first trial. Thus, even though the assigned lawyer and personal counsel worked together smoothly and evaluated the case identically, the insurance company prevailed with a different goal. It is not wise to retain personal counsel for the purpose of trying to change an insurance company's decision not to defend a case. Advantages of personal counsel lie more in other areas.

POSSIBLE CONTRIBUTIONS OF PERSONAL COUNSEL

1. A personal attorney can assist assigned counsel in preparing the defense, particularly in complex or difficult cases where a single attorney is all the insurance company will authorize and there are obvious limits to how much that attorney can do. Assigned attorneys should approve and welcome personal counsel and encourage them to assist in the defense. If personal counsel is not welcomed by the assigned counsel, the personal attorney should stay out of the defense and confine his or her activities to other areas.

2. In defensible cases, personal counsel should do all that can be done to argue against arbitration and mediation. As in the case cited above, there are arguments and tactics that both defense attorneys agree are warranted in the goal to acquit completely but that assigned counsel is not free to utilize because the insurance company controls the strategy. In such instances, personal counsel can sometimes be effective in preventing a less than desirable outcome for a defendant deserving complete acquittal.

3. A personal attorney can present the strongest case possible to the insurance company against premature settlement. Sometimes personal counsel can be stronger and occasionally even more effective than the assigned counsel operating under the restraints of employment.

4. A local personal attorney can provide knowledge of potential jurors after the jury venire has been released by the

clerk of the court's office. When assigned counsel is from another venue, there is a special need for local counsel for this important function.

5. A personal attorney can help prepare the defendant for cross-examination by spending quality time in going over his or her deposition and having him or her answer practice questions. Particularly if it is the defendant's first courtroom experience, an assigned lawyer often underestimates the fear his client may be harboring about cross-examination. Personal counsel can and should provide additional help in preparation of the defendant. This is one of the areas where having personal counsel can be most advantageous. With the concurrence of assigned counsel, additional help can be rendered in the preparation of defense expert witnesses. In the experience of the author, the most often neglected duty of assigned counsel is the preparation of expert witnesses and cross-examination is the part that needs the most additional help. Personal counsel should really specialize in this endeavor and be well worth the cost to a defendant in this service alone.

6. When it becomes clear that the case is going to be settled, a personal attorney should advise his or her client that a courtroom defense is not going to be possible and explain possible settlement strategies. The most glaring need is that someone with fiduciary responsibility exert all of the influence possible. There are many ways a settlement can be structured. In most cases this does not make any difference to the insurance company or the plaintiff as long as the amount of indemnification stays the same. How a settlement is reported to the NPDB can make a world of difference to a defendant physician, however. For example, if the defendant physician is incorporated and there is more than one physician in the corporation, settlement can often be made in the name of the corporate entity or even some institution rather than in the name of the individual physician. The Health Care Quality Improvement Act (HCQIA) does not require insurance companies to report payments made for medical malpractice on behalf of some corporate entities and institutions, only those made on behalf of individual physicians.

Similarly, when there are multiple entities being sued jointly, there are often numerous possibilities for structuring the final payment so that one individual is not singled out. It is against the law to make a settlement contingent upon dropping an individual, but there is plenty that can be inferred within the law to cause parties to think along such lines, and a personal attorney may be the only person aware of the need to do so.

7. Finally, when settlement has been agreed upon and the final report has to be made to the State Board of Medical Examiners and to the National Practitioner Data Bank,[2] it is the prerogative of the defendant practitioner to submit a carefully worded statement regarding the nature of the accusation, their response to it and the reason for settlement. Personal counsel should assist with preparation of this and should ensure that the strongest possible response is submitted. It is particularly important that the statement carry strong wording that liability was never admitted and that settlement was agreed to only as a matter of financial expediency, etc. In fact, if true, the statement can make it clear that the defendant only agreed to settlement under pressure from the insurance company and continues to maintain innocence of the charges of medical malpractice.

SUMMARY

At first blush, it simply does not seem fair to even suggest that a physician who has paid extraordinary malpractice insurance premiums, often for many years, should have to pay a personal attorney to be on his or her defense team. And most of the time he or she will not need the services of a personal attorney. The purpose of this chapter is to make a defendant doctor aware that the role and goals of an assigned attorney and their insurance carrier employer may, at times, be in some conflict with the defendant's goals. If so, the services of a personal attorney may be justified. Many, if not most, assigned attorneys are able to represent a defendant's interests and those of the insurance carrier at the same time. When this is not the case, as is sometimes so for any number

2. National Practitioner Data Bank for Adverse Information on Physicians and Other Health Care Providers, 45 C.F.R. §§ 60-60.14 (1993).

of reasons, it may be worth the additional expense to retain personal counsel, at least for a short period of time.

It should be remembered that retaining personal counsel does not have to be continuous and certainly not all-encompassing. There are very specific times such as during jury selection, appearance at trial, or, most often, during settlement that a personal attorney can come on board for a short time or for a specific purpose and, by so doing, keep defendant's out-of-pocket expense reasonably low.

There are many factors to be considered in retaining personal counsel, but probably none more compelling than how the defendant and those close to him or her feel about the quality of assigned representation. In the final analysis, professional confidence and personal satisfaction are imperative legal assistance requisites when a physician has to endure the pain of frivolous malpractice allegations. Anything less should be addressed and retention of personal counsel for short periods or specific purposes may be all that is needed, particularly when there is already a long-standing relation between the client and personal counsel.

In order for a physician to work smoothly with any attorney, it is necessary for both to recognize certain basic differences in their education and mental processes (Peacock 1994). Truth for physicians rests in authoritative experience and the scientific method or reproducibility. Truth for an attorney is what a jury will find as truth. There can be a vast difference. Attorneys live by the Rules of Evidence, which rigidly control what they are able to introduce into evidence and argue. Physicians know almost nothing about the Rules of Evidence and frequently misinterpret an attorney's actions as not letting the doctor have his say. Similarly, physicians live in a world of risk; literally every decision a physician makes involves balancing risk factors. Attorneys, in contrast, live in a phantom world of a "reasonable prudent person," and as a result, may not be able to appreciate the inevitable risk factors in the practice of medicine. A successful venture in the defense of a medical malpractice suit may be significantly enhanced by the ability of an attorney and a physician to recognize and accommodate for the education, background bias, and life experience of the other. Retaining personal counsel may be most valuable in its capacity to enhance such understanding and tolerance of the differences between two professions. The additional cost of retaining personal counsel in some instances may be justified on this basis alone.

REFERENCES

Peacock, E. E., Jr. 1994. "Doctors versus Lawyers. A Robert Burns Analysis." *N.C. Med. J.* 55:41–43.

Syverud, K. D. 1990. "The Duty to Settle." *Va. L. Rev.* 76:1113–1116.

Thomas, S. S. 1995. "An Insurer's Right to Settle versus Its Duty to Defend Non-meritorious Medical Malpractice Claims." *J. of Legal Med.* 16:545–583.

16

The Deposition—a Place of Great Danger and Great Opportunity

Lee A. Whitehurst, M.D., J.D.

I once gave a talk to the Duke Orthopedic alumnae on a topic concerning spinal surgery. Afterwards, the chairman asked for a show of hands of those surgeons present who had been sued. Most of the surgeons raised their hands. I secretly prided myself that I had not, because I was especially caring and I communicated well with my patients. Shortly thereafter, on the *20/20* television program, there was a report of a malpractice suit settlement involving pedicle screw patients. The implication was that pedicle screws were not safe because they were not approved by the FDA. In short order, I was sued by a number of my adoring patients. One patient who brought a claim against me said in a newspaper interview that she had nothing against me.

The reality is that every physician should expect to be sued and to give a deposition in his or her defense. In the 1998 AAFP *Professional Liability Survey Report,* 45% of respondents reported having had a malpractice claim filed against them. For ophthalmologists, it was estimated that in a 35-year period, 95% of all physicians will be sued and that the average ophthalmologist, over that time, can expect an average of 2.8 lawsuits (Weber

1997). The good news, however, is that in the United States four out of five medical malpractice suits either are dismissed or end in a verdict for the defense (Gorney 1999). According to statistics from the Physician Insurers Association of America (PIAA), 30% of claims against ophthalmologists result in indemnity payments, and only 5% of those payments result from a trial (Weber 1997). A lawsuit and its necessary depositions are a part of the practice of medicine. The statistics show that usually the physician is exonerated. But you will need to do your part in your defense. There is no greater opportunity to aid your cause than that presented by the deposition.

A legal maxim says, "Lawyers do not win or lose malpractice claims; physicians do." You are more important in winning your suit than your lawyer. A major battlefield is your deposition. Your preparation is crucial. This chapter will prepare you to discourage the plaintiff's lawyer and enhance your chances of winning. This chapter is intended to give you an understanding of what the plaintiff's attorney wants to achieve by taking your deposition. You will learn how to protect yourself by understanding his tactics and methods. You will learn how to prepare adequately for your deposition. You will understand how to present yourself favorably in order that the adversarial attorney will be less inclined to risk a trial. Education regarding the deposition process will give you confidence and relieve stress. Other than a jury trial itself, your deposition probably will be the most stressful part of the suit. But remember, the odds are greatly in your favor. Your deposition is a time of opportunity to help achieve your goal—so relax and prepare.

THE PURPOSE OF THE DEPOSITION

The deposition is the most important part of the discovery process. Each side in a lawsuit has the right to take the discovery deposition of the opposing party. As the defendant in a medical malpractice lawsuit, you will be required to appear at a specified time and place and to give oral testimony in response to specific questions. The questions and answers will be recorded and transcribed into a record, which may be used in a future trial. This process gives the attorneys involved a chance to gain information directly from the adversary. The opposing attorney has the opportunity to develop a framework for presenting allegations at trial. If your case does result in a trial, the plaintiff's attorney will use the questions and responses from your deposition to cross-examine you at trial. He or she will be able to predict your responses to questions since he has already asked you the questions in your deposition. He or she will use those questions which help his or her client. Our legal system provides this opportunity of depositions to both sides in a dispute in the hope that, once all of the facts are known to both sides, there will be a settlement. Settlements are best for society. Settlements prevent the expense of a trial and do not consume the resources of our court system. Your deposition will be the first opportunity for the opposing attorney to form opinions as to how you will perform at trial. It is important that you make a good first impression upon the opposing attorney, which will have a bearing upon the demands in settlement negotiations and ultimately on whether the plaintiff will risk going to trial against you (Vesper n.d.).

During your deposition, you must testify truthfully under oath. Otherwise, you are subject to perjury. The plaintiff's attorney will be taking aim, and he will intend to test you. He will test your credibility and emotional stability. He also wants to identify other possible witnesses and to learn both facts and your opinions. He hopes to set you up for the possibility of impeachment at trial. He would like for you to admit things that you have not disclosed previously. The plaintiff's attorney desires to gain enough information through the deposition process that you and your attorney will become discouraged and want to settle (Cohen n.d.).

PREPARATION FOR YOUR DEPOSITION

Your preparation should begin weeks or months before your deposition. Leaving your preparation to the last minute will expose you to risk and stress. You should be aware of the emotional and mental strain that results from being sued. The effects of the malpractice suit, referred to as "malpractice stress syndrome," have been studied and documented. Common symptoms include "irritability, insomnia, and anorexia, difficulty in concentration, decreased self confidence and decreased libido." Often a physician wrongly concludes that the malpractice suit is an indication of his or her ability to practice medicine (Reading 1987). The facts are, however, that most malpractice suits have very little to do with your ability to practice medicine. In medicine, physicians are taught to learn the truth and to share their mistakes so that better treatment for patients will result. On the other hand, in the malpractice litigation process, the plaintiff's attorney's goal is not to find out the actual truth of what happened in the operating room. Instead, it is to present your former patient's side in the most favorable light in order to win a judgment (Weber 1997). Remember that the attorney representing the plaintiff is an advocate of his client's position. The plaintiff attorney is duty bound to be the best possible advocate for his client's allegations. He is not the trier of facts; the jury is charged with determining what the truth is. The plaintiff attorney is not charged with searching for the truth. He or she is charged with forwarding her client's position. Remember these concepts as you prepare for your deposition.

You must know the medical record. Study the nursing records, consultant reports, and your own notes. Think about why you acted as you did at the time. Would you have acted differently if you would have had more information? Think about what you would say if you were asked about certain aspects of your care.

Practice your manner of response. Train yourself not to answer without thinking carefully about what you will say. If your deposition is not videotaped, the transcript will not reflect how long you took to respond after a question was asked. Take a generous amount of time to formulate your answer. The answer you give may be used against you in any trial. I once was embarrassed while serving as a spinal expert witness for the defense in a malpractice trial because the answer that I gave concerning whether other spinal surgeons were "colleagues" differed from my deposition answer. Even if you are on videotape, it is best to pause for about three to five seconds after the question is asked before you respond. This pause will help you to compose a thoughtful, concise answer. It will also give your attorney a chance to consider objections to the question (Weber 1997). The plaintiff's attorney wants you to talk. The more you talk, the more questions he will think of asking you. The more questions he asks you, the more danger you have. The plaintiff's attorney may entice you to continue talking by raising her eyebrows or by gesturing for you to continue. Resist the temptation to talk for the purpose of convincing the other side that you are right. Practice control in pondering the question prior to responding so that you can formulate a concise answer to the question asked.

You should lighten your workload prior to giving your deposition. A lighter load will give you more time to prepare for the deposition and for relaxing and spending more time in recreation with family and friends. If you are rested prior to your deposition, you will have more reserve for the rigors of the deposition and be less likely to be emotionally labile. Before the deposition, talk about feelings and concerns with people upon whom you rely (Weber 1997). Prepare to have a good night's sleep. You may want to have a physician prescribe a short-acting sleeping medicine, such as Ambien, in case you have insomnia before the deposition. Also, many people who have a "reactor"-type personality, which is associated with an increase in pulse and blood pressure in stressful situations, may benefit from using a beta blocker, such as Propranolol. An off-label usage for this drug is for public speaking. A beta blocker may make you less susceptible to the end organ response of adrenaline, which may help you to react in a calmer fashion and may aid you with clearer thinking during the deposition.

DURING THE DEPOSITION

At all times, before, during, and after the deposition, conduct yourself in a professional manner. Shake hands when appropriate; you do not need to initiate shaking hands with the plaintiff's attorney. You do not have to participate in small talk, but you must be civil and pleasant. Dress appropriately in conservative business attire. Face the examiner and maintain eye contact. Do not display emotion or say anything of which your parents, spouse, minister, rabbi, or children would be ashamed. You are being evaluated as a witness, and the plaintiff's attorney will assess how you will appear to a jury.

Do not feel pressured to answer questions when you are not sure of the answer. Instead, say that you do not recall or that you do not know or that you need to refer to a particular document. You have a right to refer to anything that will help to refresh your memory. Remember to pause for five seconds before answering.

Always be completely honest. Tell the whole truth to the best of your ability and do not be afraid to be emphatic about what you know or have sensed to be fact. However, stick only to the facts of which you have first-hand knowledge. Do not volunteer what you have been told unless you are specifically asked. Do not offer opinions unless asked, and then only give your opinion if you have definite reasons for supporting such opinions.

Always remain confident. Have confidence in the truth and stick to it. Do not let the opposing attorney plant doubt or shake you from what you know is the truth.

Do not educate the examiner. Answer succinctly each question asked, if you know the answer. Do not volunteer your reasoning. For example, you can remember a particular date because that was your son's birthday—do not volunteer that it was your son's birthday. Just give the date. Also, never reveal your feelings, such as "I was feeling badly for Ms. Jones." If you volunteer information, your examiner will have more information upon which to base more questions. Questions are potentially dangerous, and you do not want to add to the volume of questions.

Never qualify your answers with clichés such as "to tell you the truth" or in "in all candor" or "the best I can remember" or "honestly." These clichés cause unpredictable impressions in those who hear them. If you say "honestly," does it mean when you do not say it that you are not telling the truth?

Listen carefully to each question. Be patient and wait for the opposing attorney to finish his or her question. Pause at least several seconds before answering. Remember, if a video camera is not present, the record does not reflect how long you pause before answering. If you do not understand the question completely, ask that the attorney repeat the question. Compose your answer before vocalizing the answer. Answer questions slowly and clearly. Answer only what is asked. Do not volunteer information.

Be careful about giving exact information, such as dates, times, measurements, or other facts, of which you are not definitely certain. It is better to say that you are not sure or that you do not recall, if there is any doubt in your mind. An unqualified answer or a dogmatic one in a deposition, if it is not accurate, may cause you to be impeached and embarrassed at trial. The plaintiff's attorney will imply or say that you lied and the implication will be that if you lie once, you will lie again.

If you are hungry, thirsty, or tired during the deposition, ask for a break. Deposition may last for long periods of time, and you become more susceptible to mistakes when you are tired. After a break, the plaintiff's attorney may question you under oath as to whether or not you discussed your testimony with your attorney. It is preferable not to initiate discussion with your attorney, either on the record or in the presence of opposing counsel, unless it is absolutely necessary. However, at any time you may ask for a consultation with your attorney in private. The content of discussions with your attorney is not discoverable. Remember that everything you say will be recorded as a part of the deposition unless both attorneys agree to go off the record (Manson n.d.).

If your deposition is videotaped, the videotape may be shown at trial. Every facial movement will be available for the jury to examine. You must appear credible at all times. You must always be polite. Never appear sarcastic. Do not exaggerate or purposively conceal information to specific questions. Do not appear to be uncooperative. Do not argue with the opposing attorney. Do not respond with anger or rudeness to bad manners or to what you might construe as insults from the opposing attorney. The opposing attorney would like for you "lose it." He would like for you to appear arrogant and ill-mannered. Recently I attended a deposition of a noted plaintiff's expert taken by a young, aggressive defense attorney. This attorney indicated to me prior to the deposition that he was planning to derail the expert's testimony by asking him questions that would challenge his credentials and credibility. His tactic was effective in upsetting the expert. Although the expert's testimony was well grounded in medical science, the defense attorney scored points by causing the expert to lose his temper. If you give the appearance of being fair, earnest, warm, sincere, and honest, you will help yourself greatly towards a satisfactory outcome (Vesper n.d.). Remember that one of the most important aspects of your testimony is how you conduct yourself when you are asked questions. Always be a lady or gentleman.

The litigation process is long and grueling. However, it will pass. The deposition is a necessary part of the process. Be patient. Prepare yourself as well as possible. Relax and look for the benefits. You will learn from it and your character will be strengthened.

REFERENCES

Cohen, E. E. n.d. "Anatomy of a Medical Malpractice Claim." Westborough, Mass.: Eastern Dental Insurance Company.

Gorney, M. 1999. "Coping with the Bad News—Part I." *The Doctor's Advocate* (1st quarter).

Manson, M. A. n.d. "Surviving the Deposition." OHIC Insurance Company.

Reading, E. G. 1987. "Malpractice Stress Syndrome: A New Diagnosis?" *Md. Med. J.* 36(3):256–257.

Vesper, T. J. n.d. *Guide to the ATLA Deposition Notebook*, 2nd ed. Washington, DC: Association of Trial Lawyers of America.

Weber, P. 1997. "How to Survive a Malpractice Suit." *Review of Ophthalmology* (July).

17

Participating in Your Own Defense

Louise B. Andrew, M.D., J.D., F.A.C.E.P.

Attorney Barton L. Post described the following scenario, one of the most satisfying in his 30 years of medical malpractice defense.

His client, a neurosurgeon, had been named a party to the case in a "shotgun" fashion by a "certifying" expert witness because his name appeared in the hospital chart, despite the fact that he had no factual or legal connection to the patient whose family brought the suit. This fact was made known to the attorney well in advance of the deposition, with requests for his release.

> At the deposition, when the lawyer asked my client to state his name for the record, my client identified himself, and then he stated that everyone, including the plaintiff's lawyer, knew the case lacked merit. He noted the lawyer's repeated refusal to terminate the case voluntarily. He then told the lawyer that if he wanted questions answered, he would need a court order. Then he declared that we were leaving the deposition and returning to my office to start a countersuit. That is what we did.

This physician defendant was a model of participatory defense! He agreed to drop his countersuit against the plaintiff attorney's firm when the firm agreed to fire the attorney.

147

We should all be so lucky. Not every case will be entirely frivolous, and not every frivolous case can be so easily and happily disposed of. But every physician who is involved in a malpractice claim has a key decision to make: am I an active participant, or am I a pawn in a process that is not of my making yet could prove my undoing?

The former approach is highly recommended. Here is my own story:

As a brand new attending fresh out of residency at Hopkins, I was required to supervise residents in the Emergency Department at Baltimore City Hospitals by being available to them if they wished to bring cases to me. Some did, others didn't. One particularly arrogant senior resident never did. So when one of his patients returned to the department unexpectedly DOA, he was immediately named in a lawsuit which made its debut in the *Baltimore Sun*. Reviewing the case, I could find no fault in the care that was provided (her death was ultimately a mystery), so when the prominent attorney who represented the resident asked me if I was willing to be deposed in the case, I did not hesitate to do so (although on what basis, I was not informed). I was given no preparation by the attorney, but apparently did well in the deposition, as evidenced by the fact that the plaintiff attorney became angrier and angrier as the questioning proceeded. Nearing the end of his rope, he asked to see my copies of the medical record (no one bothered to tell me not to bring them, and always overprepared, I had them with me neatly catalogued in case I needed to reference them). At the bottom of the page, he spied my signature (in those days attendings signed all records generated while we were on duty). Gleefully, he added my name to the list of defendants. Careless xeroxing had previously obscured my name, and thus my connection to the case.

It did not take me long to decide that I needed separate representation from the resident, and I demanded an attorney from another firm who was at least as prominent as the attorney who had needlessly implicated me in the resident's case. The case was ultimately settled, the details are forgotten, but I decided then and there that someone needed to be able to teach enough details of the law to physicians to keep us safe from this flawed legal system, and that type of legal mistake, which of course was one of the things which prompted me ultimately to become such a teacher.

Lesson learned: you can't trust lawyers to "handle the case," any more than patients should trust us to just "handle the illness," In both instances, it is a joint venture, and the person with the most at stake is the person most motivated to work towards the eventual outcome. In this chapter, that is you.

How can you become an active participant in your own defense? First off, it is not necessary, nor even necessarily desireable, to go to law school. (Though for me it was great fun!) What *is* necessary is that you be prepared, available, and willing, and that you become knowledgeable about those aspects of medicine which will help your attorney to defend you successfully. And enough aspects of law to defend yourself, if necessary, from the attorney!

What do I mean by "be prepared"? Well, first, be realistic. The likelihood of your being sued at least once in your career is astronomical. Many specialists will be sued multiple times. Malpractice claims are an unpleasant but unavoidable fact of the practice of medicine in the 21st century. So while doing everything in your power to prevent involvement in suits, e.g., remaining up to date in your field, documenting clinical encounters and related matters thoroughly and appropriately, and maintaining good patient and staff relations at all times, you need also to spend some time actually planning what you will do *when* (not if) you are sued.

YOUR DEFENSIVE STRATEGY

Begin planning for your first claim as you plan your practice policies. How do you handle calls from attorneys, or requests for medical records, which are often the first clue and almost always precede the actual filing of the case? How will you accept service of process when a claim has been filed? Your office staff should have a written procedure including what to do if you receive the court documents by mail, in person, or via paper airplane through the back window (don't laugh, this has happened). *When* and where will you actually have the time and privacy to review the complaint? The policy should specify this, as well as such details as what will happen to the patient's records, X-rays, and other tests. What about records of phone conversations? And how will all of these things be protected from pilferage or alteration by others?

When will you notify your malpractice carrier? This answer is painfully clear. *Before* the patient or an attorney makes any claim, *as soon as* you have any inkling that something may have gone wrong. The reason is equally painful. Policies may vary, but if your policy is claims made, as most are, your coverage for any claim, potential or real, will not begin until you notify the company of the possible existence of a case. If the policy should expire before you have notified the company, unless you have purchased "tail" coverage, you may be entirely responsible for defense or judgments in the case. Don't just call the carrier. Write down the notification of potential litigation, with as much detail as possible, and fax as well as mail the details with return receipt requested, to your carrier.

What do you do when you *know* there is a case pending against you? Start bugging the claims representative. Find out whom they are appointing to represent you. Tell them (in writing) who you want to represent you, if you have knowledgeable legal contacts in the community. If you are being covered for malpractice by another entity, such as a hospital or clinic, bug the risk manager. Let him or her know you are not just a passive defendant. Be sure that they know you require separate representation. Get an appointment to meet with the attorney as soon as possible.

In the meantime, make a detailed summary for yourself and the attorney. Title the document "confidential attorney correspondence, prepared in anticipation of litigation." Write down everything you can remember about the case and the patient, referring to the medical records as well as your own memory. If your records are woefully handwritten, dictate a translation for inclusion in this document. Try to be as chronological as possible, but do not make up dates or times if you are unsure of them. Try as best you can to remember and record the exact wording of conversations you may have had with patient, family, staff, or others regarding this patient or interaction. Note in your summary all possible additional sources of information, such as hospital records, phone conversations, consultation notes, imaging reports, etc. If there are other individuals who might have knowledge of some of the facts surrounding the case, e.g., the patient's employers, neighbors, your former staff, etc., add their names and last known contact information to the document.

Make sure that you have, and understand, your malpractice insurance contract. It will contain important details about your representation, such as your right to determine whether to settle your case or go to trial, and the limits of your coverage. The latter will be made much more obvious than the former in the contract, but both are important details which will become obvious later. Take the contract with you with any unclear areas highlighted when you visit your attorney. If the contract is at all ambiguous, ask your claims representative or personal attorney to interpret the contract for you. Hopefully, you will have long since done this (at the time you purchased the coverage), and with luck it is a fair contract, considering that you have probably paid dearly for it. You will be glad you had legal review of the contract of coverage when you obtained it, if you need your own lawyer to reinterpret it to you at this time! But if your insurance is provided by another entity, such as your clinic or hospital, this may be the first time you have actually examined the contract. Do it now, before the inevitable questions arise.

MEETING WITH YOUR ATTORNEY

On the day you meet the attorney, be polite and cooperative, but remember that part of the reason for this initial interview is that it is your first opportunity to determine the attorney's fitness to represent you, just as a patient may interview you initially to see if you are the physician they want to do their procedure or take their case. Be respectful, but direct. See the chapter devoted to this topic. I will sprinkle a few of my learnings in this chapter.

In my first case, the first attorney assigned to me was a junior partner. She was nice, but in no way measured up to the senior partner from another firm representing the resident. I demanded, and ultimately got, her senior partner as my counsel. In my last case, my interview with the attorney was a warning to me which I did not heed. I asked the attorney what his experience was in dealing with medical malpractice cases. He replied that he had actually not had any experience with med mal, but that he had handled a number of legal malpractice cases dealing with mis-handled medical malpractice cases. In retrospect, I should have realized that this was akin to allowing the pediatric pathologist to treat your kid because he would knew what the pediatrician should have done. I also did not pick up on just how happy he was to have me as an attorney physician client. But back to how to participate in your defense.

Let's assume you have satisfied yourself that the attorney is competent. Make it clear to the attorney that you know his duty is to represent you, not the insurer, and that you are prepared to hire personal counsel if this ever comes into question. Like doctors, lawyers hate to be second-guessed. A really secure, experienced attorney should be comfortable, if not happy, with this suggestion. However, if your attorney really seems to welcome the possibility of cocounsel, it could be a tip-off, as it should have been with me, that the attorney really is unqualified and is hoping for some guidance through unfamiliar territory.

Make it clear to the attorney during this first meeting that you do not intend to be a passive defendant. You are available to meet and answer questions, you will assist in procuring responses to discovery, related medical information, and potential expert wit-nesses, and you want to attend all case-related events at which your presence could be helpful. Ask the attorney what meetings this might entail, and at the proper time, to explain to you the ad-vantages and disadvantages of attending pretrial conferences, depositions of all parties, settlement conferences, etc.

Politely request that copies of all significant documents relat-ing to your case be forwarded to you discreetly, but in a timely way. Be specific that you do not want any document to go out in your name or any correspondence regarding your case if you have not been informed about it and been given an opportunity to review it if you desire. In these days of instant communications, there is no excuse for an attorney just to respond to a motion on the eve of the deadline without running it by you first. Requiring them to run it by you will help them to avoid procrastination.

Then, of course, you must follow through on your requests. Multiple meetings may require your absence from practice. Mountains of documents may be generated. Groves may be sacrificed. You will have raw material for a splendid bonfire when this is all concluded. But you will not be "fat, dumb, and happy," blissfully ignorant of important decisions being made about your case and therefore your future, and you will not be blindsided by an incompetent attorney (nor, it should not be missed, will you be forced to retrieve all of these documents through expensive discovery if it eventually becomes necessary for you to sue the insurer or your counsel for negligent representation).

As has been mentioned in other chapters, you are not the only defendant in this case, even if you are the only *named* defendant. Your partners, both personal and professional, have also been involuntarily drafted to help you with your defense. Take the time right now to speak with each of them about what you are feeling, how you are handling it, and what sacrifices will be necessary on their part to help you through the crisis. Tell them you may need more understanding and verbal support when you appear to be taking things harshly. You will need more time to attend to your legal case, and also to get away from it all to recharge for the next phase. And you may need professional support, in the form of a counselor or group, to keep you healthily processing what is happening to you. All of these needs will come to some extent at the expense of others who are in some way attached to you. Acknowledge their sacrifice. Let them know how much you appreciate both this and all the other ways they have supported you through the years. And tell them explicitly that once this case is over you intend to make it up to them. For your colleagues particularly, reassure them that you will stand by them in their hour of need just as they are standing by you now.

Confirm with your attorney what can safely be shared about the case. Some response to inquiries made by your family, partners, and office staff will be necessary. Different responses will be appropriate for differing audiences. And if you have the incredibly bad luck to be involved in a high-profile case, you might even want to consult with a professional about how to handle media inquiries or adverse publicity generated.

YOUR RESPONSE TO THE CLAIM

Every claim for malpractice requires a response to the claim within a certain period of time, in the absence of which the court will enter a judgment against the defendant (you). So the first item of business is that your attorney will need immediately to draft on your behalf a response to the complaint. He or she may wish to enter what is called a "general denial," which is basically refuting every allegation in the claim. Or it may be appropriate to confirm and deny varying parts of the claim, or even to defer response on some issues until more information is known. Find out when this response is due, and ask to review it before it is filed. This may help to avoid retractions later, and when you are going over the document may be a good time for your attorney to begin to share with you some of his or her strategies in the case.

Soon after, or even accompanying the originating complaint will be a slew of requests for what is called "discovery," which is the generic term for various types of demands for information from your opponent in a lawsuit. The theory behind discovery is that once all or much of the information regarding a case is on the table, the parties themselves will be better able to judge their chance of success in court, and may be willing to settle without clogging up the courtrooms. In practice, discovery is an extreme inconvenience, almost bordering on harassment, and it is definitely so used by all members of the bar. "Paper them with three sets of interrogatories and requests for admissions" is an opening battle cry in most tort claims. Interrogatories are long, detailed lists of questions which can cover almost any topic which is "reasonably calculated to lead to relevant evidence" concerning the case. So they may ask you to list some pretty ridiculous things, like the names and number of all patients you have ever treated with this type of condition.

In my second case, I just took my taped dictation to the attorney's secretary. You don't have to go this far, but you do have to be sure that the responses are factually correct, as they will be attributed only to you. Any errors in them may be ascribed to your lack of good-faith response, and you could either lose your case or be charged with contempt of court if the errors are both significant and judged to be intentional. Your attorney has the responsibility for making sure that the responses are legally sufficient and that they do not reveal more than is required by the law.

Requests for Production of documents, which are just what they sound like, can be equally tedious. They may require you to produce all of your tax returns, insurance binders, hospital or insurance application forms, archived hospital or office policies and procedures, or just about anything else which might foreseeably lead to additional evidence. Your lawyer is skilled at handling these requests. But just like interrogatories, they are actually addressed to you, and the responses will be legally ascribed to you, so it behooves you to review them with your attorney, understand exactly what is being requested, and, if production is legally required, to dig up the documents somehow.

THE ART OF DEPOSITION MANAGEMENT

Next will come depositions. Question your attorney carefully about his or her philosophy regarding depositions. Some prefer to depose all parties and experts early, so as to get maximum information early in the game. Others prefer a waiting strategy, hoping that by learning key information in other ways (e.g., interrogatories), the need for depositions (and the accompanying expense) might be reduced. A deposition, as you have learned elsewhere, is a formal quasijudicial interview that is conducted under oath and is recorded and transcribed by a court reporter for later use. The party requesting the deposition is responsible for paying the costs, which can be substantial. In the case of the typical medical malpractice defendant, the costs are borne by the insurer. So if your attorney seems to be delaying deposing a key factual or expert witness in the case, find out why. It may be strategic legal maneuvering, or it may be that the attorney is attempting to minimize costs. This is more likely if the attorney is working on a capitated basis with the insurer, which is a key fact you need to be aware of early in your representation. It may mean that corners are being cut.

Attend any depositions you can, of the patient, family members, and expert witnesses. This can be a time-consuming and possibly uncomfortable situation, but it is very good for you in a number of ways. One, it helps you to size up the memory, intelligence, and honesty of the plaintiffs. Two, it may help to keep them honest, if you look at them incredulously as they relate things which never happened or deny things which did. Three, it lets them know that you are not afraid to confront their allegations and to refute them when your turn comes. Four, it gives you a bit of practice as to how you will feel when sitting in a courtroom in front of strangers with falsehoods being said about you. Five, it gives you an idea of the style of your attorney and theirs, in preparation for your own deposition if it has not yet occurred. Last, if the deposition is of a "professional expert" (see the related chapter), you will learn effective deposition and testimony tactics from someone with experience.

When it comes time for your deposition, make it clear to your attorney that you will require extensive preparation beforehand. The attorney should spend at least several hours on several occasions preparing you, and more if you are anxious, are not a good actor, or do not adapt well to confrontational situations. If your attorney does not have the time to do this personally or in sufficient detail that you are comfortable with testifying, there are consultants who can do deposition and court preparation in conjunction with and on behalf of the attorney.

Ask your attorney how much literature research is appropriate before your deposition. Some recommend extensive knowledge about the medical science in the case, so that you are on a sure footing with your scientific responses. Others recommend ignorance so as not to risk giving any usable scientific information to the other side. Ask what their strategy is, and why. Of course, any preparation you do, you must be prepared to reveal.

The deposition is a critical component in any litigation, and it can make or break your case. See the related chapter on depositions. Your attorney should be able to give you a very good idea of the type of questions that will be asked, and the manner in which they are likely to be asked, by the opposing attorney. If you have attended some of the preceding depositions, you may both have an idea of the deposition style of the opposing attorney. But there are important differences in the way the attorneys will handle their own clients as opposed to the opponents'. With the plaintiff, the plaintiff attorney will be gentle and supportive. Your attorney will (should) be challenging and forceful. With you, your attorney will be direct and affirmative. The plaintiff's attorney will be attempting to do only one thing: convince you to settle.

How will he or she do this? Knowing this strategy is an important part of your preparation. Your attorney may have some knowledge of this attorney from previous interactions. If it is a first experience with this attorney, though, you may both need to fall back on general approaches. The opposing attorney is doing several things by taking your deposition. First, he or she is sizing you up as a witness and defendant. While attempting to get more details out of you than is already known in the case, or to learn more about the medicine if he or she is not well schooled clinically, the attorney is carefully assessing whether you have any natural abilities as a witness, and whether you have any triggers, or "tells," which can be used against you in court. Second, you are being pumped for information. The attorney is hoping to wheedle out of you any details that he or she was unable to discern from the records or from previous discovery in the case. He or she will be persistent, creative, and sometimes devious in asking the same question multiple times and in multiple different ways, hoping to catch you in a new admission or a misstatement which can later be used against you. Third, the opposing attorney is sizing up your attorney, learning whether or not he or she is experienced in trial law, is fluent in evidentiary rules, and is a fighter or a cooperator. There will be skirmishes between the lawyers in most depositions. This is primitive posturing, similar to what animals do to defend their turf or their mates, or to discourage actual combat. Expect and ignore this.

How do you participate in your defense in deposition? Dress professionally, and behave according to your dress. Be cordial, but maintain a professional distance (slightly more than your usual professional distance; remember, this is not your turf). Be aware that the plaintiff or family may be present. With them be doubly polite, but equally distant. There is no formal seating protocol, except that the court reporter must be able clearly to hear your responses and frequently may use lip reading to ascertain them, and thus may legitimately request to be directly next to you. Outside of this constraint, you may ask to sit anywhere. You do not have to give a reason as to why you want a particular seat. It is your right to be comfortable. You will probably want your lawyer nearby, but it is a matter of personal preference, which should be decided between you before entering the room.

Before entering the room, you should also have eaten, preferably something containing protein and without much carbohydrate or caffeine. You are allowed to bring whatever food or drink you need to maintain your comfort level. Personally, I recommend slow-dissolving non-sugar hard candies, which allow one to look thoughtful while sucking, and deter the tendency to answer too quickly without taking that critical moment in preparation. Bring an extra layer of clothing to combat the sympathetic tendency to decrease circulation to skin and extremities in times of stress.

Ask your attorney specifically what else to bring and not to bring to the deposition. Your notes, records, and other documents are all fair game for the opposing attorney (as I learned for myself) if they are present in the room. Ask about the rules regarding any notes you take during the deposition. Let your attorney carry any documents that may be needed for reference during the deposition.

Before responding to anything other than "Will you please tell the reporter your name, title, and address?," repeat to yourself whatever it is that has been proposed as a question. Ask yourself, "Was that a question?" "Tell us what happened" is not a question, it is a command. You do not have to follow commands. Listen for a question, and if none is asked, ask for one. Then (if there is no objection from your attorney) answer only what is asked. "Will you please tell us what happened?" is a question. "I will answer any specific question you ask to the best of my ability" is a reasonable answer. If the question is too broad, as they tend to be on fishing expeditions, ask for more specificity. "What specifically would you like to know?" is a reasonable response. And so on.

Of course the attorney is human and will be looking for shortcuts. Block them. The attorney is probably not a doctor and will be looking for medical education. Stifle that all too common humanitarian impulse to share, and don't dispense any. The attorney may not be very experienced and may be trying some new or hastily composed questions or boilerplate, inapposite questions on you. The attorney may throw out long, convoluted hypotheticals that even he or she can't follow. Ask for such questions to be repeated. If the attorney has to ask the court reporter to read them back often enough, he or she will stop for fear of looking foolish. Lengthen the attorney learning curve, let his or her tactics backfire. Tell the attorney if a question doesn't make sense to you, but don't tell why. If you don't understand the question, you cannot answer it, period. It is not your job to tell them how to rephrase the question so that a normal human doctor could understand and answer it. If the attorney says, "Doctor, help me here," stifle your laughter and put on a stone face as the attorney realizes the lunacy of what he or she has asked.

If the attorney makes a mistake with medical terminology or usage, use your judgment as to whether to call attention to the error here or wait until court. If it is a foolish enough mistake, you can fluster and sometimes shorten the deposition, especially if the attorney's clients are intelligent and are in the room. If not, just allow the attorney to maintain his or her ignorance, but make a note of the misunderstanding for possible future use.

For the duration of your case, there will be fits and starts of activity. Be prepared to deal with this, and tell yourself that it is no worse than raising children going through phases. Be knowledgeable about deadlines, such as for making responses and naming experts, and bug your attorney if these are approaching and there is no sign of activity.

PROCURING THE BEST EXPERTS

Malpractice cases often hinge on the quality of expert witnesses. Be active in soliciting experts on your own behalf. If someone has done research and written about the subject of your case, they are potential witnesses. If you know of respectable members of your community who do expert witness work, suggest them. If your attorney seems to be going for a stable of the usual experts, be sure that you go over that list and warn of potential conflicts of interest before time is wasted on securing someone who really shouldn't be testifying in your case. In my last case, the attorney attempted to engage one of my former students as an expert on my behalf. I redirected him to more appropriate sources of expertise. I do recommend attending your experts' depositions as well as those of your opponent. Presumably you will have no need to keep your witnesses honest, but if they have experience, it will be helpful for you to observe how they handle difficult questions. Also, you may realize more applications of their expertise to your case than was originally apparent, allowing you and your attorney to utilize them better.

A WORD ABOUT SETTLEMENT

I will assume for the rest of this chapter that your case is one that will be tried, because other chapters address the issue of when it is best to settle. But I will say that even if your malpractice carrier reserves the right to settle without your permission, you should be an active participant in the decision as to whether or not to settle. There are reasons other than legal merit which might induce a physician to settle a case, such as if the stress of a trial is judged to be too great to undergo, as in the case of illness in the physician or a close family member. But when settlement is being contemplated, always investigate the ramifications of reporting to the National Practitioner Data Bank (NPDB). Such reporting is required when settlement is made on behalf of a physician. This report will remain on your record indefinitely and will need to be explained every time you apply for privileges, licensure, or insurance coverage. Some insurers may use the fact of reporting as a reason to deny you coverage or dramatically increase your rates. Although it is supposed to remain confidential, there is a constant clamor for the database to become public record, so even a nuisance settlement may someday be reproduced as evidence of your purported unfitness to practice.

At some point in all but the most trivial cases the insurer may ask you to sign a document stating that you are personally responsible for any judgment that goes beyond policy limits (check to see if such a statement might be required by your contract of coverage). The insurer is, of course, trying to protect its assets and discourage you from thinking about suing them if the judgment does indeed go over limits. If you are nervous about signing (for example, worry that your attorney may not represent you as aggressively if you have acquiesced to this fact), then it might be time to consider getting personal counsel. Although personal counsel's contribution to the case might be minimal, sometimes just knowing that there is another attorney who is looking out for your interests and has not even the slightest potential for conflict because he or she is *not* being paid by an insurance company is a security blanket that is worth your investment.

PARTICIPATING IN THE TRIAL

As the court date approaches, get plenty of exercise (for stress reduction) and rest, and pursue extra pleasurable activities such as sports or social gatherings, or attend to a neglected hobby. Far from detracting from your preparation (remember, you have been participating since day one of all of this), you will be building up a reserve of energy and confidence to take with you into court. On the day or days just prior to trial, go over all the details in the case again with a very fine-tooth comb. Whenever a physician gives testimony, as irrational as it seems, the physician's knowledge of the case (which by now may be years old) may be used by the jury as a means of determining how diligent he or she was during the events in question. When testifying in court, be sure that you are quite familiar with what you have said in deposition, so that if there are any discrepancies you will be prepared to deal with them. New factual information may have come forward between deposition and trial, or you may have done some research which validates something which happened for which you previously may have had no explanation.   There are many reasons for changes in testimony between these stages, and it is a destructive myth that nothing can be changed between deposition and trial for fear of impeachment. However, in some jurisdictions, if there are substantial changes in testimony before trial, there is an obligation to inform the court in a timely way.

Go to bed early after a protein-rich meal (remember eating fish before exams?) and have your usual breakfast, whatever that may be. Dress professionally, but not in any way which would imply that you are a rich doctor (the expert witnesses can do this). Drive and park carefully. You never know when approaching a courthouse which ordinary citizens may in fact be your jurors. Be cordial to everyone you see, but not overly so. Sit where your attorney designates, and bring something on which to take notes. Attend carefully to all of the court proceedings and testimony, but do not react to anything that is said in a disrespectful way. If you should encounter the plaintiff in the courthouse, make eye contact, nod your acknowledgment, and say nothing. Communicate with your attorney in whatever way has been decided between you. Find out from your attorney whether you are allowed to converse with your own expert witnesses, and if so, when. Be there throughout the trial. Once the jury identifies you, it will help you for them to know that you care enough to be here to see that justice is done. Your presence may also help insofar as that anyone who testifies dishonestly will realize, seeing you there, that this dishonesty is not going unheeded. Some physicians have advocated bringing other physicians who are well known in the community into the courtroom. Besides the obvious scheduling difficulties, there are serious drawbacks to this approach. Certainly, wearing white coats or buttons would invite serious juror alienation. It is a good idea for family to accompany you, as it will help them to support you both during the trial and afterwards, to have a realistic idea of what the experience has been like for you, and let the jury know that you have the support of significant others.

Just as for deposition, you should have careful preparation by your attorney for your court testimony. Preparing themselves for trial is a difficult ordeal for most attorneys. Ask your attorney to do whatever part of the preparation of you he or she can do, weeks prior to trial. Then only a brush-up session may be needed on the day or days prior to your testimony. If your attorney is unable to provide extensive preparation, yet you feel you need extra time to prepare with someone coaching you, ask for a consultant.

YOU ARE YOUR OWN BEST WITNESS

When you are called to the witness stand, you may feel a bit weak in the knees. This is natural, normal stage fright. All of the best actors acknowledge it and use it to improve their performance. Walk confidently, and be sure that your seat is comfortable and that you have water before you nod to the judge indicating your readiness to proceed. Take the oath or affirmation confidently, as if you were assuming an office. Look the officer in the eye as you do.

Be aware that the attorneys now are staging a play that they have been preparing for months, if not years. They will have props, lighting, even special effects. The plaintiff will use a number of tricks designed to put you on the defensive and make you look less attractive to the jury. If you have been observing trial for several days, you will be aware of some of these tricks, as they may already have been used on your expert witnesses. You will respond to questions in much the same way you did at deposition, but you will be slightly more cooperative. You will not intentionally irritate the attorney, but you will still generally answer only questions that are indeed questions. If you are not asked actual questions, *politely* ask for a clarification. For example, if the question is "tell us about the night in question," ask the attorney to be a bit more specific. You're happy to oblige, but what exactly is he asking you to try to recall? This will give you more time to compose your response and give your attorney time to object if the question really is overly broad. The jury, meanwhile, will begin to suspect that the attorney is fishing.

In court, when the opportunity arises, you can finally release that profound impulse to teach. You can teach the jury all of those things you want them to understand about the clinical issues in order to fairly decide the outcome. You want them to recognize you as the most knowledgeable and authentic witness in the case. After all, you not only know the medicine and science involved in the case (probably in excruciating detail), but unlike any of the other experts, you were *there*. You knew how the theoretical science would or would not apply to the actual human patient, and you used that knowledge in whatever the circumstances, in an attempt to make the patient well. You may have watched the initial response, and even changed your treatment accordingly. The "expert" did not.

Bear in mind that the jury is composed of human beings who also have been, and will be, patients. They want to believe that medicine is an advanced science that will be used to their benefit when their time comes, and they want for a physician they *like* to be available to apply that science to them (along with a humanitarian touch) when the need arises. Your job, in addition to teaching them what they need to know to decide your case, is to make them want you, or someone just like you, to be their doctor.

The trial bar uses jury fantasies extensively. They play on the juror's sympathies, asking the jury to put themselves in the shoes of the plaintiff. The really good thespians try to portray themselves as "feeling the pain" of the plaintiff. At trial, you can also use the jurors' fantasies of safety and certainty in medicine to your benefit, and without acting. You can do this simply by demonstrating your caring, competent, and concerned self. In order to have a good and caring physician available to them when they need one, jurors must protect physicians like you from junk science and false or inflated claims based on sad but peripheral stories of healing gone awry. So help them to fulfill this aspiration by teaching them good science, as well as the limitations of that science, and how you attempted to apply science to a body which is by no means always predictable in its response. In so educating them, you are giving them a very good reason to protect you. Impart to them through your concern about their complete and accurate understanding of the case, that you are a caring and compassionate physician who in no way resembles the ignorant, careless, unfeeling, or malevolent monster whom you are being portrayed as by the plaintiff.

If the plaintiff has suffered a terrible outcome and the opportunity arises to express your concern and dismay over that outcome, use it honestly. If the plaintiff has done something to cause or worsen the outcome despite your advice or best efforts, state how sorry you really are that he or she made that choice. If the plaintiff is simply out and out lying, try to show not anger, but rather disbelief and disappointment that anyone could be so dishonest or misguided or motivated by greed. Use your best teaching skills and bedside manner with the jury. Look the jury members in the eye, one by one, as you speak to them. The plaintiff's attorney will be on the opposite side of the room, trying to force you to look at him or to get the jury to look at his colorful exhibits. Ignore them. Use the power of your earnest gaze to engage the jury to look back empathically at the honest and empathic human being who is being judged on this stage: you.

Listen for any objections from your attorney, and know ahead of time what he or she is attempting to convey by objecting. It may be a simple "be careful, here," or it may be a "don't say another word until we have a bench conference" type of objection. The attorney should advise you beforehand as to how to determine the difference. If the judge should happen to ask you a question, be especially respectful and conscientious in your reply. The judge is the spiritual leader of the jury, after all, and in this room, his or her word is law. Although they don't do this often, questions by the judge are usually among the most important ones asked because they may clarify important issues based on the law which no one else has thought to ask. Such questions may be pivotal in the jury's deliberation about your future. Even more so than to the jury, don't ever talk down to the judge. One of the worst mistakes I ever witnessed in a courtroom was a witness for my ex-husband lecturing the judge about her superior understanding of childcare. If you are unsure about some aspect of court procedure, it is usually permissible to ask the judge respectfully how to proceed. He or she appreciates being acknowledged as the boss. Even if what you have asked is not an appropriate question, as long as it is asked respectfully, the judge's demurrer will be conveyed similarly.

Be polite to court staff and to anyone else you meet around the courthouse. Law, like medicine, often works in strange ways.

If settlement or other conferences occur during your trial and you are allowed to be present, I recommend attending. You have already dedicated this time to the case. Better to be there knowing what is going on than to be killing time somewhere else and worrying. You won't get anything useful done elsewhere anyway.

PREPARING FOR THE VERDICT

When closing arguments are complete, there is nothing left to do but wait for the decision. This is the hardest part of all. But you still have work to do. Use the time to visualize in detail what you will do immediately if you win or lose the case. Make plans to celebrate or to commiserate. Plan how you will convey the decision to anyone who asks. Plan how you will integrate the result into your practice and into your life. Don't think about things like appeals; it is premature at this stage. But do decide how you will change your practice in the future regardless of the outcome of this case, in order to prevent any future ordeal of this sort to the extent that you can. Think of positive changes (like having more time for relaxation and recreation) as well as more difficult ones (like learning new documentation systems, etc.) you can make in your practice, and your life, so that you can move on.

Once the decision is handed down, you can discuss further options with your attorney if there are decisions to be made (such as whether to appeal, countersue, etc.). Be sure to get a concise statement of the case, including the judgment or settlement documents and pertinent case information, for your files for future reference in credentialing applications and the like. If reporting to the National Practitioner Data Bank is required (it is required by law in case of settlement or judgment against you personally which you have not paid yourself), augment your reference file accordingly. Consult your insurer regarding future coverage.

When the case is finally over, have that big bonfire with all of the accumulated documents. Consciously say goodbye to the painful emotions as the reminders go up in smoke. Be glad that however imperfectly, we settle disputes in ways other than mortal combat.

If this is the first time you have been sued, congratulate yourself for being a survivor! If it is not, then be proud that you are a learner. And continue to be. In addition, give thought to becoming a teacher. Many others in your profession will face the same trauma that you have just been through, and most will have no preparation at all. You can be a part of a virtual mutual defense association by sharing with others what you have learned through this painful process.

18

When the Expert Is Not an Expert

Louise B. Andrew, M.D., J.D., F.A.C.E.P.

A five-week-old child was brought to the ED for decreased activity, grunting respirations, and decreased urine output. Since the child was resting quietly and breathing normally when assessed by the triage nurse, the child remained in the waiting room for about 35 minutes before being brought to the back for further evaluation. The admitting ED nurse reviewed the triage note and asked the on-duty emergency physician to eyeball the patient. Physician examination showed the child to be dusky and cool with somewhat cyanotic extremities. There was questionable neck stiffness and rales were heard in the left chest. The physician immediately ordered fluid resuscitation and oxygen was started. Stat pages were made to the pediatricians. Two pediatricians arrived to assume care three minutes after the call and eight minutes after the patient was placed in the examination cubicle. With nurses and pediatricians attempting IV access, the infant suffered an apparent respiratory and then cardiac arrest 10 minutes later. IV and intraosseous lines were attempted for another 10 minutes before being successful. Despite the resuscitation efforts, the child died. On autopsy an undetected metabolic disorder was revealed to be the cause of dehydration and unresponsiveness to resuscitation. No infection or other complicating conditions were apparent.

A claim was brought against all of the physicians and nurses whose names appeared on the chart on the basis of a Certificate of Merit signed by a former emergency physician from a distant state. He opined that neither the hospital nor any of the providers had met the acceptable standard of care.

This was a typical "shotgun" case in a state that requires pre-certification by an expert. A hired gun expert from elsewhere is utilized preliminarily to sign an affidavit that will allow the plaintiff to name every conceivable provider in a case. It makes sense from a plaintiff attorney's viewpoint, because if the negligent provider(s)—assuming there are any—are *not* named in a suit before a certain time, then the case cannot proceed against them. But to healthcare providers who get dragged into a case in which they had little or no involvement, such a case will be forever a black mark on their professional records. This generates a great deal of legitimate physician anger toward the legal system.

I know, because this was my case. The "expert" in question in the above case was coauthor of one of the original textbooks in emergency medicine. He had not practiced in nearly a decade at the time of this case. It was learned that he had lost his teaching position and had not been asked to coauthor subsequent editions of the textbook. However, he still made quite a good living as a professional expert. Local defense attorneys in our state had participated in depositions held at his apparently quite magnificent estate. The state in which this case took place had a further requirement that certifying experts must devote no more than 20% of their professional effort to medical legal work. A call to the only hospital where the expert's CV indicated he held privileges revealed that no one could remember when last he had appeared on the E.D. schedule.

A search for the expert's name in a defense database led to discovery that he had given hundreds of plaintiff depositions. In at least one case, it was revealed that a judge had disqualified him from being an expert in another state forever. Yet he was still able to sign the certificate in this state, and was in fact the only witness the plaintiff ever offered in an attempt to prove substandard care in the case.

Because there was no real case against us, ultimately all of the providers were dismissed without payment.

ROLES PLAYED BY EXPERTS

In some states, there are two roles that require the services of an expert witness. In the first, as in the case above, an expert is required by the legal system to allow a medical negligence case to go forward. A signed affidavit of a healthcare provider must be submitted to the court to indicate that there is some evidence of negligence having occurred in order for a claim to be made against another provider. The rules for this type of expert witness may, but do not necessarily, differ from credentials required of experts who will actually testify as to negligence or causation. In at least two states, Illinois and New York, the identity of this so-called certifying expert witness does not even have to be revealed to the healthcare provider whose care is being certified as falling below the standard of care (Albert 2003).

Lawyers, like many of us, are often procrastinators. So with the statute of limitations looming (that is, the legal time period within which a claim for malpractice must be made coming to an end), it is not at all uncommon for lawyers to issue urgent requests for such precertification assistance from a member of their stable of expert witnesses (those with whom they have done business before). In a case in a state requiring precertification of negligence, any records going out to the witness for review may well be accompanied with a fully prepared affidavit for the expert to sign as soon as he or she is in agreement. Experienced experts will require that a retainer accompany a request for case review or certification, so a signed check will also accompany the packet. There is no statutory requirement for a certifying expert to do anything further with the case. The expert's identity may not even be revealed in some states, so there is absolutely no risk involved. He or she may never see or hear of it again. With essentially all of the work done and paid for, do you wonder how often those packets get returned with the signed checks?[1]

The second and most common role for an expert witness is to evaluate the case formally in preparation for trial to determine whether or not the defendant's treatment conformed with existing standards of medical care, and to testify in the case if it comes to trial. Almost always, more records should be provided to the trial expert than to a certifying expert, including, for example, depositions and medical records and communications which come into the case as a result of discovery (and were not available at the time of the filing of the case). The expert has an ethical obligation to review all materials provided in a given case, and although many are not aware of this, to request additional materials (such as original copies of imaging studies, consultant notes, and any other information such as other expert reports) while arriving at an opinion regarding the standard of care in the case.

Furthermore, the expert should evaluate care in the light of what was standard practice at the time of the incident, not at the time the case is brought. An expert should not form any opinion at all until all available records and the literature are reviewed. And an expert should conform to principles of ethics of their profession and specialty, which make honesty the sine qua non of participating in the legal process.

But by definition, attorneys are advocates. They have a vested interest in the outcome of a case. Since plaintiff cases are usually taken on contingency, the plaintiff's attorney is paying out of pocket (beginning at about $350 per hour) even to ask the witness to glance at a case. Less diligent, more penurious (or less intelligent) attorneys sometimes do not provide all available information to their experts, especially those items which might not support their theory of liability. In order to save money on experts who will ultimately not support them, they may also take other

---

1.   Incidentally, this is not necessarily only a plaintiff phenomenon. In Maryland, for example, in order to defend a malpractice case the attorney must file a "certificate of defensibility" within a certain period of time, after a claim is filed. The same procedure may well be used, especially nearing the deadline for filing the certificate.

shortcuts, such as giving the proposed expert their view of the case before they even send the records for review, along with that retainer (Moss 2003).

Although attorneys are expected to advocate for their clients (Lubet 2001), the same does not hold true for the expert witness. Steven Lubet, a legal ethicist, describing the appropriate role of an expert witness, writes, "An objective expert views the facts and data dispassionately, without regard to the consequences for the client. An independent expert is not affected by the goals of the party for which she was retained, and is not reticent to arrive at an opinion that fails to support the client's legal position." He goes on to explain that "the entire system of expert testimony rests upon the assumption that expert witnesses are independent of re-taining counsel, and that they testify sincerely."

Nonetheless, Lubet admits that "It will probably come as no surprise that there are lawyers who will attempt to influence the content of an expert's testimony" (Lubet 1999). And if you have observed or participated in any substantial number of cases your-self, you have probably seen the effects of this advocacy coming out in the testimony that was provided. Unscrupulous or ignorant experts often become advocates for their side of a case, stepping far beyond the purely educational role which is prescribed for ex-pert witnesses under rules of procedure, which is simply to apply "special knowledge, skill, experience, training, or education to aid judge or jury in resolving a complex issue or question beyond the usual understanding or competence of laypersons."[2]

LEARNING TO BE AN EXPERT IN YOUR OWN DEFENSE

It is not the purpose of this chapter to teach you how to be an expert witness, but there is a very good description of the proper role of the expert witness in a 1998 Baylor University Medical Center Proceedings, which is available online (BUMC Proceed-ings 1998). Several excellent books on the topic are available through the APA Press (Brodsky 1991, 1999). I have also written about the ethics of being an expert witness in emergency medicine

---

2.   Federal Rules of Civil Procedure 702 and 703, and similar state rules.

(Andrew 2002). The fundamental responsibility of any expert witness is to educate the jury about issues that are beyond the knowledge or experience of most laypeople. Honesty and impartiality are the hallmarks of the ethical expert witness.

You will function as a "fact" witness in your own case, which means that you can be asked about the actual occurrence and other related issues. You might be asked your opinion about whether you met the standard of care in your own case, but because you cannot be considered to be impartial, this opinion will not be given as much weight as that given to an expert engaged for the purpose of helping the court to determine the actual standard (an "opinion" expert).

When you are faced with a malpractice claim, there are, as we have illustrated in a previous chapter, a number of ways you need to become active in your own defense. One avenue is to be sure that your attorney is competent and to the best of your ability, to monitor the attorney to be sure he or she is doing the legal part of the job. Another particularly effective way is to become an expert in the subject that is the basis of your case. Although you can't be qualified to testify officially as an expert witness, you certainly can and should thoroughly educate your attorneys about all of the medical nuances of the condition, some of which you will only become aware of through intensive study. Through your reading you will also become aware of those who are expert enough in the subject to have done extensive research and who have published materials. These materials can be a very good source of potential experts on your behalf.

If this is a high-stakes case, you may not want your attorney to use only the local experts with whom he or she is used to dealing. As an expert in your specialty, you are in the best position to determine whether the usual stable of experts used by your attorney are in fact appropriate experts to testify on your behalf.

In the above case, the defense attorney, without my knowledge, approached one expert who had previously been my intern and still worked at my institution, and another who was a colleague of mine from our local professional association. They were convenient and cheap because they would serve both as certifying experts (certifying in this case the defensibility of my perform-ance) and as testifying experts. Neither of them, however, had any expertise in pediatric emergency medicine or neonatal emergen-cies, which were the crux of the case. I made it clear to the attor-ney that I felt that the potential for a jury finding bias in either of his chosen experts made them unacceptable as testifying experts, and insisted on obtaining the services of two board-certified pediatric emergency physicians and a world-renowned metabolic disorders expert on my behalf. I identified these experts through reading and by networking within my national professional asso-ciation.

CHECK OUT THE EXPERTS

A competent attorney should be pleased and not threatened by your research. Nonetheless, if the attorney is working on a capi-tated basis for the insurance company, he or she might balk at the fees charged by bona fide experts. If you have done your due dil-igence in identifying experts and put your requests in writing along with your reasoning with a copy to the insurance adjuster, you will be less likely to encounter resistance from your attorney. After all, if the insurer ignores your advice and loses your case, they are in a vulnerable position with respect to you. You could sue them for not mounting a vigorous enough defense in your be-half.

Once the plaintiff has identified their expert or experts, your attorney should begin to explore the expert's background and qualifications as grounds for possible disqualification or im-peachment. You can sometimes be very helpful to him or her in this process. Study the curriculum vitae of the expert. Does this person even qualify as an expert in the field involved in the case? Some state statutes require such expertise. Check yours. If the ex-pert is from your specialty, there is no one more qualified to judge his or her credentials than you.

Is there anything questionable about the expert's qualifica-tions? For example, is the medical school one with a good repu-tation? Can graduation be confirmed via the AMA or Federation of State Medical Boards? I have heard of cases of persons who were not even physicians living very nicely as "medical expert witnesses." Did the "expert" complete a residency or fellowship in an appropriate specialty, and did he or she achieve board certification promptly? Does he or she claim to be a member or fellow of a professional association? Does this imply continuing membership in the association, or maintenance of board certification in the specialty? All of these details are things that the defense firm should be willing to investigate further—for example, by verifying such training and certification through the AMA or Federation of State Medical Boards.

If the designated expert belongs to any medical specialty professional association, there may be ethical principles by which he or she is bound, and may therefore be held, by other members, such as you. Some associations have developed admirable expert witness policies,[3] affirmations, and procedures for evaluating and disciplining members who offer rogue expert testimony. Check the website of any associations in which the expert claims membership for applicable policies.

There may be guidelines for expert witness behavior, affirmation statements of member willingness to abide by guidelines and other ethics policies, and ethical review policies available to apply to members who stray beyond these guidelines. Be aware that in order to use ethical or disciplinary policies to review the behavior of an expert, the complainant (you) must be a member. Not a member? Join. Some societies, such as the American College of Emergency Physicians, even have resources for members for litigation stress support. If the so-called expert is not a current member of the AMA or a specialty association, association policies will not apply. The expect can still be asked under cross-examination if he or she will sign an affirmation of willingness to abide by ethical policies of the association affiliated with his or her specialty. But check with the society as to whether or not the expert is a member. If he or she is claiming to be a member of any association and has never been, or his or her membership has lapsed, these are all bases for impeachment by your attorney.

---

3.   Such as AMA CEJA E-9.07, available at http://www.ama-assn.org/ama/pub/category/8539.html, AANS, ACEP, and most others.

Such misrepresentations can be used to discredit the witness in front of the judge or jury.

Is the individual licensed? Almost every state licensure board maintains a list of licensees and any actions against their licenses, including, in some states, malpractice and other claims. Check every state in which he or she is claiming licensure. A false claim of licensure or a disciplinary action in any one jurisdiction can, in addition to impugning the witness in this case, become the basis for a future licensure complaint in all of the other states. Almost all of these things are easily available online. Does the witness claim medical school teaching credentials? Faculty status at medical schools and universities is public knowledge and is worth confirming. Lapsed credentials can be nearly as damning as feigned ones.

Note: A good defense attorney will already be checking into these things. But a little reminder from you, and requests for status updates will keep them on their toes. Keep those paralegals busy. Make your investment in liability coverage pay off fully for you.

USE NETWORKING AND DATABASE RESEARCH

Use your networking skills. Check Medline for articles written by the expert, which may contain contradictory information. Do an Internet search of the expert's name in all possible combinations. Ask your professional colleagues what they know about the individual. There are very large databases of stored testimony from experts maintained by both defense and plaintiff organizations. Have your attorney search these legal databases for records of the expert's participation in previous cases, and contact the attorneys involved for any information that might not be readily apparent from the stored depositions. Some databases, such as MedicalExpertReports.com, are free as of this writing. Some societies, such as ACOG, ACEP, ACS, and AANS, subscribe to online databases such as IDEX and/or maintain their own, and will allow members to query these databases about the expert's depositions from other cases. One organization has been formed to help members inform themselves about the track records and unethical practices of expert witnesses (the Coalition and Center for

Ethical Medical Testimony, www.ccemt.org). If you learn through any of your networking efforts or through professional exchanges the names of prior defendants in whose cases the expert has participated, contact them. Usually they will be only too happy to share anything they may have learned about the expert with you.

In the chapter on counterclaims to frivolous litigation, you will learn some specific legal techniques for dealing with unscrupulous or unethical expert witnesses and plaintiff attorneys who bring cases without establishing a basis for negligence. Expert witness malpractice litigation is still relatively rare, but it is possible. A pivotal case involving just this topic is reviewed in an article by Richards and Walter ("When Are Expect Witnesses Liable" n.d.).

As previously noted, you will not be designated as an expert witness in your own defense. But that doesn't keep you from becoming the most informed physician who might enter the courtroom to testify on your behalf! Juries will judge a defendant physician based on a number of things besides the evidence that is produced in the courtroom. They will judge your dress and demeanor in the courtroom. Is this the type of person I might want to take care of me? (Does he or she listen to people, and answer their questions, the way I would want my questions attended to?) They will judge your knowledge of the specifics of this case. (Does this doctor pay attention to details such that I might be able to trust him or her with remembering the details of *my* illness or that of someone I love?) And they will judge your understanding of the illness or injury. (Does this doctor seem to be knowledgeable about the condition he or she was treating?) You can't afford not to be knowledgeable. After all, jurors will reason, if the doctor doesn't even care enough to find out *now*, after it's all over and there was a problem, then he or she probably just doesn't care about anything or anybody.

But this would never be you. You will be prepared, intellectually, physically, and psychologically, to defend yourself. Because you have read and applied the principles in this book, and are as qualified and competent a defendant as you are a clinician.

REFERENCES

Albert, T. "Doctor Fights to Know Who Advanced Suit." *American Medical News* (28 July).

Andrew, L. 2003. "The Ethical Expert Witness." *Journal of Medical Licensure and Discipline*, 89:125-131. Available online at http://ccemt.org/la.pdf.

Brodsky, S. 1991. *Testifying in Court*. Washington, D.C.: American Psychological Association.

————. 1999. The *Expert Expert Witness*. Washington, D.C.: American Psychological Association.

BUMC Proceedings 1998. 11:227-230. Available online at http://www.baylorhealth.edu/proceedings/11_4/11_4_thornton.html.

Lubet, S. 1999. "Expert Witnesses: Ethnics and Professionalism." *Georgetown Journal of Legal Ethics* 12:465.

————. 2001. "Nothing but the Truth: Why Trial Lawyers Don't Can't and Shouldn't Have to Tell the Whole Truth." New York: NYU Press.

Moss S. 2003. "Confessions of an Expert Witness" *Legal Affairs* (March-April).

Richards, E. P., and C. Walter. n.d. "When Is an Expert Liable for Their Malpractice?" LSU Law Center, http://biotech.law.lsu.edu/ieee/ieee33.htm.

19

Alternative Dispute Resolution

Albert E. Sanders, M.D.

If you are faced with a malpractice suit, there is a good probability that the judge will require *mediation* prior to the trial. Mediation is a nonbinding form of alternative dispute resolution (ADR). At the very least it is an opportunity to gather information and evaluate all of the participants in the case.

Another alternative method used to resolve a dispute is *arbitration,* which is binding. It is used when demanded by the insurance contract or by mutual agreement of the involved parties. Each side picks an arbitrator to represent it, and both select a third arbitrator. After each side presents its case, the arbitrators, proceeding under the rules of the American Arbitration Association, render judgment based on a majority vote.

HISTORY OF ADR

Alternatives to a trial for settling a dispute have been with us for a long time. They are incorporated in the Texas Constitution of 1845 ("Non-binding Dispute Resolution" 2003). The pain associated with a trial for both the defendant and the plaintiff has also long been recognized. Voltaire said, "I have been ruined twice. Once when I lost a lawsuit and once when I won one." In the 1950s, court dockets became crowded and an alternative to lengthy jury trials was necessary to administer justice in a timely fashion. In 1976, at the Pound Conference, a number of influential lawyers, judges, and law professors proposed several avenues for dispute resolution. Shortly thereafter, dispute resolution centers were established in Houston, Tulsa, and Washington, D.C. Centers are now located in most major municipalities, and the states have codified ADR legislatively. The Carter Center is an example of the ADR concept being utilized to solve international disputes. Details on the spectrum of conflicts that can be addressed by ADR can be found on the Texas ADR website (www.texasadr.org). In arbitration, a judgment rendered by the three arbitrators is binding and is a part of most business contracts. Many HMO contracts contain a clause requiring arbitration for disputes that arise. Nonbinding forms of ADR are mediation and mock trials. One form of mock trial is a summary jury trial, which allows the litigants to present their case in a limited fashion to a jury, usually of six people. Another form is a commercial venture, E-jury, in which the arguments of both sides are submitted electronically and heard by a jury. The litigants are then able to evaluate their probably of winning in an actual trial.

MEDIATION PROCESS

The most common form of ADR in medical liability cases is nonbinding mediation. Both parties with their attorneys and a representative from the insurance company meet with a professional mediator to try to negotiate a settlement. First a conference including all of the participants is held. The mediator explains the rules of mediation, the fickleness of juries, and the advantages of a negotiated settlement. Both sides briefly present the facts from their perspective. The parties then go to separate rooms with their attorneys and the mediator meets with each party presenting demands and offers, discussing facts and legal issues, and encouraging resolution. Settlement occurs in about 80–90% of all cases, though the figures for medical malpractice cases are somewhat lower. If the parties cannot reach agreement, the case will proceed toward trial. Mediation is the most likely form of ADR that you will be involved in, so it is worthwhile to look at its various components. These include:

1. Premediation planning;

2. Conducting the conference at the beginning of the mediation session;

3. Working with the mediator as he performs his shuttle diplomacy;

4. Maintaining a dialogue with the plaintiff if mediation fails.

PREMEDIATION PLANNING

Considerable time needs to be spent with your defense attorney prior to the mediation. If at all possible, you should be present for all depositions. The plaintiff's expert witness may not be as critical if you are facing him. The opinions of the opposing experts should be examined for faulty conclusions. The medical treatment and records should be studied. Finally, your schedule should be cleared to provide a day free from distractions.

The strengths of your case should be weighed against the strengths of the plaintiff's case. An evaluation should be made of your chance of winning or losing in a jury trial. Multiple factors are involved in this evaluation.

Case example: A 60-year-old woman who had been fused from L4 to the sacrum for spondylolysthesis with a left iliac crest graft developed a degenerative disk at L3-4. She was decompressed and fused posteriorly using a graft from the right ilium. She developed a painful pseudoarthrosis at L3-4 and the decision was made to do an anterior fusion at L3-4 using cages and a graft from the anterior iliac crest. Her great vessels were friable and she developed a small leak from the vena cava. With each attempt to control the bleeding with a suture by the vascular surgeon, the bleeding became more severe, and the patient expired. The carrier and defense attorney for the orthopedist thought the orthopedist had a defensible case. The odds of losing were increased because the vascular surgeon appeared arrogant and had a limited grasp of

English. Because of this, the carrier for the orthopedist recommended that he settle.

If multiple defendants are involved, an estimate of the percentage of any award which would be assigned to you should be calculated. An estimate of the average amount juries have awarded in similar cases is also a factor in this calculation. From these data, a realistic settlement range can be calculated. As an example, the average jury verdict for a case similar to yours has been $600,000. You have two codefendants, all with equal involvement, and your chance of losing has been estimated to be 25%. $600,000/3 = $200,000 × 0.25 = $50,000. Since $50,000 is the mean, your bargaining range in mediation would roughly be $25,000–$75,000. If the plaintiff is willing to settle in this range, it might be prudent to settle to avoid time away from your practice and exposure to a possible hostile or overly sympathetic jury. On the other hand, you may feel your case is strong and want to take it to trial. However, keep in mind that the insurance carrier will provide coverage in accordance with your contract only up to the limits of your policy. If there is a potential for a judgment in excess of your policy limits, you should seriously consider settlement rather than risk a trial. If you believe that you should settle but the carrier insists on taking the case to trial, you should consider hiring your own attorney to apply pressure on the carrier. You can also discuss the possibility of an appeal with your attorney. The plaintiff may also want to negotiate a settlement to avoid a lengthy trial and appeals process.

Discuss with your defense attorney and the insurance representative exactly how the mediation will be held. Ask them to be specific with you about your case and the strengths and weaknesses of both sides. Inquire regarding the consequences of your settling, having your name in the National Practitioner Data Bank, and how a negotiated settlement will affect your insurability and liability premium. Consider the day a learning experience. Avoid distractions. Remember, mediation takes one day and is a confidential process. A trial may take many days and is a public procedure. Spend adequate time with your attorney going over the strategy of mediation. Ask him or her how he or she will conduct the conference, and what help he or she will need from you. Make sure you have shared all pertinent data and feelings you have about the case with your attorney. All pertinent records should be assembled before the conference.

The mediation site is important and should be a neutral location. The mediation I was involved in was in the office of the mediator. The conference room was commodious and their other rooms quite adequate for both parties and their attorneys. Satisfactory space can also be obtained at hotels. One should avoid holding the mediation in the office of the plaintiff attorney, since it would give his client a perceived if not real home court advantage.

MEDIATION CONFERENCE

Be early, neatly dressed, and courteous to the plaintiff and his attorney. You and your attorney now have the one opportunity that is available to meet with the plaintiffs in an atmosphere that is not completely adversarial. Either through your attorney or directly, let the plaintiff know that you regret that in spite of all your efforts to provide appropriate care, that there was an unfortunate end result. Also let them know that you have come in good faith, are sure that they have as well, and will do all possible to reach a reasonable agreement. Studies have shown that a courteous but firm problem-solving approach is more likely to lead to a satisfactory resolution than a hard-nosed, arrogant stance. A trial is similar to football, where contact is part of the game. Mediation is more like basketball, where contact will be penalized. You will probably not change the attitude of the plaintiff, but if your position is presented in such a manner that a reasonable jury would side with you, it will be easier to negotiate with the plaintiff.

Case example: A local bar manager and several colleagues left on a deep-sea fishing trip early one morning after a night of drinking and other recreational drugs. While at sea, the manager was supposedly knocked down by the force of a rogue wave. He claimed the accident had nothing to do with his inebriated state. An orthopedic surgeon was on call for a local emergency room. He performed an open reduction and internal fixation of a fracture. The patient was discharged after three days with no obvious signs or symptoms of infection, despite questionable redness, erythema, and a discrepancy in the patient's temperature as reported by the discharge nurse. Three days later the patient was readmitted with obvious infection. A diagnosis of necrotizing fasciitis was soon made. Numerous debridements followed. An infectious disease consult was obtained. The patient ultimately suffered an above-the-knee amputation, but his life was saved. The physician chose to consent to settlement because he had not seen the patient on the day of discharge and the nursing notes were poorly written and harmful to his defense. Mediation ensued. The patient and his lawyer were extremely belligerent during the general session, even accusing the physician of altering records. The physician became so outraged he withdrew his consent and stormed out of the mediation. The process failed. Eight months later, the case settled for an amount the physician's insurer was willing to pay at the time of mediation. This case illustrates an important aspect of mediation. Regardless of the conduct of the opposing party or his lawyer, keep your cool and remember that mediation should be a time of calm negotiation and diplomacy.

WORKING WITH THE MEDIATOR

The skill of the mediator is crucial to reaching a reasonable conclusion.

Case example: The patient was a 49-year-old man with end-stage multiple sclerosis who was bedridden with progressive skin breakdown and subsequent decubiti. He was noncompliant and the family was absent during much of the patient's confinement in the nursing home. The patient's family came out of the woodwork following his demise and sued the nursing home, the administrator, the director of nursing, and many of the staff nurses. A full day of mediation was unsuccessful. However, a week after the mediation the mediator contacted each party privately. The mediator sent a blind settlement proposal to each party. Each party was instructed to accept or reject the mediator's proposal without knowing the terms offered to the other party. This unique approach resulted in resolution of this unfortunate case.

If your attorney doubts the ability of the mediator assigned to you, a substitute can be requested. It is best not to let the mediator know your settlement maximum. If you have to change your evaluation as the negotiation proceeds, it could put you in an uncomfortable position. Expect the plaintiff to make a positional or unreasonable demand to start with rather than one based on the facts of the case. Don't let this disturb you. Keep in mind your calculated value of the case when you come up with an offer and stay below this. Hopefully the plaintiff will lower his demand so that there is a bargaining range where his bottom line is less than the maximum you are willing to pay. The mediator can then help both sides come up with a number they may be unhappy about but can live with. If a bargaining range cannot be established, ask the mediator for his advice. The mediator may spend excessive time with the plaintiff. You may ask, "What is going on in the other room?" You may get information that will be of value to you. Don't worry about lunch, and do all you can to work with your attorney to keep the mediation moving.

When there is down time, work with your attorney, revising your strategy as necessary and planning the course if negotiations fail. Remember that if you have a reasonable case and continue to negotiate in good faith, there will probably be a resolution.

Case example: A 68-year-old successful insurance broker with a long-standing history of asthma and lack of optimal compliance with physicians' orders presented to a freestanding minor emergency clinic for an acute asthma exacerbation. Nebulizer treatments failed to relieve his symptoms, and the patient was transferred by ambulance to the ER of a major hospital for further evaluation and treatment. Upon arrival, the patient's condition had dramatically improved. All vital signs were stable, pulse oximetry was within nominal limits, peak expiratory pressures were acceptable, and the patient was manifesting no signs of respiratory distress and wanted to go home. The ER physician recommended admission, although he was not convinced it was needed. The patient refused. The recommendation to admit was not charted. A Medrol dose pack was ordered and the patient was discharged. On the way home, the prescription was filled, but due to unclear instructions, the medication was not taken. Three hours later, the patient experienced another acute exacerbation. His inhaler and home nebulizer failed to relieve his symptoms. In route back to the same emergency room, he suffered a respiratory and cardiac arrest and died in the arms of his wife. A wrongful death lawsuit ensued. The widow, who was an integral part of the deceased's insurance business, believed that a large portion of the targeted settlement demand should have included compensation for lost earning capacity or loss of the value of the business. The business, however, which she continued, earned more after her husband's death than it had in the five years preceding his death. Unfortunately, it required her to work much harder. Additionally, an interested third party offered the same purchase price for the business after the death as had been negotiated with her husband prior to his demise. The business had been valued at approximately $675,000; therefore, this was a pivotal issue in the case.

The defendant physician consented to settlement. Negotiations prior to mediation stalled because the widow could not understand why she should not be reimbursed for the value of her husband's business, despite her lawyer's attempt to explain the weakness of that argument. An experienced and professional mediator was chosen by the lawyers. At mediation, he spent a great deal of time with the widow explaining why the evidence would not support a jury award for the loss of profits or diminution in value of her husband's business. After hours of heart-to-heart discussions and much shuttle diplomacy, the widow and her daughter began to understand that the physician's insurer would never include loss profits or a reduction in the value of her husband's business as a part of this settlement package. Due to the skills of the mediator, the parties' negotiations ended approximately $100,000 apart. Over the next two weeks, the parties continued to negotiate and the case settled.

This case illustrates several points. First, parties to mediation may have unreasonable expectations going in. This can defeat the purpose of the process. Second, an objective mediator can help explain the strengths and weaknesses of a case that even the parties' own lawyers cannot seem to get across to their clients.

MAINTAINING A DIALOGUE

A sign of a good mediation is when both parties conclude their business feeling they have gotten the short end of the stick. The plaintiffs are dissatisfied that they have accepted less and the defendants feel they have paid more than the value of the case. If an agreement cannot be reached, recall that in the days before mediation, many cases were settled on the courthouse steps. Let your attorney know that in the time remaining before trial you want to remain reasonable. If the case does go to trial, remember that the time spent in mediation has not been wasted and that you are much better prepared to help conduct a vigorous and reasonable defense before a jury.

Case example: A middle-aged man sued his surgeon, the hospital, and the manufacturer of the spinal implants used in his surgery. He claimed the alleged negligence caused injury to his spinal cord, which resulted in impaired bladder control and decreased sex drive. All defendants denied liability and damages. Two separate mediations were conducted.

Mediation was complicated due to the number of parties' involved, alleged degrees of liability, as well as theories of liability. At the conclusion of the second mediation no agreement was reached. However, the parties continued to negotiate separately with the plaintiff. After a short period of time, this resulted in settlement for all the parties. This happens with some frequency.

Sometimes mediation day is the first step toward the resolution of a case.

REFERENCES

"Non-Binding Dispute Resolution." 2003. Report. *The Advocate* 23 (Summer).

20

Attending Trial

Richard J. Nasca, M.D.

In most medical malpractice cases, going to trial is unnecessary. Oftentimes some type of settlement is agreed upon prior to
trial. Many insurance companies have the right to settle without
the doctor's permission (Thomas 1995). Many hospitals agree to
settle a case to avoid the publicity of a trial. It is prudent to avoid
a trial in jurisdictions where sympathetic juries commonly give
large awards in medical malpractice cases. However, in some
cases the doctor defendant will need to go to court. The purpose
of this chapter is to prepare you for that experience by describing
the process in some detail.

PRETRIAL

The case is usually assigned to a county or city courthouse in
the jurisdiction where the patient lives or where your office is located. It is rare that a case will be moved out of the jurisdiction in
which the event or treatment was carried out. A judge is assigned
to supervise the case from start to finish. The city or county clerk
of the court will schedule all deadlines and events connected with
the case. Unless there is good cause, it is wise for the defendant
and his attorney to cooperate with the court set dates. Any requests for postponement must be made for good reason and in the

form of a motion to the presiding judge. It is necessary to complete all depositions prior to the assigned deadlines set by the court. After the discovery phase is completed, the judge decides the pretrial motions of both parties. The attorneys involved present any special agreements to the presiding judge. For example, there may be an agreement known as high-low. Both attorneys agree upon a high dollar amount limit if the case should be decided in favor of the plaintiff, whereas if the case is won by the defendant, the low dollar amount is paid out. The purpose of this agreement is to protect the defendant against a judgment exceeding the dollar amount of his or her medical malpractice insurance coverage. I believe that a high-low agreement is a good tactic which can protect the defendant from the potential of a runaway jury award in an emotionally charged case.

PREPARATION FOR TRIAL

The defendant should be fully versed in all aspects of the medical records. It is wise to review your deposition as well as the depositions of the plaintiff and the plaintiff's experts. Any literature quoted should be freshly reviewed. Prior to trial, radiographs, photographs, and other graphic material to be used should be checked for availability and relevance. Nothing is more embarrassing than to show up with an X-ray folder in which key radiographs are missing or nonrelevant to the case.

Be prepared to explain in simple terms what was done to the patient. Do not hide behind medical terminology. Your dress should be conservative. Expensive or flamboyant clothing and fancy jewelry are to be discouraged. Make eye contact with the jury and speak directly to them as you would speak to a patient in your examining room. Do not become upset or provoked by the questions asked by the plaintiff's attorney; this would be playing into their hands. Keep your cool and stay alert to traps set by open-ended questions posed by the plaintiff's attorney.

It is wise to spend several hours with your attorney in preparing for your court appearance. Your attorney is your mentor and guide through this difficult process (Danner et al. 1996). You must have confidence and listen to and abide by your attorney's advice. If you lack confidence in your assigned attorney, you need to ask for a replacement well in advance of the trial. You and your attorney must be able to communicate and have rapport with one another. You must be totally honest with your attorney and admit any deficiencies in diagnosis and treatment. An experienced medical malpractice defense attorney with a fund of medical knowledge will know the weak points in your case. These deficiencies should be discussed and defended, if possible, but not ignored.

PICKING A JURY

Picking a jury is the first order of business at trial (Bern 1986). The judge will provide a brief overview of the case to the jury pool of 40–50 people prior to jury selection. This is intended to provide limited information to potential jurors who will be interviewed. Potential jurors are dismissed for cause if they have any personal or professional relationship with the plaintiff, defendant, experts, or the attorneys. Each attorney is given the opportunity to interview each potential juror. A good defense attorney will frame his questions to a potential juror to fit the circumstances of the defendant's case. A certain number of peremptory challenges (strikes) are given to each attorney. Your attorney may consult with you about his or her picks. You should pay close attention to the demeanor of the potential juror and how he or she answers the questions asked by your attorney. Often subtle biases become apparent during this questioning process. Analytical people, such as engineers and scientists, make excellent jurors. Teachers, business professionals, and self-employed individuals who are responsible for the day-to-day operation of their businesses are usually good jurors. Potential jurors will be asked if they can be impartial in reaching a final decision regarding the case. It is wise to pay close attention to their answers and to their demeanors. Race and gender may play a role in jury selection. The judge may dismiss a potential juror for cause at his or her discretion. For a civil case, 12 jurors and 2 alternates are chosen from the jury pool. Prior to empanelling the jury, the judge provides instructions on how the trial is to be conducted. The jury may elect a foreman prior to the opening of the trial, during the trial, or prior to final deliberation.

Your role during jury selection should be one of assistance to your attorney only if asked. Close attention to the process of jury selection is in your best interest and should be taken as a serious part of the trial. You must remember that these individuals will be deciding on the merits of the case and will make the final decision regarding your guilt or innocence. The jurors may submit questions through the presiding judge during the trial. The judge may or may not direct that the appropriate participant answer these questions, especially if the answer is important to the outcome of the case. It is estimated that the outcome of 30% of all malpractice cases is directly determined by jury selection (O'Connell and Pohl 1998).

OPENING ARGUMENTS

Opening arguments consist of statements made by the plaintiff and defense attorneys regarding the circumstances of the case. They will also discuss how they are going to go about proving the guilt or innocence of the defendant. The degree of or lack of damage suffered by the patient is also presented during this time. Plaintiff's counsel will take this opportunity to detail what occurred during your care of the plaintiff and the subsequent suffering which has resulted from your treatment or lack of it. He or she will discuss why it is necessary to bring this case to a court for resolution. The plaintiff's attorney will avoid issues and facts which cannot be substantiated during trial (Bollinger et al. 1996). Both attorneys will define medical terminology and procedures to the jurors. If surgical procedures were done, they will familiarize the jury with the type of the procedure so that the jurors have a step-by-step understanding of what went on before, during, and after the operation. The plaintiff's attorney will indicate where you deviated from the standard of care in performing the procedure and the harm that resulted to his or her client.

It is also important to detail the plaintiff's injuries and permanent disabilities. It is also common practice to indicate what other doctors would do in a similar case.

The plaintiff's attorney must prove that it is more probable than not that the defendant's negligent acts caused the plaintiff's injury. If there are any weak points in the plaintiff's case, they are usually mentioned by their attorney during the opening statements.

The defense attorney will present a solid and plausible defense theory, which the jury may understand and use during deliberation. The defense attorney must avoid making statements that cannot be proven during the trial. Defense counsel will educate the jury on the medical facts of your case during his or her opening statement (Bollinger et al. 1996). The defense theory often depends upon an understanding of the diagnosis, medications, and procedures.

The defense counsel should speak to the jury regarding the details involved in your evaluation and treatment of the plaintiff during these opening statements rather than later, after they may be confused about a critical issue or procedure. However, he or she should not burden the jury with facts that may be confusing, irrelevant, or extremely complicated. The defense must recount in some detail the causes, circumstances, and results of the treatment which resulted in the plaintiff bringing action against you. Counsel should provide the jury with information on the individuals who were responsible for each facet of the plaintiff's care and treatment (Bollinger et al. 1996).

In the opening statement the defense counsel must explain why the defendant's conduct did not violate the standard of care or cause the plaintiff to suffer the alleged damages. The defense must indicate that the care rendered to the plaintiff was reasonable and proper and did not cause the plaintiff harm (Bollinger). Jurors should be instructed not to allow their sympathies to affect their assessment of the facts. However, if they do, you entrust they will favor your client.

PLAINTIFF'S EXPERTS

Plaintiff's experts are chosen for their expertise and their ability to perform well in a courtroom setting. In most cases these individuals will be in the same specialty as the defendant physician (Manos 1991). The expert should be knowledgeable about all aspects of the case. He or she should be familiar with the standard of care in the city or county where the case is being tried. The plaintiff's expert should function as a teacher of medical fact and reason. It is important for the defense attorney to check on the reliability of statements made in the plaintiff's expert's deposition prior to going to court. For example, a surgeon was being sued for a complication following a procedure. The expert indicated that he had done 40 similar surgical procedures a year. A subpoena to the hospital medical records department indicated that the surgeon had not done any of these procedures in the last three years. This information was pivotal in the defense of the surgeon being sued for the complication. There are some experts who make a living testifying against other doctors indiscriminately, and these individuals should be disciplined for this behavior. However, there are other experts who testify with integrity because they believe that the standard of care was violated and malpractice did occur. Experts should be cautioned to avoid being advocates on behalf of those for whom they are testifying. A good plaintiff's expert should have firm medical documentation to support his or her testimony. The plaintiff's expert should avoid personal opinions and professional jealousies.

Experts who provide undocumented medical opinions and erroneous testimony in their depositions can often be made to look foolish in the courtroom by a defense attorney knowledgeable about the particular field of medicine under discussion. The defense attorney may question the plaintiff's experts regarding the money they generate from testifying, the usual charges for depositions and court testimony, and whether or not they advertise their availability in legal journals. Most intelligent juries are sensitive to issues of bias and credibility. It is incumbent on the plaintiff to utilize experts with impeccable credentials and no significant bias.

DEFENSE'S EXPERTS

The success of one's defense may depend on the effectiveness of his or her chosen expert. The doctor being sued should provide his attorney with a list of qualified experts in his specialty, or at least review any list of experts provided by the defense attorney. The defendant doctor should not attempt to contact or influence in any way his defense expert. One should seek individuals who are well respected in the field of medicine at issue and who have impeccable credentials. The defense attorney must present his or her expert's qualifications in some detail, thereby cementing their credibility and reliability. Although physicians in academics are often called to be experts, individuals in private practice can be very effective in the courtroom. A balanced personality and a good demeanor are important characteristics of an expert. Again, the defense expert should act as a teacher imparting truth and knowledge to the jury, not as an advocate for the doctor being sued. The defense expert should be conversant with the treatment rendered by the defendant and all the appropriate literature regarding the diagnosis and treatment under question.

TREATING PHYSICIANS AS WITNESSES

Plaintiff may call on physicians who have treated the patient to subtantiate the patient's injuries, degree of disability, and need for further care (Adams and Dorf 1992). The treating doctor is considered an impartial witness and usually carries great credibility. These individuals can cause irreparable harm to the defense if they testify that the defendant did not perform according to the standards of the community, mismanaged the patient, or did not follow through on acceptable treatment options. Treating physicians need to substantiate their testimony with documented evidence that the defendant did not practice according to the standard care. For example, a treating surgeon may indicate that he found a nerve to be cut during a reoperation. To substantiate this statement, a pathology report confirming a neuroma would be necessary. On the other hand, the treating doctor could provide a great deal of support for the defendant by testifying that the standard of care was met and that he and other doctors in the community would support the defendant in all aspects of the care rendered to the plaintiff. The defense attorney should take care to present the credentials of the treating doctor favorable to the defense in a similar manner to those of the expert witness.

PLAINTIFF'S CASE

After introducing the plaintiff to the jury, the plaintiff's attorney will ask the plaintiff to describe the medical condition(s) for which he or she sought your medical care. The plaintiff will be asked to give a detailed recap of the encounter with you and the treatment you rendered. The plaintiff must establish credibility and communicate directly to the jury.

He or she must describe the disabilities and limitations which resulted from your treatment. The plaintiff may wish to present a videotape of a day in his or her life or submit photographs taken before and after your treatment. Plaintiffs may call coworkers as witnesses to corroborate their disability status.

Plaintiffs are cautioned by their attorneys not to exaggerate their complaints, become adversarial with the defense attorney, or demonstrate outbursts of unusual emotion. Plaintiffs need to be instructed to answer the defense attorney's questions thoroughly and not deny or fail to disclose previous medical history relevant to their case.

Plaintiff's attorney will usually grill the defendant physician thoroughly during initial examination. The defendant must be tolerant, cooperative, nonargumentative, and pleasant in spite of the harassment. A defendant who becomes emotional, defensive, and uncooperative presents a poor image to the jury and reduces his or her chance to prevail and win the trial. The defendant must avoid providing the plaintiff's attorney with information or statements not substantiated by the medical record, current literature, and accepted local practices. The defendant must be cognizant of statements made in depositions and take care not to impeach him- or herself during questioning at trial by not giving responses similar to those given in pretrial depositions. Often the plaintiff's attorney may ask the same question at different times in a slightly different manner in order to trip up the defendant. It is prudent not to answer a question that you do not understand. Hypothetical questions can usually be objected to by the defense and will be sustained by the judge. It is wise for the defendant physician to speak directly to the jury and not the judge when answering questions. When you are asked to read a statement or portion of your deposition, read it word for word and do not summarize, editorialize, or embellish it.

THE DEFENSE'S CASE

The defense attorney will usually spend a significant period of time questioning the plaintiff. Statements made by the plaintiff regarding the particulars of your case will be revisited in some detail. For example, the patient may deny or forget to mention that the defendant advised the patient to stop smoking prior to surgery. Suppose the patient developed a pulmonary complication following surgery, which is directly related to the smoking. The defense attorney will often ask the patient to read that portion of the medical record which indicates that smoking was discussed with the patient and that he was advised and agreed to stop smoking prior to the operation. Good medical recordkeeping is vital in defending a physician being sued for malpractice. The defense experts will be asked to review for the jury the appropriate indications for the treatment rendered and whether or not the defendant met the current standard of care. The experts should be prepared to document and discuss why they agree that proper treatment was provided. They will also be asked to discuss any complications that occurred and whether the defendant was negligent in causing these. The defense experts should be familiar with the percentages of commonly occurring complications with the procedure under discussion and their management.

EXHIBITS

Radiographs, videotapes, photographs, drawings, and anatomical specimens should be carefully chosen for presentation to the jury. The doctor defendant can be especially helpful in selecting useful and significant visual material to be used (Manos 1991).

If X-rays are to be presented, proper illumination must be available in the courtroom. Enlargements of photographs and drawings are necessary and should be available. Complex anatomical structures can be presented by use of plastic models, and in some cases 3-D imaging is helpful. Proximity of anatomical structures often encountered in the surgical field should be presented to the jury for orientation and their appreciation of the environment in which surgeons are required to work. Documentation by way of photographs, X-rays, or videotapes of unusual or unexpected pathology is often very valuable in defending intraoperative treatment decisions. Occasionally a surgeon will create one or more models of what was encountered during the procedure. More than a few jurors have been impressed by these models. No visual material should be discarded, and there should be no attempt to suppress, ignore, or hide this information.

CLOSING ARGUMENTS

Closing arguments are vital ingredients in winning cases. These arguments provide the opportunity for both attorneys to convince and sway the jury by the forceful presentation of their theories developed during the trial. The attorneys should analyze the evidence and present to the jury their conclusions based on what a prudent person would understand to be reasonable and true.

The plaintiff's attorney will usually thank the jury for their attention and patience in hearing his or her client's case. He or she will review the evidence presented and relate this to the applicable law in the case. In a medical malpractice case, the plaintiff's attorney will discuss in some detail the concept of the standard of care, how it relates to the case under discussion, and how the defendant physician deviated from the standard. A litany of the plaintiff's disabilities, pain, and suffering will be presented.

Lifestyle changes allegedly resulting from the defendant's care will be brought to the jury's attention once more. A specific dollar amount of compensation will be requested and related to the law, which entitles the plaintiff to be reasonably and fairly compensated for damages.

The closing argument of the defense attorney must convince the jury that the defendant's care of the patient was within the standard of care and that the defendant provided competent care. The defense attorney should review for the jury the key points of the plaintiff's and defense's expert testimony. He or she should indicate that there are different methods of treatment all of which are within the prevailing standard of care in the location where the care was rendered. Defense counsel should emphasize that the defendant doctor is a qualified practitioner who chose to follow the same course of care recommended by the defendant's expert (Bollinger et al. 1996). It is proper for the defense to take issue with the amount of the plaintiff's demand for damages. The attorney for the defense should indicate to the jury that a verdict for the plaintiff will not only result in a monetary loss for the defendant but will also tarnish the defendant's reputation as a competent medical caregiver. Defense counsel should thank the jury for their attention.

JUDGE'S INSTRUCTIONS TO THE JURY

The judge will issue instructions to the jurors regarding the questions to be deliberated. These questions will also be reviewed by the attorneys for the plaintiff and defendant. The question format will be presented to the jurors for their deliberation.

For example:

Question No. 1: Was the defendant guilty of practicing below the standard of care or did the defendant deviate from the standard of care?

If the answer to Question No. 1 is no, the jury is finished deliberating.

If the answer to Question No. 1 is yes, the jury is instructed to proceed to:

Question No. 2: If the defendant did practice below the standard of care, was this the proximate cause of damages to the plaintiff?

If the answer to Question No. 2 is no, the jury is finished deliberating

Question No. 3: If the answer to Question No. 2 was yes, the jury must decide on the amount of damages.

The jury is required to return a verdict if it can unanimously agree on one. If the jurors cannot agree on a verdict, the foreman can request further time for deliberation and further instructions from the judge. At all times the jury should try to be as objective as possible. The law requires the jury to render a decision based on what a prudent person would decide, and on the evidence and testimony presented.

Your attorney and you, the defendant, will stand when the judge and jury return with their verdict. In the vast majority of medical malpractice cases, the jury will find in favor of the defendant physician. However, in certain parts of the country, overly sympathetic juries may be common, and the defendant doctor may not prevail. Awards may be quite generous, especially in "bad baby cases" and in surgical cases with poor outcomes.

You and your attorney, anticipating a trial in a jurisdiction with a history of sympathetic juries and potential for a runaway jury, may file a motion for change of venue. It is rare that a case will be moved out of the jurisdiction in which the event or treatment occurred. The courts have a cadre of judges. When a case is filed, it is assigned to a judge who is responsible for ruling on each motion presented. He or she is responsible for setting the ground rules of the case and for conducting the trial. In many jurisdictions, the judge will meet with the attorneys prior to the case going to court. The judge may recommend that the case be sent for mediation in anticipation that a mutually agreeable settlement can be reached prior to trial. If the case goes before arbitration, the decision of the three arbitrators is binding on all parties but an appeals process is available. Judges are to be impartial and are charged with being sure the trial is conducted in an acceptable manner, according to principles of law and local jurisdictional customs.

If you should lose, you can request that your attorney file a motion requesting the judge reduce the award since the amount awarded is out of line with the facts of the case. All judges have this power.

REFERENCES

Adams, M. B., and G. W. Dorf. 1992. *Medical Malpractice Case Management in Discovery: A Defense Perspective.* 435 PLI/ Lit 23. New York: Practising Law Institute.

Bern, M. J. 1986. *Selecting Juries in Medical Malpractice Cases.* 302 PLI/Lit 97. New York: Practising Law Institute.

Bollinger B. G., K. A. Giampa, and A. M. Ialongo. 1996. *Trial Technique*, ch. 15. Springfield, Ill.: Illinois Institute for Continuing Legal Education.

Danner, D., L. L. Varn, and S. J. Mathies. 1996. "Medical Malpractice Checklists and Discovery."*J. Legal Med.* 17:463.

Manos, E. S. 1991. *Handling Your First Medical Malpractice Case: Fundamentals of Case Management.* 421 PLI/Lit 297. New York: Practising Law Institute.

O'Connell, J., and C. Pohl. 1998. "How Reliable Is Medical Malpractice Law?" *J. Law & Health* 12:359.

Thomas, S.S. 1995. "An Insurer's Right to Settle versus Its Duty to Defend Nonmeritorious Medical Malpractice Claims." *J. Legal Med.* 16:545–583.

21

Settlement of Medical Malpractice Cases

Roger L. Young, J.D.

INTRODUCTION

The outcome of a medical malpractice lawsuit can be determined in one of two ways. An arbitrator or a jury can hear the evidence and make the decision who wins and who loses, or the plaintiff and defendant can negotiate a settlement of the claim. In the former approach, the parties to the lawsuit surrender the power to decide the outcome to a person or group of persons who are essentially strangers to the dispute. In the latter approach, the plaintiff and the defendant retain control of the ultimate outcome of the lawsuit. Litigation is necessarily a win-lose situation, whereas negotiated settlements are win-win opportunities. The selection of the appropriate approach to resolve a lawsuit is driven by many factors, which must be evaluated on a case-by-case basis.

COMPETING INTERESTS

Every medical malpractice lawsuit represents convergence of many and often dramatically competing interests. The most obvious of these competing interests are the plaintiff's perceived need for compensation for an injury that he or she feels is the result of a healthcare provider's negligence versus the provider's desire to seek vindication that the care provided was within the standard of care.

THE PLAINTIFF'S PERSPECTIVE

Plaintiffs are frequently not the kind of people who sue lightly. In fact, many make it a point to emphasize just how devastated they are about what has befallen them—be it the loss of a loved one or a life-changing, devastating turn of events that they feel could and should have been avoided. Often their lives have been permanently changed in ways that preclude them from earning a living or doing activities that they previously enjoyed. They see no solution to what they perceive to be their desperate situation.

THE HEALTHCARE PROVIDER'S PERSPECTIVE

The healthcare provider is placed on the defensive and is angry that their patient has turned on them by filing a lawsuit. The initial reaction is "How could this patient and or family for whom I provided what I believed to be good care do this to me?" The doctor may feel that the complication or end result was out of his or her control and he or she should not be held accountable or blamed for a bad outcome. Many physicians think juries are not knowledgeable enough to decide a medical malpractice case on its medical merits.

They would prefer to have a jury of their peers decide these cases. Most physicians worry about the attendant adverse publicity and the possibility of being reported to the National Practitioner Data Bank and the potential impact that such a report will have on their ability to maintain hospital privileges and remain competitive.

THE LIABILITY INSURANCE COMPANY PERSPECTIVE

The liability insurance carrier wants to minimize indemnity payments and defense costs, but at the same time wants to be perceived as a company which will stand by its insureds when they are under siege. Insurance companies used to handle claims the way they felt was appropriate based upon their assessment of the relevant legal and economic factors involved in the case. In the old days, the liability carriers would settle cases with or without the concurrence of the insured physician. Such a practice infuriated many physicians, who felt betrayed. As competition for market share increased, the insurers sought ways to differentiate themselves. One marketing strategy was to include a clause in a policy that required the physician's permission to settle a case, so that the physician had a voice in the process. This settlement permission clause is included in most modern policies. It makes good sense from a marketing perspective, but often allows a physician's ego or stubbornness to get in the way of good decision-making.

PLAINTIFFS' LAWYER'S PERSPECTIVE

While most plaintiffs' lawyers are driven by the desire to help people in need or to represent people in an environment where the system would otherwise ignore or minimalize them, the reality is that lawyers must choose cases that will result in fees sufficient to pay the bills and justify the expenditure of time and resources necessary to prosecute a medical negligence action. The plaintiff's lawyer probably took the case on a contingency basis and must prevail to recover the considerable expense money that he or she has inevitably advanced as well as to earn a fee (a percentage of the total settlement or verdict).

It makes no economic sense for an attorney to file a medical malpractice lawsuit that has no basis. Most clients with medical negligence claims do not have the financial resources to fund the litigation necessary to assert a claim against a physician; therefore, the attorney must advance the costs of litigation as the suit progresses. Litigation costs in a medical negligence case can vary in a range from several thousands to tens of thousands of dollars (and even several hundreds of thousands of dollars in rare cases).

Plaintiffs' medical negligence lawyers recognize that medical negligence cases are strongly defended by highly capable defense lawyers. They know there is no such thing a free ride in such cases. The statistical reality is that patient plaintiffs lose about 70% of the time when a jury decides who wins and who loses.

From the lawyer's perspective, a lawsuit is the application of the law to the facts of a given situation. It is not intended to belittle the physician, nor to prove that a physician is not worthy of the title. The purpose of a medical malpractice lawsuit, like any other lawsuit, is to assert a claim for compensation for injury or death that could have been avoided if the standard of care had been met.

These factors quickly lead to the conclusion that a plaintiff's lawyer would be foolhardy to file a claim that did not have two basic characteristics: first, that the chances of prevailing on liability be substantially positive (based upon the input of the physicians who review the case prior to filing); and second, the damages be of sufficient magnitude to produce a recovery large enough to cover the litigation expenses and the attorney's fee and leave enough to make the outcome financially worthwhile for the patient. Anything less compelling amounts to an unacceptable gamble for the plaintiffs' lawyer, since the outcome is usually against the plaintiff if the case must be resolved by jury trial. As a result, most good plaintiff's lawyers would rather not accept a case in which it is clear from the beginning that it will have to be tried in front of a jury—not out of fear of going to trial, but because it usually indicates that the case has inherent weaknesses that will ultimately benefit those defending the case.

DEFENSE LAWYER'S PERSPECTIVE

The defense lawyer must strike the proper balance to serve two clients—the doctor who has been sued and the liability insurance carrier who pays his bills. The defense lawyer's primary allegiance is technically to the client, but because the insurance company pays the bills, it will be the driving force behind many strategic decisions, such as when and if to settle a case and how much the case is worth. The defense lawyer realizes that most doctors take lawsuits personally and are not willing to admit that they have failed to meet the standard of care in a given situation. Consequently, the defense lawyer assigned by the insurance carrier often has a difficult role to play.

MEDICAL COMMUNITY PERSPECTIVE

The medical community is an unnamed participant in most medical negligence litigation. Various professional organizations at all levels have taken strong positions against "frivolous lawsuits." Individual physicians and many medical organizations have lobbied state and federal legislative bodies to address the "malpractice crisis" by limiting the amounts that are recoverable for pain and suffering. They also claim that juries cannot be trusted to do the right thing because of high verdicts by juries. Some professional groups make it extremely uncomfortable for those physicians who are willing to offer expert testimony for the plaintiff in malpractice cases. Some malpractice groups blame lawyers who represent patients for the "crisis." The battle plan is to attack and modify the legal system that has served us for 200 years—not perfectly, perhaps, but better than any other.

RULING SETTLEMENT IN OR OUT

ASSESS THE COMPETING INTERESTS

The starting point in considering whether a medical malpractice lawsuit should be settled is to recognize the competing interests of the direct and indirect participants in the litigation and put these interests into proper perspective. In theory, a lawsuit is a search for the truth. If so, unvarnished truth should be the ultimate arbiter of the competing perspectives. The resolution of a lawsuit should be driven by the dispassionate application of the law to the facts of the situation. Resolution should not be based on a "winner-takes-all" mentality, but rather should reflect a fair outcome for everyone involved.

OBJECTIVELY EVALUATE WHAT HAPPENED

A sober, objective assessment of what happened is the next step in the analysis. This assessment amounts to evaluating the physician's performance against the standards of practice recognized among his peers—fellow medical practitioners. The courts of every state require expert testimony to define those standards and whether or not they have been met in a given situation. Lawyers do not set the standards and cannot testify that they have been met or broken. Hence, *the viability of a case is determined by physicians, not plaintiffs' lawyers*. Therefore, it is prudent to remember that it is another physician's evaluation of your performance that provides the basis for the lawsuit.

SEPARATE THE WHEAT FROM THE CHAFF

It has become commonplace to denigrate medical malpractice lawsuits as frivolous. Frivolous lawsuits are held out as a burden on society and an impediment to prosperity. This term has frequently been applied to medical malpractice lawsuits, resulting in a diversion of attention from the real issues involved. Although lawsuits are particularly unpleasant for the defendant physicians, that does not make them frivolous—even if a jury decides in favor of the defense.

The legal dictionary defies "frivolous" as "So clearly and palpably bad and insufficient as to require no argument or illustration to show the character as indicative of bad faith upon a bare inspection."

All states have a procedure for dealing with truly frivolous lawsuits. In most jurisdictions the procedure is called a motion for summary judgment. If a defendant considers a lawsuit to be frivolous and without merit, he or she may ask the court to review the available evidence and determine that there is no genuine issue as to any material fact. Upon making such a finding, the court can then dismiss the lawsuit. If no such motion is brought by the defense, it is a reasonably good indication that the lawsuit is not frivolous.

One of the positive changes resulting from the last wave of medical malpractice legal reform has been the requirement for lawyers to certify prior to filing a lawsuit that the medical records relevant to the case have been reviewed by someone who could qualify as an expert witness (a physician—usually in the same specialty or a closely related specialty) who is willing to testify that the care was negligent. Some states require an affidavit from the expert physician to be attached to the complaint. Other states simply require the lawyer to certify that this requirement has been met.

It is important to recognize a valid claim and prepare to deal with it appropriately. Denying the reality of the situation at best delays the inevitable and at worst exposes everyone involved to needless angst and anguish. The fact that a suit has been filed usually reflects that there is at least one physician who believes the suit is meritorious. The bottom line is that one should deal with reality and not be distracted by the rhetoric of others.

WHY TRIALS HAPPEN

A jury trial is the inevitable result in three common scenarios. First, if the plaintiff is just plain wrong on the factual/medical analysis of the situation. Second, if the plaintiff wants too much money for the damages that can be proven. Third, if the case is in the gray zone and could go either way when the jury deliberates. Most plaintiffs' lawyers are reluctant to take a case in the gray zone because they are the ones that often go to trial. (Remember, the plaintiff loses 70% of the time, so it makes sense for the defense, especially the insurer, to accept the risk of a gray zone case and see what happens, unless the financial risk is so great that even a 30% chance of losing is unacceptable.) If you find yourself in one of these three scenarios, settlement may not be appropriate; however, settling rather than trying a case in the second or third scenario may reflect the insurance company's attempt to save money at your expense in terms of time and stress.

THE RISK OF THE JUDGE

The trial judge is required to be independent, unbiased, and fair. It is the judge's responsibility to maintain order in the courtroom and to ensure that both sides receive a fair trial. It is the judge who decides if, what, how, and when evidence will be presented to the jury. The judge also rules on countless issues that arise during a trial. Most of the decisions of the trial judge are discretionary, meaning that they will not be overturned on appeal unless it can be shown that the judge acted arbitrarily or capriciously in making a particular ruling. Different judges may exercise their discretion differently and yet still be within the bounds of propriety. No lawyer can know for sure how a judge will rule in every situation. As a result, the judge's ruling always introduces an element of uncertainty to both sides during trial and therefore must be considered in balancing the pros and cons of settlement.

THE RISK OF THE JURY

For all of their faults, juries tend to do the right thing most of the time. Even when the jury bases its decision on the wrong things, it frequently makes the right decision! Jurors can intuitively sense when an expert witness is not being truthful, or is simply stretching his assessment of the case too far to reach a predetermined result. Plainly put, juries usually find a way to separate the wheat from the chaff. After all, it's hard to get an unanimous verdict from any group of 6, 8, or 12 people who know nothing about the case when they take their oath to receive and weigh the evidence and measure it by the law, as explained to them by a judge. Accordingly, it would be foolhardy for a lawyer knowingly to use less than fully credible expert witnesses or to base a case on some tangential theory of liability.

A trial by jury is theoretically a trial by one's peers, who listen to the evidence and render a verdict based upon what they hear and see during the trial (to the extent that they understand) and the instructions (to the extent that they understand) given to them by the judge at the conclusion of the presentation of evidence. In fact, a jury is a group of 12 strangers to both sides who come to the courthouse with their own personal prejudices, biases, and preconceptions that will impact on how they evaluate the evidence, regardless of how hard they try to decide the case in accordance with the judge's instructions. Frequently, jurors would much rather be doing something other than sitting and listening to testimony and considering evidence during trial.

As soon as both sides have finished presenting evidence and making arguments, the litigants' power to affect or control the outcome ceases to exist—unless a settlement is reached during jury deliberations. No matter how well a case is presented or how well qualified an attorney might be, a jury is empowered to do what it considers appropriate. There is no certainty when it comes to jury verdicts. Truthful lawyers on both sides will admit that they have been unexpectedly surprised by a jury decision on numerous occasions.

Thus, the uncertainty of what can happen at trial is an incentive to resolve cases before going to court, where everyone loses some measure of control over the ultimate outcome.

THE COSTS OF LITIGATION TO A DEFENDANT PHYSICIAN

The amount of time devoted to litigation can vary significantly, depending upon the nature of the case and the degree to which a physician chooses to be involved in the details of preparing the defense. A defendant physician must make significant time commitments to prepare for and attend depositions and to ready oneself for trial. Review of medical records, depositions of the plaintiff's experts, and review of current and relevant medical literature will be necessary in preparing one's defense. Phone calls and meetings with the defense attorney, consultants, and insurance adjusters may require a significant amount of time away from a practice.

A physician must consider the personal costs of litigation in evaluating whether or not to settle a case. The costs in terms of time, money, and stress are significant and increase with the length of time the case stays in litigation. Frequently, professional liability policies provide for only nominal compensation to the physician while away from the practice for reasons related to the litigation, so time away usually amounts to money lost.

STRESS OF LITIGATION

The physical and emotional stress of defending a suit may be overwhelming for some individuals. The duration of litigation, which may last three or more years before resolution, the anxiety regarding the outcome, and the exposure to an intensely adversarial process may be such that it might make sense for a physician to agree to settle the suit in order to gain peace of mind and the ability to practice medicine without such distractions.

THE RISK OF BEING PROVEN WRONG

If, after review of all the records, depositions, and other evidence, it becomes apparent that you do not have a case that is easily defended or has a good chance of prevailing in front of a jury, it would make sense to resolve the matter. **It is prudent for a defendant to ask the defense lawyer for an unvarnished assessment of how defensible the case really is.** Most defense lawyers have sufficient experience to recognize a problem case and would welcome an opportunity to share such an assessment when it is directly solicited. Anything less than a strong declaration of the soundness of the defense should be interpreted as a potential indication that the lawyer thinks settlement could be appropriate.

THE RISK OF A VERDICT IN EXCESS OF LIABILITY COVERAGE

In some cases, it may be prudent to settle within policy limits rather than to go to trial and put personal assets—or the assets of your partners—in the event of a verdict in excess of available coverage.

THE RISK OF ADVERSE PUBLICITY

Going to trial usually draws the attention of the local medical community to the case. They often come to trial to show support for the physician, but I suspect that there is a certain amount of doubt about competency in the minds of colleagues as they become more aware of the case. There is also the risk of media involvement, which could expose not only the physician but also the family, group, or hospital to public scrutiny and/or censure.

THE VALUE OF PRIVATE COUNSEL

The decision to settle a malpractice suit is not easy. Under certain circumstances, it makes sense to consult with personal counsel who is familiar with the challenges of such litigation. The attorney hired by the insurance company to represent you will undoubtedly be competent, but because of an inherent conflict of interest he or she may not be in the best position to advise you with regard to settlement. Talk to an attorney you can trust to give you straightforward advice about what is in your best interest. Such a consultation will not be covered by your insurance company, but reliable, independent, objective advice is worth whatever it will cost if it helps you determine the course of action that is appropriate for you. See Chapter 15.

22

Matters before the Medical Board

Robert M. Clay, A.B., J.D.
H. Diane Meelheim, B.S.N., M.S.N., J.D.

GENERAL ADVICE

When dealing with a medical board in any matter, whether it be applying for a license or responding to a complaint or formal charges, total honesty is always the best policy. It has frequently been said in jest that the medical board will forgive you for being an axe murderer if you have been rehabilitated and if you honestly confess what you have done, but they will never forgive you for a lie.

You will need the advice of an attorney who is familiar with the rules and regulations and regularly practices before the medical board in all but routine licensing matters. Most physicians will have contact with a medical board only when they apply for a license or when they register their license in accordance with the state requirements. The staff attorneys who work for the medical board are generally quite good about giving out information about attorneys who can be of assistance to physicians facing hearings and other matters before the medical board. You will not find these attorneys by looking in the telephone book, because they generally do not advertise their services.

LICENSING MATTERS

Most state medical boards require similar information before an applicant can be granted a license. The requested information concentrates on the applicant's education and training, with particular emphasis on other states that have granted a licensure, either while in training or on a permanent basis. There will be questions regarding any investigation of which the applicant has been the subject, as well as any lawsuits or claims that have been made against the applicant. If in doubt, it is advisable to interpret the questions as broadly as possible or to ask for clarification as to the meaning of the question. It is important to remember that most medical boards use common terms differently, and for that reason the applicant may inadvertently be viewed as less forthcoming than circumstances may require. For example, one applicant failed to disclose that he had been accused of cheating in medical school and allowed to withdraw without the investigation coming to any conclusion. There was no question on the application that specifically addressed that sort of accusation. When a background check revealed it, the board felt the applicant should have revealed it and denied him a license. He subsequently retained an attorney to intercede, in order to be allowed to withdraw the application without prejudicial information becoming a permanent part of his record.

Physicians who are applying for a state medical license (whether allopathic or osteopathic) should become familiar with each state's requirements at least a year before planning to begin work in the state. Generally there is no way to speed up the application process after the paperwork leaves the physician's hands. Consequentially, all efforts should be made to complete the application and provide all the required materials before the form is mailed in order to assure processing on the part of the receiving state medical board in a timely and efficient manner.

There is no single national medical license. The Federation of State Medical Boards (FSMB) has developed a subscription data repository called the Federation Credentials Verification Service (FCVS). Physicians who anticipate making multiple state applications during their professional careers may choose to subscribe to this service. Almost all state medical or osteopathic boards belong to the FSMB, and almost all will accept the FCVS. A few states require the FCVS certification in order to complete an application. The FCVS allows physicians to deposit information generally required by all states with the FCVS. The FCVS performs the primary source verification of the data and prepares a certificate of verification. When applying for a license, the physician requests the FCVS to send a copy and a certificate of verification to the medical licensing board in the state where the physician is seeking a license. Often the data can be sent electronically. This will significantly decrease the time required for the process.

One important point of which an applicant must be aware is the extent to which the different state medical boards network and exchange information. Almost all medical boards report actions taken by the boards to the FSMB Board Action Data Bank (BADB), which banks data from all the participating boards from the beginning of their respective recorded history to the present. This is in contrast to the National Practitioner Data Bank (NPDB), which has data only from its creation in 1986 to the present. All medical boards query the BADB for information regarding license applicants and compare the actual application with the report generated by the BADB. Most boards also query the NPDB before making a recommendation regarding action on an application. In addition to the cross-checks against these two databases, the boards also perform a primary source verification on all data reported, especially if the applicant has not chosen to use FCVS. Should data not be verified, the consequences can be severe. One applicant falsified documents quite convincingly regarding his attendance at a prestigious medical school. The applicant had not applied for a training license during residency. This individual subsequently applied for a permanent license. The Medical Board actually checked with the medical school in question, as well as a nationwide resource that lists every medical school graduate in the United States. The impostor was identified and exposed.

Because of the networking and exchange of information among the different state boards, it is vital that you understand that any time you are refused a license by any state board, that information will be available to the medical board of any other state to which you may apply. The same is true about states in which you have turned in your license while under investigation. That sort of information will follow you wherever you go. Therefore, it is imperative that you seek competent legal advice before allowing the denial of a license to go unchallenged or turning in a license while under investigation.

Even if the applicant has chosen to use a credentials verification service, each state will include a portion of the application which is unique to that state alone. Some states require a jurisprudence exam.

Others may include special education in some other area of special interest. In order to reduce unnecessary delay in the granting of a license, the applicant should read and carefully complete the requirements for the application. It is unwise to delegate to an employee the job of completing your application for a medical license. This increases the likelihood of error or misstatements.

Following several noteworthy incidents which caused some boards embarrassment, most medical boards now perform a criminal background check on each applicant. The applicant will be asked to submit fingerprint cards with their application. If the cards are not properly executed, delay will result while the cards are resubmitted and processed. If the physician applicant fails to note details of a criminal or arrest history and the incidents are detected by criminal background check, the physician applicant will receive heightened scrutiny and perhaps delay or denial.

Boards are also required to submit information to the Department of Health and Human Services. If an individual applicant has defaulted on federal student loans or has failed to make child support payments, this information will be conveyed to the board. Most boards also query the National Practitioner Data Bank and the Health Insurance Portability and Accountability Act (HIPAA Data Bank). It is also mandated that the medical board report any actions to both data banks.

COMPLAINTS TO THE MEDICAL BOARD, SETTLEMENTS AND PAYMENT OF VERDICTS

These matters are, for the most part, benign proceedings that, if promptly and frankly addressed, are not likely to lead to adverse consequences.

Settlements and Payment of Verdicts. The laws of some states require a report to be made to the medical board of any settlement of a medical malpractice case or payment of any verdict for monetary damages in such a case. The laws of most states require that any suit when it is filed must be reported to the medical board. This will prompt the medical board to address an inquiry to the physician involved. The board may request records and/or a letter of explanation. Your response should be succinct, calm, and very reasoned. If you are represented by an attorney, your attorney should be involved in preparing your response. It is important that you respond within the time limits set by the request.

Complaints to the Medical Board. Nowhere is it clearer that there is no common lexicon among state medical boards than when one discusses complaints and medical boards. Each state has a variant of a complaint, ranging from the actual beginning of a formal legal process similar to a criminal grand jury charge all the way to allegations which have no substance and require only a minimal investigation. In a state taking the latter view, a complaint would, for the most part, initiate a benign inquiry. A prompt and frank response would most likely resolve the matter and not lead to any adverse consequences. In such a state, the complaint may be in writing and may be made by members of the public who are either patients or family members of patients. They usually write to complain about the treatment or lack of treatment of the patient. Quite frequently, the complaint will result from a bad outcome, such as infection after surgery, or unexpected death during treatment. Sometimes the complaint will arise out of simple rudeness, according to the perception of the complaining party. More likely than not, most complaints of this nature are initiated as a result of poor communications. Other types of complaints that can be quite serious are those that involve *boundary violations*. These violations occur when the practitioner crosses over the accepted boundary into an area which may cause potential patient harm, such as in sexual or financial matters. Also, practitioners who enable or permit the practice of medicine by unlicensed individuals will find that this is also a very serious allegation which draws attention from the boards around the country. In addition, prescribing over the Internet or prescribing on demand without forming a proper physician-patient relationship with the requisite records is sure to bring the practitioner to the attention of the board wherever the individual is licensed. Less frequently, the complaint may be made by another physician or healthcare provider. This type of complaint is generally viewed as requiring heightened investigation and attention. The licensee will be notified, generally by letter from the medical board, of the complaint and will be requested to send a written response to the complaint within a specified period of time to the board. It is advised that your proposed response be reviewed by an attorney familiar with practice before the medical board before it is sent to the board. Your response must be calm and reasoned, no matter how inflammatory the complaint may have been. It must directly address the issues raised by the complaint. It must avoid personalities and pejorative comments. It must show your professionalism. In some states the board may investigate complaints with no notice to the licensee. If no probable cause is found, the complaint may be closed with no notice to the licensee. Nevertheless, the complaint remains on the licensee's record and can be discovered by other states who request information about the licensee.

BOARD INVESTIGATOR INVESTIGATIONS

In some states, the board hires investigators who perform investigations at the request of the board. In other states, the investigators may be a part of a state investigator agency. In either scenario, the agents may be sworn law-enforcement officers and may carry a weapon and a badge. A few states use investigators who are there merely to ask questions and may deliver subpoenas for the board. If the board has the statutory authority to employ and direct its investigators, it may send one of its investigators to your office to question you about a complaint or bad result. The investigator may demand to audit a number of your other patient records. The investigator may arrive with a subpoena requiring you to produce these patient records instantly. You must do so or risk the loss of your license. Depending on the nature of the complaint, the records can usually be quickly copied and returned to your practice. The investigator is not required to inform you that you have the right to have your attorney present during questioning by the investigator, and usually will not do so.

However, you do have the right to have your attorney present during the questioning. You can safely refuse to be questioned until your attorney can be with you. Ideally, you should have an attorney familiar with the workings of your state medical board. If such an individual is not readily available, contact the attorney who regularly represents your practice. It is recommended that you be interviewed with counsel present. You should authorize your regular attorney to consult with an attorney who regularly appears before the medical board. This individual can quickly fill your personal attorney in about what you are required to do. The investigator will most likely make notes about the interview. Following the interview, the investigator will prepare a written report for the board, which may or may not be accurate, depending on the experience and skill of the investigator. Remember, you should have a witness (preferably an attorney) at the investigator interview

INFORMAL INTERVIEWS

A few boards conduct a conference called an informal interview. These conferences are conducted when the board would like additional information about an occurrence or incident. The board would like to discuss the matter with you and make their concerns known without taking the matter to a formal hearing with charges against you. This is an important part of the board proceedings. If you are invited to an informal interview, you will be told that you have the right to be represented by counsel, and it is wise for you to bring your attorney to the interview with you. Your attorney may prepare you for the interview but is not allowed to speak for you during the main portion of the interview.

The attorney will generally be offered the opportunity to add his or her comments near the end of the interview. You must answer the questions of the board members yourself. It is recommended that, with the help of your chosen counsel, you anticipate and prepare answers to these queries. It is also wise to prepare and bring packets of materials which you and your attorney believe will explain your situation. Deciding what should be presented is best determined by an attorney with practice experience before the board. Boards in some states only conduct formal investigations. Depending on the state, those records will be made public. North Carolina is unique in conducting "informal interviews" that are not made public.

FORMAL CHARGES

Having formal charges filed against you by a medical board is one of the most serious matters that can confront a member of the medical profession. It means that a board consisting of the doctor's peers (other physicians) has determined that there is substantial evidence that the doctor:

1. Has been guilty of misconduct; or

2. Has provided medical care below an acceptable standard of care; or

3. Is lacking in basic knowledge; or

4. Is impaired in some way which affects the doctor's ability to diagnose and treat patients safely.

Any one of those four charges, if substantiated, provides justification for the board to suspend or limit a physician's license to practice medicine in that state.

The seriousness of the charges is compounded by the breadth of the statutory authority granted to the medical board. Most state statutes grant to the medical board the power to revoke the license of any physician who is found to have violated the state medical practice act. Most states have adopted, to some extent, a model act which details that discipline can be voted by the board or disciplinary panel for lack of competency, ethical violations, or a belief that a practitioner is unable to diagnose and treat patients safely or competently. Most states have a bootstrap provision which allows any other state where a physician is licensed to take a similar action based on the first state's decision. Some physicians have been lulled into complacency, thinking that since they do not intend to practice in the state where charges are filed, they need not actively defend, only to find that they face similar actions in all states where they hold a medical license and practice.

The proceedings, which are defined and governed by the state's administrative procedures act, are usually started by the issuance of written formal charges by the medical board or investigative panel for the board. These formal charges are then served on the doctor who is charged, the respondent. Depending on the state statute, the formal charging document may be brought to the doctor's office by a process server or sent by certified or registered mail. Immediately upon receipt of the charges, you must take steps to form a defense team and start it in motion. Many insurance carriers who write liability policies for physicians will provide defense coverage for charges before the medical board or similar trial body. Usually there is a dollar limitation, such as $25,000, of coverage the insurer will provide. You will be responsible for the rest if your defense requires more than that. Your insurance carrier can verify the amount of coverage and will usually assign an attorney to represent you. If you do not have such coverage, you will be responsible for paying for your own defense.

The proceedings are generally governed by the same rules that govern medical malpractice suits in the superior courts of the state. Discovery is available to both sides as a matter of right. Interrogatories and requests for production of documents can be served on the board and by the board's attorneys on the doctor charged. In this fashion, reports prepared by the investigative staff of the medical board, including statements they have recorded, can be reviewed. The depositions of the accuser(s) can be taken as well as depositions of the doctor and the doctor's staff and any other witnesses.

Before the hearing, there may be a meeting of the board attorney or attorney general, the defense attorney, and the board president or a representative of the board, executive director, or assistant executive director. Each state will conduct portions of this process differently. For this reason, you should have an attorney familiar with your state procedures and methods preparing and mounting an effective defense in your behalf. A prehearing stipulation will be drawn up, agreeing on such facts as are not disputed, and each side will list their witnesses, their exhibits, and the issues they contend the board should consider.

It is not always necessary that the matter be resolved by a hearing before the board. The attorneys for the board and the respondent can meet privately and discuss a resolution by agreement. If it turns out that there is a punishment that the board is willing to accept and that the physician is willing to have imposed, then a consent order is prepared and can be entered. Most of the time, a consent order, will require the physician to admit some level of wrongdoing and will become a public record.

The hearing itself will conducted like a civil medical malpractice trial, but without a jury. Each state forms its hearing panels in a different manner. Most states have a charging authority similar to a grand jury and a different trial panel. Some states use an administrative law judge as the trier of fact. In North Carolina, which is a little unusual, some members of the Board will have participated in the investigation. However, all members of the Board (unless recused) will have participated in the decision to bring the charges. Typically, the president of the board will rule on objections to evidence, unless the state provides for a presiding officer such as an administrative law judge. Regardless of the jurisdiction and which rules are followed, a hearing regarding a practitioner's medical license is a most serious matter, and you need the best and most experienced legal counsel that you can obtain.

The hearing will generally, regardless of the jurisdiction, be open to the public as long as witnesses have not been granted the right to testify in confidence.

Sometimes there will be coverage by reporters and by video cameras from TV stations in the hearing rooms. Typically, the attorneys for the board will present their evidence first. However, since the same rules govern the hearing as govern civil malpractice trials, you can be called as a witness by the attorneys for the board and compelled to give testimony. This is unlike criminal trials, where the defendant cannot be compelled to testify. The board attorneys will introduce the record of the patient(s), who may testify. In certain circumstances, the patients are allowed to give their testimony in a closed portion of the hearing, so that they are not exposed to public scrutiny, unless they elect to be. Your attorney will be allowed to cross-examine the witnesses called by the board and to present witnesses for your side.

The board members are allowed to question all the witnesses who testify. Although most boards contain lay members, in many states a majority of the board members are licensed physicians. Your attorney should make sure that you know the history of the members of the board. You must remain aware that although they will hear opinions from witnesses about the care given, they will be using their own experience and training in coming to a decision. They will be judging your testimony, and the testimony of other witnesses, from the perspective of their training and experience. The more you know about them, the better chance you have of giving testimony which will not offend them and which may convince them.

Each side will call expert witnesses. Most often they will simply be other practitioners with similar training to your own, and not writers of textbooks or teachers of great reputation. Often the question the board must decide is whether your actions were within an acceptable standard of care, and expert testimony will be required. You may also express an expert opinion as a part of your own defense. Sometimes, in cases alleging improper physical or sexual contact with a patient, it may be necessary for the physician to be evaluated by a physician or psychologist who has training and experience in this area to testify as to whether the physician is a sexual predator and likely to be guilty of such conduct in the future.

At the end of the presentation of evidence, your attorney will be allowed to make a closing argument, and the attorney for the board will have the same opportunity. Following the closing arguments, the board will clear the hearing room and deliberate the case and reach a result. Sometimes hearings are broken into two parts: a *liability* part and a *punishment* part. If the board decides that the doctor has been guilty of a violation, then it will proceed with the punishment phase, during which the board attorneys will offer any evidence they may have to suggest that the doctor is a repeat offender or that the actions in question were egregious. They will argue for a particular punishment. Your attorney can offer evidence of good acts, mitigating circumstances, and the like, and argue for light or no punishment. The burden of proof lies with the board's attorney to prove that the physician violated the medical practice act. Different states require different levels of proof. A few states require a showing of proof beyond a reasonable doubt. Most require that the greater weight of evidence prove the facts of the case and some require clear and convincing proof.

If the board reaches an adverse result, it can take many forms. The board can issue a *letter of concern* that basically tells you to clean up your act, or else. The Board can issue a *reprimand,* either public or private. Both of them become part of your permanent record. The board can *take your license,* but immediately *reinstate* **it** upon conditions stated by the board. The conditions can vary with the circumstances. For example, you can be required to attend continuing medical education in some specific area, or to achieve competence in some area in which you are perceived to be deficient. Your license can be limited and you can be confined to some geographical area, or you can be forbidden to perform some operation or therapy. The board can take your license for a stated period, after which you will automatically get it back, with or without conditions. The board can take your license for an indefinite period of time. In that last instance, you will have to wait for some period of time before you can even apply to get your license back, and there is no guarantee that you will get it back once you make an application. Only one state, New York, has a separate agency to issue licenses which is different from the discipline arm. Punishments allowed by law vary greatly from state to state. Many states have the ability to levy a fine. Some may issue a warning, place the doctor on probation, or require remediation or competency assessment. If you have licenses in several states, the other states will learn of your loss of license and will commence action in their state to take similar actions.

APPEALS

In many states, an appeal from the decision of the board only addresses whether there is any evidence from which the board could make its conclusions, and the court to which you appeal does not have the power to make a different decision, unless there is no evidence to support the decision of the board. In many states, the process of appeal is fairly expensive and may take a year or more. The decision of the board to revoke a license will likely be given immediate effect and will remain in place during the appeals process, which means that the doctor cannot practice. It is possible to petition the board or the court to whom you appeal for a stay of the revocation pending the appeal, but most times it is unlikely to be granted.

The bottom line is that in most states the medical board has a great deal of power. You cannot defy the board with impunity. In most instances, the board requires the physician to persuade its members of the correctness of his or her position by sound and *humble* responses rather by challenges. In order to be successful in keeping your license to practice medicine, you must employ, trust, and cooperate with an experienced attorney who is familiar with the rules and procedures of the medical board and is respected by its members.

23

The Criminalization of Medical Errors

Thomas R. McLean, M.D., J.D., F.A.C.S.

INTRODUCTION

Prior to 1990, physicians were rarely tried for medical errors. For the most part, in those instances when physicians were criminally prosecuted for activities related to the practice of the profession, the charges were limited to narcotics trafficking, sexual abuse of patients, and fraud. And while it is true that from time to time a physician was convicted of manslaughter,[1] such a conviction was often overturned on appeal.[2] The paucity of physicians who were criminally convicted for medical errors is most likely related to several facts: (1) egregious conduct that would rise to the level of a criminal act was rarely observed in physicians who were practicing their profession; and (2) even when such conduct was detected, because physicians were held in such high esteem by society, the judicial system was willing to bend

The author wishes to thank Edward P. Richards, Harvey A. Peltier Professor of Law, Paul M. Hebert Law Center, Louisiana State University, for reviewing this chapter and making recommendations that improved the chapter's readability.

1.   *State v. Reynolds,* 22 P. 410 (1889).
2.   *United States v. Millen,* 594 F.2d 1085, 1087 (6th Cir. 1979).

over backward to find a way to let the truly criminal physicians off the hook.[3]

Those days are gone. In the past decade, prosecutors have shown increasing willingness to file charges against physicians for medical errors (Gic 2002; Feinberg and Saxton 2002; Albert 2001a, b). Consider what happened to Dr. Wolfgang Schug (Milligan 1999). After he started an 11-month-old on antibiotics for what appeared to be otitis media, the child deteriorated. Realizing that the child needed a higher level of care, Dr. Schug made a tactical error: he sent the child to a tertiary care center by private vehicle rather than by ambulance or helicopter. After the child died en route, the local prosecutor charged the doctor with manslaughter. Although the charges against Dr. Schug were ultimately dropped, the criminal accusation did irreparable harm to the doctor and his career.

Nor is Dr. Schug's experience with the criminal justice system an isolated event. Increasingly, physicians are being charged with criminal actions when their patients die from narcotic overdoses (Albert 2001a). Worse, many physicians who are criminally charged do not even fare as well as Dr. Schug, because they are convicted and have to serve jail time. Dr. Naramore served jail time after being convicted for both attempted murder for prescribing an excessive dose of a narcotics to a patient, and manslaughter for the method he used to extubate a second, brain-dead patient;[4] Dr. Wood served jail time after he was convicted of manslaughter when one of his patients died of a potassium overdose;[5] and Dr. Gerald Einaugler, who mistakenly ordered a patient to receive tube feedings via a peritoneal dialysis catheter, was convicted of both manslaughter and criminal endangerment after his patient died.[6] Interestingly, this phenomenon of holding physicians criminally liable for medical errors is not isolated to the U.S., as it has been reported in Japan and England ("Five Sentenced" 2001; Rosser 2001).

---

3.   *People v. Burpo,* 647 N.E.2d 996 (Ill. 1995).
4.   *State of Kansas v. Naramore,* 965 P.2d 211 (Kan. App. 1998).
5.   *U.S. v. Wood,* 207 F.3d 1222 (2000).
6.   *Einaugler v. Supreme Court of New York,* 109 F.3d 836 (2d Cir. 1997).

While placing physicians on trial for medical errors appears to be on the increase, few physicians are aware of this phenomenon. Accordingly, this chapter examines the criminalization of medical errors.

Before we begin, a word of caution is necessary. Criminal law exists in its own perplexing world. Because this book is being written for physicians, some of the complex workings of the criminal justice system have been simplified. This chapter will not impart enough knowledge for physicians to defend themselves against a criminal accusation. It is imperative for any physician who is criminally charged to retain an experienced criminal defense attorney as early as possible. Frequently this means that an attorney should be consulted when a search warrant is executed. In fact, if a physician has even a reasonable belief that he or she is the subject of a criminal investigation it is recommended that a criminal defense attorney be retained immediately.

TORT LAW VERSUS CRIMINAL LAW

Anglo-American law recognizes that certain actions are "wrong" because they result in injury. Wrongdoers, moreover, are required to provide compensation for the injury that they caused. The law has developed two basic compensation systems: tort law (including medical malpractice) and criminal law. (A third system of compensation, know as administrative law, does exist, but its discussion is beyond the scope of this chapter.) Although tort law and criminal law are both compensation systems, these bodies of law have different purposes, procedures, and remedies.

Tort law is applied in situations where one individual injures another. Injuries associated with these private wrongs may include bodily, economic, and/or dignitary injuries. Most of this book covers tort law and how it is designed to redress injuries that arise during the course of medical treatment. Under tort law, an injured party must bring a legal claim and demonstrate that: (1) the defendant owed the plaintiff a duty; (2) the defendant deviated from the standard of care; (3) the defendant's deviation caused the injury; and (4) the injury resulted in damages. Each of these four elements must be demonstrated by the preponderance of the evidence (i.e., >50% certainty). The chief remedy is a cash award. Because only money changes hands in tort litigation, a defendant is not guaranteed a jury trial; however, most jurisdictions do provide a mechanism for jury trials in medical malpractice actions.

By contrast, the purpose of criminal law is to redress injuries done to society as a whole. Anything that destabilizes society is wrongful conduct that is to be redressed through the criminal justice system. Since murder, rape, and robbery all increase the level of fear in society, thereby destabilizing society, they are criminal acts. Unlike tort law, where the injured party has to initiate proceedings to recover compensation, in a criminal action it is the prosecutor, who is a special agent of the government, who brings an action against the defendant. In general, to obtain a criminal conviction, the prosecutor must prove: (1) the defendant engaged in a wrongful act (this is known as the *actus reus*); and (2) the defendant performed the wrongful act with criminal intent (this is know as the *mens rea*). Both of these elements must be proven beyond a reasonable doubt (i.e., >95% certainty). Because a criminal action results in an injury to the whole of society, jail time is considered to be the most appropriate form of compensation for serious criminal acts. Because a defendant in a criminal trial may be sent to jail, thereby depriving the defendant of liberty, criminal defendants charged with felonies are guaranteed a trial by jury.

THE ORIGIN OF A CRIMINAL COMPLAINT

A criminal action against a defendant begins with the filing of a criminal complaint. Whether a criminal complaint against a physician is filed is at the discretion of the prosecutor (Feinberg and Saxton 2002). The discretionary authority that is granted to a prosecutor is broad, and it is generally exercised when the prosecutor has formed a subjective belief that a defendant is guilty of a criminal act. The prosecutor must also be able to frame a physician's actions to fit a standard criminal complaint. Because the practice of medicine requires the need for physical contact between a doctor and a patient, a prosecutor can potentially frame a medical error to fit a number of standard complaints. These may include manslaughter (creating a reckless situation that results in death), negligent homicide (failure to perceive that a patient has been placed in a reckless situation that may cause death), assault and battery, sexual assault, drug dealing, and failure to comply with laws designed to protect the elderly and vulnerable (known as endangerment statutes).

To a degree, the evidence needed to prove criminal liability is similar to the evidence needed to prove medical malpractice liability. This is especially true in situations where the *actus reus* has a causation element; for example, murder requires that the prosecution demonstrate that the defendant caused the victim's death. Because medical causation is complex, an expert witness is needed to translate medical science into terms that a judge and juror can understand. Thus, expert witnesses are generally necessary in criminal cases that turn on a medical error. Still, despite some similarity in the allegations and the need to put on expert witness testimony to prove causation, criminal and tort cases that are concerned with medical errors have two significant differences: a criminal conviction requires a demonstration of criminal intent, and criminal law has its own unique procedure.

CRIMINAL INTENT

Tort law does not speak of criminal intent; rather, it speaks of fault. In a medical malpractice suit, fault, which is also called negligence, must be demonstrated before a physician can be held liable. The concept of fault roughly translates to, the physician should have known better; i.e., the physician made a stupid mistake. In contrast, in order for a physician to be held criminally liable for a medical error, a prosecutor must demonstrate that a physician made more than a stupid mistake. Criminal intent means that the defendant must have acted in a "reckless" or "knowing" manner. "Recklessness" means that the defendant performed the act in such a way as to create an unreasonably dangerous situation. (For example, firing a gun into a crowd creates an unreasonably dangerous situation.) "Knowing," on the other hand, means that the defendant was consciously aware that a particular outcome would follow from an action. To a physician who is trying to help a patient, the idea that he or she would intentionally create an unreasonably dangerous situation, let alone know-ingly do deliberate harm, is almost unfathomable. And yet in recent years physicians have been convicted of just that: acting in a reckless or knowing manner so as to harm their patients.

For physicians, the concept of criminal intent can be both a blessing and a curse. Because it must be demonstrated beyond a reasonable doubt, criminal intent has often proven to be a great defense. Generally, when a physician makes a medical error in treating a patient, it is difficult for a prosecutor to convince a jury that the physician made anything more than a stupid mistake. Thus, because demonstrating criminal intent at the level of reck-lessness or knowingness is objectively difficult, it is probably the main reason physicians are usually found not guilty when they are charged with a criminal act after committing a medical error.

But criminal intent can also be a curse to physicians because of the way it is demonstrated, which is left to the discretion of the prosecutor. This means that the evidence used to demonstrate that a physician acted with criminal intent does not have to be scien-tific. The prosecutor does not have to discuss a consecutive series of patients treated by a physician; just a few bad outcomes out of years of practice will sometimes be deemed sufficient to demon-strate criminal intent. Admittedly, such a nonscientific approach to criminal intent must seem unfair to physicians. Still what we deem to be fair depends on the way that we think. Because law-yers and physicians do not think in the same manner, it's not sur-prising that what is deemed fair to lawyers is not necessarily fair to physicians. Because there is no minimal standard for the dem-onstration of criminal intent, all that is really needed for a demon-stration of criminal intent is a sad story and a persuasive prosecutor. On the other hand, for physicians the minimal scien-tific analysis a court should consider would be a consecutive se-ries to which some statistical analysis was applied. And while the physician can put on a consecutive series and statistical evidence to rebut the prosecution's argument, the physician's defense attor-ney needs to be as persuasive as the prosecutor because many ju-rors will not understand advanced statistical arguments.

Finally, the prosecutor's job is further facilitated by new laws, like the so-called endangerment statutes. The purpose of these statutes, which are often placed in the public health code, is to protect those members of society who cannot protect themselves. Vulnerable individuals include nursing home and hospitalized patients as well as others who are unaware of their surroundings. When a physician makes a mistake that harms such a patient, prosecutors have shown an increasing willingness to use endangerment statutes to punish what otherwise would have been a stupid medical error.

EXCLUSIONARY HEARINGS

The second significant difference between a criminal action concerning a medical error and a medical malpractice action is the procedure used. In a criminal action, because society is the injured party, it is society which brings an action against a criminal defendant. Society is, of course, the ultimate deep-pocket opponent. Potentially, society could outspend, outinvestigate, and outwit even a truly innocent defendant. Because of this inherent potential for unfairness, the criminal defendant is granted multiple procedural safeguards. These safeguards, which flow from the Fourth and Fifth Amendments, prohibit the government from acting in a tyrannical fashion. In general, these rights mandate that the government use proper police procedure to collect evidence against a criminal defendant. If the government does not follow the proper procedure, then at a pretrial hearing the evidence can be suppressed. An important implication of limiting society's ability to utilize illegally obtained evidence is that criminal proceedings are often won and lost at the pretrial exclusionary hearings.

PHYSICIANS AS MURDERERS

Physicians, like any other person in society, are answerable in criminal court when they commit murder outside of the scope of their practice.[7] And some physicians, like the notorious

---

7.   Rizzo (1996); Thompson (1976); *State v. Sheppard,* 135 N.E.2d 340, *cert. denied,* 352 U.S. 910 (1956).

Dr. Michael Swango, do intentionally commit murder. During a 15-year period, Dr. Swango used potassium chloride injections to intentionally kill as many as 60 of his patients. Ideally, when a physician makes a mistake leading to a death of a patient, the mistake is scrutinized by peer review, perhaps a medical malpractice trial, or occasionally by a state medical board. But increasingly today it seems that prosecutors are not willing to view a medical error as the result of stupidity; rather, they see it as an act completed with criminal intent. Recall that criminal intent requires that a defendant must demonstrate at least recklessness, which is the creation of an unreasonably dangerous situation. To illustrate what prosecutors have considered reckless medical practice, we need to view the practices of Drs. Naramore, Wood, and Einaugler through they eyes of the court.

CIRCUMSTANTIAL EVIDENCE OF CRIMINAL INTENT

After two of Dr. Naramore's patients died, the State of Kansas brought criminal charges against the doctor. In the first case, a terminal cancer patient with a precarious respiratory pattern was given a narcotic to alleviate the patient's suffering. Although the patient did not die, the doctor (a family practitioner by training) was charged with attempted murder after the patient's respiratory status further deteriorated. In the reported case, Dr. Naramore does not appear to have made even a stupid mistake in managing this patient. What was clear from the report, however, was that Dr. Naramore was on uneasy terms with this cancer patient's family. Still, within weeks of this event, Dr. Naramore did make a mistake in managing a patient. In this second case, Dr. Naramore was providing care for a patient who had sustained an intracerebral bleed. After two other consultant physicians found the patient to be brain-dead, Dr. Naramore prepared to extubate the patient so that nature could take its course. The doctor's mistake in extubating this patient was to use a paralytic agent. (Dr. Naramore testified that the reason he used the paralytic drug was to suppress any reflexive movement that might occur with the endotracheal tube's removal.) Unfortunately for the doctor, it appears that someone had an axe to grind. Dr. Naramore's use of the paralytic agent was construed to be evidence that the patient was not brain-dead at the time of extubation. Accordingly, the prosecutor began interviewing the hospital staff and the patient's family and gathering the doctor's medical records in order to review his practice.

When Dr. Naramore was convicted of both crimes and sentenced to serve concurrent terms of 5 to 20 years, he became the first physician to be convicted of murder for a medical error by State of Kansas in 100 years. Dr. Naramore's trial provides two lessons. First, except in an egregious situation, a prosecutor will not bring a traditional criminal action against a physician for a single medical error. If all that a prosecutor has is a single medical error, it will be hard for the prosecutor to convince a jury that the physician did anything more than make a stupid mistake. By bundling several stupid mistakes together, the prosecutor can infer that a physician was more than stupid because a bundle of several stupid mistakes constitute evidence of a pattern of reckless behavior. Dr. Naramore's management of the patient with the intracerebral bleed in isolation would not have warranted the criminal charge. Only by combining Dr. Naramore's faulty decision to use a paralytic agent to extubate a brain-dead patient with comments of an unhappy family could the prosecutor hope to show that Dr. Naramore had acted with criminal intent.

The second lesson to be learned from this case is that the criminal justice system does make mistakes. When Dr. Naramore appealed his case, the court observed that a "few facts, or a multitude of facts proven, all consistent with the supposition of guilt, are not enough to warrant a verdict of guilty." The court then took notice that the expert testimony given in Dr. Naramore's trial demonstrated that there was not even a consensus, let alone evidence that was beyond a reasonable doubt, to indicate that the doctor was reckless. Because there was room for reasonable doubt, the appellate court reversed the guilty verdict. Still, while Dr. Naramore ultimately gained his freedom, the doctor had served some time in jail, spent substantial sums of money, and had his license to practice medicine revoked. In short, the doctor's career was ruined. This is a rather high price to pay for a medical mistake.

EGREGIOUS CONDUCT

U.S. v. Wood demonstrates the exception to the above rule: If a physician's conduct is sufficiently egregious, a physician can be charged with murder for a single medical error. In this case, Dr. Wood was treating a patient with symptomatic hypokalemia. Dr. Wood ordered the patient to receive a high concentration of intravenous potassium to avoid the patient's experiencing a life-threatening arrhythmia. The nursing staff, however, citing hospital policy, refused to administer the potassium as ordered. So Dr. Wood took it upon himself to administer the potassium. Unfortunately, even though Dr. Wood did not administer the potassium at an excessive rate, shortly after the infusion was started the patient died.

In the aftermath, Dr. Wood was charged with premeditated murder. The "egregious" medical error in this case was not necessarily that the doctor gave too much potassium or that he took it upon himself to administer the potassium. Rather, it was the doctor's failure to listen to the warning that was given by the nursing staff. In the eyes of the law, charging ahead with a planned course of action after a warning to the contrary is evidence of recklessness. But recklessness alone is not enough to demonstrate that an act was performed in a premeditated fashion. Premeditated murder would require a "knowing" level of criminal intent coupled with evidence that there was a plan to commit murder. Accordingly, the jury was only willing to convict Dr. Wood of manslaughter. Dr. Wood was sentenced to 5 months of imprisonment, 36 months of supervised release, and a $25,000 fine.

Dr. Wood appealed his conviction on the grounds that his being charged with premeditated murder unfairly prejudiced him. The appellate court agreed with the doctor and ordered a new trial. However, the court tacitly acknowledged that convicting a physician on a manslaughter charge for a medical error was not offensive. Fortunately for Dr. Wood, his fate improved when the government did a cost-benefit analysis for a new trial. By the time the new trial was scheduled to begin, Dr. Wood had already served 22 months of house arrest (Walton 2000). So even if Dr. Wood were formally convicted of manslaughter, he was unlikely to spend more time under arrest. When this outcome of new trial was weighed against the cost of new trial, the government elected to drop the case. Still, because Dr. Wood's license to practice medicine had been revoked, he would not be able to practice medicine for another 15 months and only then with supervision because at that point he had not practiced medicine in seven years.

STATUTORY LAW FACILITATING THE CRIMINAL CONVICTION OF PHYSICIANS

The final case to be reviewed examines a new threat to physicians: patient endangerment statutes. Dr. Einaugler, a family practitioner, provided care to nursing home patients. Dr. Einaugler's legal problems began with a medical error: he ordered one of his patients to be fed via a peritoneal dialysis catheter that he believed to be a gastrostomy tube.[8] After the patient had been given tube feedings for an undisclosed period of time, a nurse called the error to the doctor's attention. Dr. Einaugler then consulted with a nephrologist, who recommended that the patient be transferred to a hospital. But for unexplained reasons, 10 hours elapsed between the time of the consultation and the time that Dr. Einaugler gave the order to transfer the patient. Despite surgical intervention, the patient ultimately died of peritonitis.

Feeding a patient through a peritoneal dialysis tube was stupid, but the court, to a large degree, ignored this mistake. The unforgivable mistake here, as in *Wood*, was Dr. Einaugler's failure to respond promptly to a warning. This was the egregious conduct that supported the upholding of the doctor's manslaughter conviction through multiple appeals.

Most of the appellate court's review of this case, however, concerned Dr. Einaugler's conviction for violating New York's endangerment statute. This statute, and similar statutes in other states, makes it a criminal offense for a healthcare provider to *willfully* fail to provide needed medical care. The New York statute used to convict Dr. Einaugler reads as follows: "to provide timely, consistent, safe, adequate and appropriate services, treat-

---

8.   *People v. Einaugler,* 618 N.Y.S.2d 414, 415 (1994).

ment, and/or care to a patient or resident of a residential health care facility while such patient or resident is under the supervision of the facility, including but not limited to: nutrition, medication, therapies, sanitary clothing and surroundings, and activities of daily living."[9]

Statutes like the one Dr. Einaugler ran afoul of have become increasingly common (Albert 2001b). (These statutes, which are known by various names across the country, are designed to protect vulnerable patients, i.e., those who lack the mental capacity to protect themselves.) While some endangerment statutes only classify the offense as a misdemeanor (i.e., punishable by less than a year in prison); endangerment statutes in some states, like California, are considered to be felonies (i.e., punishable by a year or more in prison).[10]

Although many physicians are unaware of these endangerment statutes, they are important for three reasons. First, the courts do not view these statutes as criminalizing medical errors because they must be *willfully* violated. Second, it is arguably easier to convict a physician under endangerment statutes than traditional criminal actions because the jury does not have to label a physician who is providing patient care as a murderer. Third, the proliferation of these statutes is an unmistakable sign that there has been a shift in the way the public views physicians. Regrettably, it seems physicians are no longer held in high esteem.

CONCLUSION

After spending a little time in the Czar's prison, Dostoevsky observed that you could tell a lot about a society by how it treats its criminals. If Dostoevsky were reincarnated as a modern American physician, he would probably observe that one could tell a lot about a society by whom it labeled as a criminal. A sociological shift has occurred over the last 30 years in the United States, which not only involves how healthcare is delivered, but also how physicians are perceived. Physicians are increasingly

---

9.   N.Y. Public Health Law § 2803-d(7).
10. Cal. Pen. Code § 368(b) (2001), MCLS § 750.145n (2001).

being viewed as providing medical care in a reckless manner, as evidenced by an excessive number of medical mistakes or a single egregious mistake. Of perhaps even greater concern to the general public is the perception that state boards of medical examiners do not discipline reckless physicians. Consequently, physicians are increasingly being tried criminally for medical errors. This trend is likely to continue and even increase as the government enacts criminal statutes to protect the vulnerable members of society. To reverse this trend of prosecuting physicians for medical errors, the medical community needs to convince the public that they are conducting themselves with undivided loyalty to their patients. In particular, physicians who are on state boards of medical examiners need to be seen as patient advocates who are willing to discipline dangerous physicians. These changes, of course, will take time.

In the interim, if you should become the subject of a criminal investigation, you should (1) retain legal counsel as soon as possible and (2) during the time a warrant search is executed remember that you have a right to remain silent. Hopefully, if you are someday criminally charged for a professional mistake, this chapter will make the criminal justice system seem a little less perplexing.

REFERENCE

Albert, T. 2001a. "Death Fuels Brouhaha over Oxycontin Prescribing Practices Elder Abuse: Failure to Properly Manage Patient's Pain." *American Medical News* (20 August).

———. 2001b. "Malpractice or Murder? Criminalization of Medical Errors Is a Troubling Trend." *American Medical News* (22/29 October).

Feinberg, R., and J. W. Saxton 2002. "Crime and Medicine." *Health Lawyer News* 6(7):4–9.

"Five Sentenced over Surgery Mix-Up." 2001. *The Daily Yomiuri* (21 September).

Gic, J. A. 2002. "The Criminalization of Health Law Malpractice." In *Medical Malpractice Update 2003,* ed. D.J. Block. New York: Aspen.

Milligan, R. J. 1999. "Criminal Liability for Medical Judgment." Available at http://library.lp.findlaw.com/articles/file/00380/ 004309/title/Subject/topic/Leg.

Rizzo, T. 1996. "Green Gets Life Sentence." *Kansas City Star* (31 May).

Rosser, N. 2001. "Police Probe Boy's Death in Operation." *Evening Standard* (8 August).

Thomson, T. 1976. *Blood and Money*. New York: Doubleday. Walton, R. 2000. "Doctor Avoids Manslaughter over Patient's Death." *Tulsa World* (28 July).

24

Reaction to a Claim: How a Malpractice Claim Affects You

Richard J. Nasca, M.D.

You have just arrived in your office and are preparing to see your afternoon patients. Your secretary informs you that a uniformed process server from the sheriff's department is in your waiting room. He elects to serve you in your waiting room in front of your waiting patients. The deputy hands you the malpractice claim document (summons) and you return to your office embarrassed and angry. Next to losing a loved one, this is one of the most gut-wrenching experiences you will encounter. It is hard to believe that someone you attempted to help and care for could now make such a claim against you. You take another peek at the claim as you try to regain your composure. Reality transcends denial, and you realize that you are the defendant and cannot ignore your need to deal with the claim.

But what you do about those patients in your waiting room? After you regain your composure, like a good doctor you begin seeing these patients. All these people know what you have just experienced in your waiting room. A few perceptive patients will wish you luck. The majority will pretend they never saw you served or your reaction to the deputy handing you the complaint.

After office hours, you read the complaints in detail. You again experience anger and betrayal. You place a call to your malpractice insurance carrier to inform them a claim has been filed against you. However, you are not able to reach a live voice and resort to leaving a message. This adds further to your frustration and anger. Again you silently wish the claim would go away or resolve itself quickly, but you realize this is only wishful thinking.

A torrent of thoughts and questions flood your mind:

What you tell your wife and children?

Do you discuss this claim with your partners and your colleagues?

Will this claim ruin your career in medicine?

How are you going to deal with the demands on your time that this problem will require?

I believe it is prudent to discuss this complaint in brief with your wife and children if they are old enough to understand. You should indicate that you have a claim which has been filed against you and you need their support and understanding during the difficult and long period of time during which you will need to be involved in your defense. You need to explain that this will cut into family time. You might warn them that if your case is reported in the local newspaper, it may result in loss of your reputation and prestigious position in the community. Although it is difficult, you should instruct them to refrain from any comment. Also, you should tell them that an award for the plaintiff could result in loss of your own money if it exceeds the limits of your insurance coverage.

You do have an obligation to inform your partners and other physician employees that a claim has been filed against you.

It would be advisable not to discuss the claim in detail with your partners or colleagues since these discussions are not privileged. Although talking to close associates is tempting and may make you feel better temporarily, you should resist such discussions. Only conversations with your assigned and personal attorney, spouse, physician, counselor, or clergy are privileged.

You may already feel defeated or worry that this claim could ruin your career. If so, you should consider the following statistics: Overall, plaintiffs won just 30.5% of medical liability cases in 2002.[1] Of the 7% of cases proceeding to a jury verdict, the defendant won 82.4% of the time.

You must accept the fact that you will need to expend extra effort and time in preparing your defense in this case. You should assume a proactive and not a passive role in all legal proceedings. You must listen to and trust the recommendations of your attorney. If you do not feel your attorney has your best interests at heart, you should discuss your concerns with your adjuster and request a change in representation.

Once you convince yourself you did indeed do the right things for the patient who has brought claim against you, you should evaluate how others involved in your defense will perceive your quality of care. Positive feelings about why and what you did will negate a lot of doubts and anxieties. However, if you see deficiencies in your decisions and care you should accept them and prepare to deal with them. You will be able to deal with the negative emotions a great deal better if you can be objective and truthful about your actions.

Let's consider how you deal with the emotions of anger, embarrassment, betrayal, denial, frustration, and wishful thinking.

It is certainly reasonable to experience *anger* after being served with a medical malpractice claim. However, you must not fixate on this negative emotion but rather transform it into useful energy needed to prepare your defense. You must put your negative feelings on the back burner and leave them behind so you can proceed forward with the task of defending yourself.

---

1.   *Jury Verdict Research* (2002), 18. The plaintiff recovery rate at trial varies from 20% as reported by the Physician Insurers Association of America to 23.4% as reported by the U.S. Department of Justice. PIAA (2002).

The feeling of *embarrassment* is not unexpected considering the circumstances under which you received the claim. At this stage, you should hold your head up high. You must realize that you need not feel any guilt since there has been no judgment against you but merely accusations. Remember that these complaints and accusations against you will need to be proven to the jury based on the evidence. In a civil case, the burden of proof is on the plaintiff to show that the greater weight of evidence (more than 51%) indicates you were negligent or failed to meet the minimum standard of care.

Another natural reaction is to feel *betrayed* by the individual whom you believe that you treated with respect and concern and to the best of your abilities. You must understand there is no turning back or appeal to the plaintiff to reconsider action after a claim is filed. Be aware that a number of plaintiffs believe or are told that the doctor never takes the claim personally. Nothing, of course, could be further from the truth. Although you may wish to publicly deny all the claims made against you by your former patient you must prepare yourself to deal with all the issues covered in the claim. No matter how frivolous or far-fetched the counts are against you, you and your legal team must deal with them emotionally as well as logistically. It would help if one could realize that hyperbole is the norm in malpractice claims and that to take all of them personally is a waste of precious emotional energy.

Frustration in dealing with a malpractice claim is to be expected. You must remember that you are no longer the captain of the ship. You must accept the need to take direction from your appointed or chosen counsel. It is similar to the need to take advice and direction from another physician when you become ill or injured. At times you will question their tactics and maneuvers. You will resent the delays, cancellations, inconveniences, and infringement on your time. You must learn to deal with the roller-coaster ride of the legal journey, which typically runs by leaps and starts. You will experience highs and lows as the process unfolds to its completion. You are used to dealing with serious medical and surgical disease. Approach your defense with the energy and enthusiasm you exert in practicing medicine. You must be intellectually and emotionally prepared to deal with the reality that you have a malpractice claim against you, which, like a serious diagnosis, will not vanish.

In summary, you should try to eliminate negative thoughts and emotions. You need to direct your energies toward your current work and responsibilities and not let yourself get mired down by the claim. Self-pity and anger will not result in anything of positive value, so reject the urge to dwell on them. Take a positive, proactive stance, be reasonable and cooperative, and trust that your defense of the claim will prevail. Remember you have a statistically better chance of winning than losing.

REFERENCES

Jury Verdict Research's Current Award Trends in Personal Injury. 2002. LRP.

Physician Insurers Association of America (PIAA). 2002. *PIAA Claim Trend Analysis.* Rockville, Md.: PIAA.

25

Managing Medical Malpractice Stress

Louise B. Andrew, M.D., J.D., F.A.C.E.P
John-Henry Pfifferling, Ph.D.

Although malpractice claims are a completely predictable hazard of medical practice in the 21st century, medical training rarely addresses the harmful effects of malpractice litigation. What follows is what you need to teach yourself to begin to transform the experience.

The impact of a medical malpractice suit on the physician, and on his or her family, produces pervasive symptoms of medical malpractice stress (MMS). Even the term *malpractice* elicits stress in physicians, because it is so often a misnomer. Physicians understand that many so called malpractice cases are nonmeritorious maloccurrences caused by systemic errors, or unpreventable bad outcomes associated with disease or illness processes rather than any negligence. But malpractice is frequently equated in the public eye with physician negligence. Because of the stigma associated with negligent injury, intense shame as well as tangible negative consequences are felt by those physicians who have been sued, regardless of the outcome of the case. Malpractice litigation uniquely mines the vulnerabilities of physicians, and it thereby causes more disruption of the practices, lives, and families of physicians than to any other type of professional.

Physicians who are sued usually perceive the suit as an assault on their own integrity. Sued physicians report reactions such as the following to describe the emotional rollercoaster of the experience:

- "Over the weeks, months, and years of the suit I felt waves of shame and betrayal."

- "Very annoying and humiliating . . . an affront to my competency."

- "An embittering experience."

- "Now I watch myself react to patients with a subtle distance."

- "I had a frantic, furious reaction, and now I realize my practice is no longer worth the sacrifice."

- "It was the most stressful experience in my life. It reinforced my commitment to leave medicine."

- "No one, not even my close colleagues, offered to support me."

- "I still have moments when I consider how I would castrate the plaintiff's attorney."

- "No one seemed to understand how I felt . . . betrayed, shamed and vulnerable."

INITIAL RESPONSE TO RECEIPT OF A MALPRACTICE CLAIM

The process of shaming begins with receipt of a claim. Process servers are notoriously devious, portraying themselves as patients or other legitimate colleagues before thrusting papers into the hand of a trusting physician, stating, "Doctor, you have been served!" The claim, while a legal requirement, is also the first tool in the plaintiff lawyer's arsenal. Clinical competence and therefore physician self-worth are directly attacked in the complaint, which typically contains words such as "care beneath the standard required by law, obvious neglect, willful and wanton," so as to increase the drama of the presentation. Reading such a claim, the physician is immediately plunged into a dark drama for which he has no preparation, and feels particularly vulnerable since so much of the usual control in his familiar environment is not available.

In the medico-legal drama, physicians are forced to become actors on an unfamiliar stage. Language, scripting, the cast of characters, and the rules of the game are alien. Added to this strangeness is fear and uncertainty of the personal and professional outcome. Even the physician's family may share in this insecurity at times and wonder if the claims could be true. The physician is not used to being in a passive or reactive role, so stress is magnified. Even if there was error, the typical physician has no idea whether his or her behavior was legally negligent or not. The "stranger-in-a-strange-land" phenomenon may induce the physician to accept more fault than may be warranted.

More so than any other professionals, physicians usually feel that their worth as a person depends on their professional competence and prestige. So a malpractice claim is not just a business matter, it has the impact of a serious personal violation. Therefore, a first step in the management of medical malpractice stress is to acknowledge that you have bought into this myth ("I am what I do"), and possibly lived it for much of your professional life. This is a good time to begin to affirm, over and over, your own self-worth aside from your professional role. Professional success is nice—but it is not you.

In addition to playing into personal insecurities, a claim of medical malpractice pulls deeper strings. It plays into the high achievement which is selected for in medical students, and into a time-honored belief system inculcated and internalized in medical training: "Good physicians do not make mistakes," and its corollary, "Those who make mistakes are not good physicians." This outmoded, but still prevalent, belief system based on perfectionism fosters denial. Attorneys frequently use it to get physicians to blame one another. This makes their job considerably easier.

The myth of perfection is that bad outcomes do not happen in the absence of mistakes. It is based in the hope that bad things don't happen to good people, the knowledge that medicine is the best defense we have against dying, and the belief that our medicine is the best there is. This myth is certainly not taught in medical schools, but it is so common in the general population that many medical students bring it with them into training. Most of the time this myth is effectively suppressed. But when a bad outcome does occur, especially when an untoward event is being investigated or a claim is filed, the myth comes back to haunt most physicians. Rumination and poor reasoning may ensue ("I must have erred or caused the bad outcome"). This is another myth which makes the plaintiff lawyer's job easier: the jury believes it, and even the physician may slip into it when self-esteem is at a low ebb (such as after receiving a malpractice claim or a terrible outcome), admitting to fault when none may actually exist. Be on guard against this.

At the scientific level, we know that no physician can predict bad outcomes, and we cannot always take a clinical path that always leads to good results. A good physician can only do what an educated and earnest, yet fallible, human being can do at the moment, and learn from that experience. With the best intentions, education, preparation, and execution, sometimes miraculous things happen, sometimes tragedies occur, and sometimes very little happens. Good science tells us that the enormous variables involved will often preclude clear delineation of cause and response. But when we are feeling badly about our patient's misfortune, compounded by allegations of incompetence or evil intent, science takes a back seat to emotion. Put it back in the front. And add a seatbelt of compassion. Remember why you went into medicine (not to cause misery or make money), reflect on all that you have done and all the sacrifices you have made to prepare yourself to do so, and begin to tally up all of the good you have brought to the world as a result.

TYPICAL SYMPTOMS OF MEDICAL MALPRACTICE STRESS SYNDROME

In retrospective analyses of sued physicians, regardless of the outcome of the suit, almost all report physical or stress reactions (Charles et al. 1985; Wenokur and Campbell 1991). Even when the case results in dismissal, physicians experience the process as a trying ordeal. Physicians are poor at reassuring themselves that they are worthwhile human beings, and since perfectionism and self-criticism are reinforced in training and practice, overwhelming sad and angry feelings accompany litigation and may linger on long afterwards.

Common symptoms include:

Isolation: Most physicians feel alone in their efforts to vindicate themselves. This feeling of aloneness often persists, in spite of having an attorney on the case. Traditionally, sued physicians rarely seek support from colleagues. Colleagues admit they hesitate to reach out to help for fear of compounding the shame, or do not know what they could offer.

Negative self-image: Regardless of the stage in the suit, many experience a sense of defeat (grief, sadness, and anger). During the suit, and after, sued physicians sense less self-confidence, lower self-esteem, and recurrent bouts of shame. Many experience a "re-wounding of their self-esteem" from shaming events (such as denigration by a Socratic attending on rounds, or Morbidity and Mortality conferences) which occurred during residency and medical school. Often they forget all the good, conscientious, and noble work they have done before the suit.

Massive emotional impact: Many physicians experience anger, free-floating tension, increased negative moods, depression-like fatigue, frustration, and violated sleep (insomnia). Many report depressive symptoms lasting longer than two weeks, even in those who previously had never experienced depression. Physicians describe various types of negative rumination affecting their ability to focus and concentrate.

Anger syndromes: Many sued physicians, regardless of legal outcome, report anger clusters, including unexpected anger outbursts, irritability (with seemingly slight provocation), frustration, or dull or negative affect, as well as physical symptoms.

Physical symptoms: These may be wide-ranging, but frequently include gastrointestinal, or chest pains mimicking MI symptoms. New onset of peptic ulcer or coronary disease and or exacerbation of preexisting disease are not uncommon.

Fatigue syndrome: Many report changes in concentration, decreased libido, changes in appetite, apathy, and exhaustion or fatigue.

Social symptoms: Physicians tend to heed their attorneys' warnings literally and shut down communication with others. Spouses have reported they feel like they were suddenly cut off from normal communication, as were the physician's children. Interactions with patients become less satisfying. Patients may come to be viewed as possible plaintiffs, even after years of comfortable relationships. Colleagues are viewed as potential additional sources of shame since they *might* have handled the case in a different manner which *might* have had a better outcome. Even the physician's own attorney is not always perceived as a reliable ally, since he or she may be viewed as a primary protector for the carrier. So the physician in litigation may receive far less social support than is the norm even for physicians. Isolation and fear are thus compounded.

Absence of symptoms: Few physicians report no symptoms. Little data is available on the characteristics of these "resilient" physicians. Further research is needed on this group, to determine whether there are immunizing factors (for example, availability of peer or professional support, family or religious affiliations, previous claims, successful defense, etc.) that might offer protection from the MMS, or whether denial is the explanation for these outliers.

RESULTS OF MEDICAL MALPRACTICE STRESS

Changed practice styles: Many sued physicians report profound reluctance to see known plaintiffs or their families, patients with seemingly high litigation risk, or those with poor prognoses. Many report a loss of empathy for some or even most patients.

Most report increased obsessiveness in record-keeping and an increase in the frequency of ordering tests, including ordering invasive tests or those with a low likelihood of affecting the diagnosis. There may be guilt associated with the compulsion to practice more defensive medicine. Many decrease their performance of certain procedures, especially those where their own sense of control over the procedure is minimal or the results are not extremely predictable and overwhelmingly positive. Some will forgo opportunities to learn new procedures because of their heightened fear of suboptimal results.

Changed life plans: A sense of professional isolation carries over to all other relationships. The litigation process typically drags on for about four years. Each stage in the suit may take place after weeks or months of inactivity, bringing back each time the emotions of the earlier stages. This process is analogous to vicarious retraumatization. As physicians complain or shut down about the bitterness they feel, they can become estranged from their natural support network. Without checking out their assumptions, many physicians feel that their significant others (life and/or long-term medical partners) cannot completely understand or empathize with the deep violations associated with a malpractice claim. Ruminating about the case can tend to cause the sued physician to detach from family and community and to shrink from contributing to strategic practice decisions. Every medical community relates instances of early retirement or successful suicide associated with involvement in medical malpractice litigation.

TYPICAL EMOTIONAL REACTIONS TO A CLAIM OF MEDICAL MALPRACTICE

If you are sued, expect to:

- Be personally angry

- Feel disillusioned

- Magnify self-doubt, question your own competence

- Experience persistence of negative feelings

- Feel isolated, frustrated, and unjustly singled out

- Experience guilt *even if* your performance and professionalism was faultless

- Experience symptoms or episodes of illness or depressive
affect

- Lose some ground in your practice, although rarely permanently

- Feel your personal identity is challenged

Don't expect:

- Compassion and support from colleagues, especially if
they have not (yet) been sued

- Immediate understanding from family, friends, and partners

- Support from administrators, if insurance coverage may be
jeopardized, rates increased, or more parties brought into
the case because of your defense

- A change of heart from the plaintiff or their attorney (that
decision is past)

- That your attorney will just handle the case with you taking a back seat

- That the jury will be educated, or able to view the case
from a logical, scientific perspective: even best-inten-
tioned jurors are not peers

- That your peers (PR committee, licensure board, or future
employers) will necessarily side with you, particularly
when not all of the details are apparent

- That the jury will *not* consider your character and its consistency, particularly your apparent truthfulness and diligence-they want to feel secure that there are good doctors to keep them safe

MECHANISMS FOR SUCCESSFUL MANAGEMENT OF MEDICAL MALPRACTICE STRESS

1. **Use of support/self-help groups.** Some in the medical community have recognized a need to deal with and reduce the isolation, negative emotional consequences, and costs of ignorance about the effects of litigation. They have begun support groups that foster mutual aid, discussion in a safe environment, and true collegiality. Impetus for these groups came from patient-inspired support groups and the initial efforts of the Illinois and Pennsylvania Medical Society pilot programs on litigation stress support and education.

Advantages of self-help/support groups include:

- Physicians are given a sense of some emotional security, even when they perceive their practice to be falling apart and/or are being tried in the press.

- The fear of catastrophe is lessened by sharing the survival stories of others.

- Successful role models are provided in the group. Valuable advice and insight as to how to handle this life event are provided by group members.

- There is an opportunity to establish a new network of friends to replace those who either shun or who have been advised not to speak with the sued physician.

- Support groups can provide the physician with an emotional outlet, as well as a way to positively channel the negative energy by speaking with and helping others.

- Groups confer an educational forum. They provide some aspects of education and coaching on litigation, legal processes and arcane requirements, the legal culture, family stress, and individual coping assistance.

- When family members are permitted and encouraged to attend, self-help groups offer support to all involved.

Note: Attorneys and risk managers appropriately warn against sharing details about ongoing cases in support groups, because an accounting of such conversations can become part of the legal record through the discovery process. This does not mean that feelings and techniques cannot be discussed, and these are often the most useful knowledge gained from such discussions.

2.   **Establishing a personal survival tool kit.** Successful coping with medical malpractice stress requires adoption of a set of skills and practices which can be learned and practiced:

- The ability to distance your core identity from both the suit and the process. Recognize that you are only an actor involved in a drama which is not of your making and not under your control. The summons and the legal process are scenes in a legal action; the arcane script has been written by long dead (and morbid) "poets," and only part of your professional persona is (involuntarily) involved.

- Adopt as your mantra: "I will not allow this temporary intrusion into who I am and what I do to change me except for the better. I will not give away my power, my self-esteem or my livelihood. I can learn from everyone and everything. This is a unique educational opportunity, and I will use it."

- After assuring yourself that your legal team is competent and knows how to access you, leave the legal maneuvering to them. You will not have time to learn to be an expert in malpractice law. Nonetheless . . .

- You must schedule time for your legal team to work on whatever is necessary to build and conduct a strong case. This may require reducing your patient load or shifts worked during certain phases of the case.

- Taking an active approach to the case is necessary. Avoidance and procrastination are never useful and may be dangerous in dealing with legal situations. Now is not the time to be independent. Ask your legal team for suggestions as to how you can assist in the process. You may be able to use this case as a strategy to learn collaborative and cooperative skills. You may be able to use what you learn to benefit others.

- Become educated in and comfortable dealing with the tactics of the plaintiff's attorney and the time and scheduling difficulties required by legal proceedings.

- Add more buffering (support) to your life during this period. Ask for support from colleagues beyond your family, even though it requires risk-taking. There is no toxic dose of support, counseling, or coaching during the stress of medical malpractice litigation. Do not allow yourself to become more isolated. Seek more input from outside your usual circle. Take a class, join a club, play for a change.

- Remind yourself repeatedly that the threat of litigation is a well-established occupational hazard of practicing medicine. Physicians prevail in over 60% of cases. In the long run, the typical suit will not harm you irreparably and will probably teach you something useful. It will, however, be a substantial distraction in the short run. The trick is to find the learning in the process. If this is your first case, you can soon affirm: "I am now a real doctor, I have survived this (odious) rite of passage." If it is not, you can say, "What I have learned before, I will apply now."

- Maximize to the extent possible your pleasurable downtime activities during this experience. Increase your pleasure producing experiences. These experiences are the internal pharmacy of your brain. (Ornstein and Sobel 1989). It has been shown that the risk of a second malpractice claim in the early period after learning of the first is high. Unmitigated stress-related behavior is hypothetically the cause of the second claim. The strain of a malpractice case should be taken as a prescription for more ease-producing activities.

- Use reframing techniques to maintain a positive perspective on the stresses of the litigation experience. For example, preparation for testimony before a jury can teach you to improve your ability to communicate with families or audiences. (If your attorney does not offer to prepare you for testimony, or you feel inadequately prepared, ask for referral to a knowledgeable consultant in litigation preparation.)

- Use this experience to learn more about the commonality of this problem and efforts at reform. Get active: lobby for Good Samaritan protection for healthcare professionals, patient compensation funds, "bad baby" funds, expert witness reform, and other alternatives to the present flawed system (www.commongood.com).

- Regularly ask, "How can I use this crisis to enhance my survivorship skills and techniques?" If you are your own worst critic, learn new (and nonmedical) skills both for distraction and to enhance your feelings of success.

- Take care of yourself. You are exemplary of the care you give. Your continual good care for others is only as effective as your regular self-care and self-respect.

- It is now a wise time to expand your ability to be more at ease with uncertainty and ambiguity. Practice what helps you deal with the state of "not-knowing." Is it an inner voice that allows you to do the best you can do? Is it practice of some meditative, mindfulness state? Is it letting go to destiny or a higher power? Is the ultimate outcome of anything really under your control?

- If you continue to experience depression, anger, or distress, concentrate on what needs are unmet. Are you exercising? A personal trainer, an expressive martial arts class or an aerobics class might be appropriate. Do you feel symptoms? Get that long-overdue physical. Anxiety, insomnia, or symptoms of depression? Use this opportunity to get counseling for one of life's most stress-provoking experiences. Take time to rest more, play more, treat yourself kindly, count your strengths and accomplishments. Self-care is now a priority; it is not a luxury.

3. **Specific do's and don't's.**

Do share the burden:

With your medical malpractice carrier.

- Notify them of any potential claim, *immediately,* in accordance with your policy.

- Notify them immediately of any subpoena, contact by an attorney, or request for records or review of case in which you participated.

With your attorney.

- Know the case thoroughly, and provide all the details you can from the outset.

- Don't conceal anything, and don't change *anything* in the documentation—it is a surefire way to lose the case.

- Ask questions about his or her deposition and trial tactics, and those they anticipate from the plaintiff's side.

- Insist on careful preparation before deposition and testimony.

- Insist on obtaining the best witnesses on your behalf.

- Attend as many depositions and courtroom proceedings as your attorney allows, so that you will be well informed.

With your family.

- Tell them you've been sued.

- Share your pain and feelings, and ask them for support through the ordeal.

- Ask them for their suggestions for dealing with the stress involved and remaining close during the process. If you have been emotionally or physically unavailable prior to the initiation of the suit, ask for forgiveness and work at fostering intimacy. Recommitting yourself to your family can be a gift from this trauma.

- Do not take out your anger and feelings of victimization on your family. Yes, you may be frustrated; but because they are there when you are feeling vulnerable, you must be careful not to alienate them. Tell them what you are feeling. Don't assume they will know.

Do strongly consider sharing:

- Feelings with a counselor—legally protected/privileged communications are possible with lawyer, clergy, physician, professional counselor, or therapist as well as your spouse.

- Feelings with your journal or tape recorder, a support group, or via art or writing.

- Feelings about the stress of dealing with alleged medical malpractice and general comments about *the process* and the *experience* with safe colleagues.

- Needs for some extra consideration in scheduling for trial preparation, appearance time, or down time to deal with the stress of litigation with your practice colleagues.

Don't share with others outside this circle:

- Avoid the temptation to speak to others (about the specifics of the case), no matter how peripheral. Nearly every discussion is discoverable (you must reveal it in court if asked), except as enumerated above. Don't discuss the details of the case except with your attorney or claims representative.

- *Never* answer questions made by phone or posed by anyone associated with the plaintiff's family, or their attorney. When your medical malpractice carrier calls for information by phone, have your office initiate the call. Check the number first.

Do consider hiring your own attorney/cocounsel:

- If your attorney advises that a settlement or award might go beyond the policy limits.

- For a second opinion if you feel that your attorney is not prepared to deal with your case effectively or does not have credentials in medical malpractice defense.

- If you feel that your counsel doesn't hear your concerns, prepare you adequately for deposition or trial, or clearly respond to your questions or concerns.

THE BOTTOM LINE AND KEY TO DEALING WITH MEDICAL MALPRACTICE STRESS

Malpractice litigation is now a completely predictable event in the career of any practicing physician. Use it as an opportunity to learn and practice exemplary care for yourself in time of crisis, and you will become a stronger person, a better doctor, and a model for colleagues who will follow in your footsteps.

ALWAYS REMEMBER: NOTHING CAN UNDO ALL OF THE GOOD YOU HAVE DONE IN YOUR CHOSEN PROFESSION

Homework:

Write down all of the reasons you know that you are a conscientious, competent, compassionate, caring physician *and* a fallible human being. Regularly revisit this list and affirm its truth.

Verbalize often, in a private space, why absolutely no one can take away your achievements or your good character.

Affirm that you are a survivor. Affirm your positive qualities. In view of this assault, consider your path, what you have learned, and what opportunities have emerged as a result.

Please share with us those steps that help you personally counteract the distress of the litigation experience. As you acknowledge and then transcend the ordeal, consider helping others as a peer counselor, an activist, or a change agent.

Self Assessment for Medical Malpractice Stress syndrome
© 2005 Louise B. Andrew, M.D., J.D.

I am involved as a defendant in litigation and I am experiencing or feeling

☐ Anger or irritability which is affecting my satisfaction with life

☐ Sense of reduction or loss of control in aspects of my work or life

☐ Singled out, isolation or tendency towards distancing from my peers

☐ Over- or underactivity relative to my usual pattern

☐ Anxiety or depressive symptoms

☐ Changes in appetite or eating habits

☐ Insomnia or poor-quality sleep

☐ Changes in libido (particularly reduction)

☐ Emotional distancing from patients or office staff

☐ Tendency towards withdrawal from family, friends, group activities

- ☐ Concerns about my competence or abililty to make decisions
- ☐ Hesitation to take on difficult problems or demanding patients
- ☐ Compulsion to order more testing of patients
- ☐ Less willingness to take on administrative decisions or activities
- ☐ Thoughts about changing careers or limiting practice
- ☐ Physical symptoms which are different or worse from normal
- ☐ Fatigue, or reduced energy levels
- ☐ Loss of enjoyment in practice
- ☐ Loss of interest in recreation
- ☐ Drawn towards mindless pursuits, e.g., television, Internet
- ☐ Frustration that no end is in sight
- ☐ Stymied by the system from dealing directly with the problem
- ☐ Questions about value of persisting in medicine
- ☐ Instrusive thoughts or compulsions
- ☐ Alone in efforts to vindicate myself from an unfair accusation
- ☐ Helpless or hopeless to change the course of events
- ☐ Impulse to do something drastic or dangerous
- ☐ Thoughts about benefit of ending it all

Although it is normal to feel some of these things in the face of a malpractice claim, if you are experiencing as many as five of them, then the stress of litigation may be starting to impact your professional as well as your personal life. It is highly advisable to discuss your feelings about what is happening to you with an experienced professional, who may recommend supportive intervention. This is one of the most stressful events in the life of any physician. **If you have felt any one of the last five items, you must seek professional help immediately.**

REFERENCES

Andrew, L. 1996. "Litigation Stress." *Straight Forward Magazine*.

Andrew, L., and J.-H. Pfifferling. 1992. "Starting a Litigation Support Group for Physicians." Durham, N.C.: Society for Professional Well-Being. www.cpwb.org; 919-489-9167

Barge, B., and K. Fenlason. 1989. "Dealing Effectively with Malpractice Litigation: A Human Factors Guide." Risk Management Services Division, St. Paul Fire and Marine Insurance Company.

Charles, S. C., and E. Kennedy. 1985. *Defendant: A Psychiatrist on Trial for Medical Malpractice*. New York: MacMillan.

Charles, S. C., J. R. Wilbert, and K. J. Franke. 1985. "Sued and Non-sued Physicians' Reactions to Malpractice Litigation." *American Journal of Psychiatry* 142:437–440.

Chedd, G., A. Liebman, A. Markowitz, F. Gale, R. Pearlstein, and J. Kirk, eds. 1998. *The Malpractice Suit: A Survival Guide for Physicians and their Families*. Videotape and guide. Eidetics.

Danner, D. 1986. *Medical Malpractice: A Primer for Physicians*. Rochester, N.Y.: Lawyer's Cooperative.

Huber, P. 1988. *Liability: The Legal Revolution and its Consequences*. New York: Basic Books.

Kane, J. 2003. *How to Heal: A Guide for Caregivers*. New York: Helios Press.

Olson, W. 1991. *The Litigation Explosion*. New York: Dutton.

Ornstein, R., and D. Sobel. 1989. *Healthy Pleasures*. Reading, Mass.: Addison-Wesley.

Port, J. 2003. "Time for a New Medical Liability Debate." Commentary, in Main Line Health (September).

Robertson, W. 1985. *Medical Malpractice: A Preventive Approach*. Seattle: University of Washington Press.

Wenokur, B., and L. Campbell. 1991. "Malpractice Suit Emotional Trauma." *JAMA* 266:2834.

26

Trends in Malpractice Litigation

Leonard Berlin, M.D., F.A.C.R.

In 1794, five years after George Washington was inaugurated as the first President of the United States, the new nation's first medical malpractice lawsuit was adjudicated by a Connecticut court. The husband of a woman who had died as a result of surgery sued the physician for operating in "the most unskillful, ignorant, and cruel manner, contrary to all the well-known rules and principles of practice," and violating "his promise to the plaintiff to perform said operation skillfully and with safety to his wife."[1] The lawsuit, the primary allegation of which was breach of contract, was won by the plaintiff. The jury found the physician liable and awarded damages of 40 English pounds.

Two hundred and ten years later our nation finds itself engulfed in a malpractice quagmire that physicians all over the nation are calling a malpractice crisis (Eisenberg and Sieger 2003). How did we reach this point? This chapter will explore this question and then address the issue of what the medical community can expect as it moves forward to the future on a road imbedded with malpractice minefields.

---

1. *Cross v. Guthrey,* 2 Root 90 (Conn. 1794). Quoted in Sandor (1957).

In order to gain a more meaningful understanding of the current state of affairs with regard to medical malpractice litigation in the United States, we must begin by looking back at the path that has led us to the present.

American law under which we are governed today derives from three sources (Sandor 1957). The first is constitutional law, founded on federal and state constitutions and interpretations given them by the courts. Second is statutory law, rules and regulations enacted by various state legislatures and the U.S. Congress. Finally, there is the common law, law that is based on judicial decisions that serve as precedents on which courts base future decisions.

Let us turn to the early settlers of the North American continent. At one time or another, many different European countries colonized the land that was to become the United States, but it was the culture, customs, and laws of England that exerted the greatest influence. During the pre-Revolutionary period, the American colonies inherited not only the English language but also its common law, and for the most part English law has remained our system of law to this day (Buckner 1999, 31–54, 68–80, 94–96, 106–113, 152–154). Only Louisiana has remnants of French law, and some Western states still have traces of Spanish law.

The common law as we know it today is therefore a legacy from the English to the United States. It is composed of published decisions of state and federal appellate and supreme courts that serve as bases on which subsequent similar cases are decided. Simply stated, the fundamental characteristic of both English and American common law is adherence to precedent, more formally referred to as the doctrine of *stare decisis* (Sandor 1957).

In 1765, British legal scholar Sir William Blackstone published *Blackstone's Commentaries on the Laws of England,* a compendium of legal principles that was to become the second-most widely read book (the first was the Bible) in the American colonies (Buckner 1999). In his book, Blackstone referred to the "neglect or unskillful management of a physician or surgeon" as *"mala praxis."* It is from this term that the modern word "malpractice" was derived (Mohr 2000).

Although the first recorded American medical malpractice lawsuit was in 1794, many malpractice cases had occurred in England before that. The 1769 case of *Slater v. Baker and Stapleton* is frequently cited as the first medical negligence case in which a court articulated the standard of care against which the conduct of a physician would be measured (Rosenbaum 2003). The standard enunciated at the time had the effect of shielding physicians from most professional liability, for not only did the Court rule that a physician could be found liable only if another physician testified that his conduct breached the standard of care, but the Court also held that the only physician who could testify regarding the standard of care of a defendant-physician was a physician in the defendant's own locality.

One of the earliest state supreme court decisions in the United States setting forth the standard of care for physicians was rendered in 1832, again in Connecticut. A physician was accused of negligence for "unskillfully and carelessly making an incision into the plaintiff's arm to insert [smallpox] vaccine, such that she suffered great pain and her arm was irreparably injured."[2] The jury found in favor of the plaintiff, and the defendant-physician appealed. Although the Connecticut Supreme Court upheld the jury verdict, its eloquent commentary regarding not only what legal duties should be imposed on physicians but also the hardships that physicians face when sued for malpractice seem as relevant if not even more relevant in 2004 as it was 172 years ago. The Court began by reviewing the defendant's argument (*Landon v. Humphrey, supra*):

> A physician and surgeon, in the performance of his professional duties, is liable for injuries resulting from the want of ordinary diligence, care and skill. The defendant-physician contends that it ought to be borne in mind that physicians never warrant their work. They make no promise, except to do as well as they can, and as well as they know how to do. There is nothing like mechanical perfection in the healing art. The only reasonable rule on this subject—

---

2.   *Landon v. Humphrey,* 9 Conn. 209 (1832).

which is in accordance with the settled law in Connecticut, England and elsewhere—is that nothing short of gross ignorance or gross negligence will subject the surgeon to damages. What man, even of skill and talent, would undertake to practice in the healing art, if some little failure of ordinary skill or ordinary diligence, or even some trifling want of carefulness might sweep from him the whole earnings of a life of toil and drudgery? Restricted to the narrow ground of the charge, many skillful and able physicians would not escape liability a single year of their practice. "Ordinary" means usual, common. The difference between a want of ordinary or useful skill and gross negligence is essential and important. If you were to draw a line of distinction just halfway between the eminently learned physicians and those grossly ignorant, would you not hit exactly on those styled ordinary. . . . To say that a physician did not perform a certain operation with ordinary skill conveys a very different idea from the assertion that he performs it with gross negligence.

The Court then affirmed the verdict in favor of the patient:

The defendant-physician prayed the Court to charge the jury that, unless the plaintiff had proved the defendant guilty of great and gross negligence in vaccinating the plaintiff, she could not recover. The Court told the jury on this point that if there was either *carelessness*, or a *want of ordinary diligence, care and skill,* then the plaintiff was entitled to recover. The principle laid down by the Court is entirely correct. If in the performance of the operation there was a want of ordinary diligence, care and skill, or if there was carelessness, then the defendant-physician was liable.

The motion for a new trial must be denied.

Further refinement regarding the duties that physicians owe patients, and an opinion on the question of whether physicians must warrant cures, were expressed by the Pennsylvania Supreme Court in 1853. A man whose leg had become deformed and shortened as a result of a comminuted fracture of the tibia and fibula sustained during an accident sued the physician who had treated him, alleging negligence. Following a trial, the jury found in favor of a patient and awarded him $850. A physician lodged an appeal that was eventually heard by the State's Supreme Court, which reversed the jury decision and ordered a new trial.[3]

> The only question of any importance presented for our consideration is whether the trial court erred in charging that the defendant-physician was bound to bring to his aid the skill necessary for a surgeon to set the leg so as to make it straight and of equal length with the other, when healed; and if he did not, he was accountable in damages, just as a stone-mason or bricklayer would be in building a wall of poor materials and the wall fell down, or if they built a chimney and it should smoke by reason of a want of skill in its construction.

> It is impossible to sustain this proposition and it was inapplicable to the circumstances of the case under investigation. The implied contract of a physician or surgeon is not to cure—to restore a fractured limb to its natural perfectness—but to treat the case with diligence and skill. The physician deals not with insensate matter like the stone-mason or bricklayer, who can choose their materials and adjust them according to mathematical lines; but he has a suffering human being to treat, a nervous system to tranquilize, and *will* to regulate and control. The evidence before us makes this strong distinction between surgery and masonry, and shows how the judge's inept illustration was calculated to lead away the jury from the true point of the cause. . . . The question is not whether the doctor had brought to the case skill enough to make the leg as straight and long as the other, but whether he had employed such skill and diligence, as are ordinarily exercised in his profession. For less than this he is responsible in damages, but if he be held to the measure laid down by the trial

---

3.   *McCandless v. McWha,* 22 Pa. 261 (1853).

court, the implied contract amounts on his part to a *warranty of cure* for which there is no authority in law.

We have stated the rule to be reasonable skill and diligence, by which we mean such as thoroughly educated surgeons ordinarily employ. The law demands *qualification* in the profession practiced—not extraordinary skill such as belongs only to few men of rare genius and endowments, but that degree which ordinarily characterized the profession.

The trial court judge in his charge fell into error in stating the amount of skill required in the treatment of the case. We reverse for that reason. When we decide the legal point, we are done with it. We are not authority on questions of surgery. Our hands are abundantly full of questions which belong to our own profession, without volunteering opinions on sciences which relate to others.

Seven years later, in a malpractice lawsuit that also alleged that a physician had negligently reduced a fracture, the Illinois Supreme Court outlined the duties of a physician in similar wording:[4]

When a person assumes the profession of physician and surgeon, he must, in its exercise, be held to employ a reasonable amount of skill and care. For anything short of that degree and skill in his practice, the law will hold him responsible for any injury which may result from its absence. While he is not required to possess the highest order of qualification, to which some men attain, still he must possess and exercise that degree of skill which is ordinarily possessed by members of the profession.

From that point on, courts in every state in the nation consistently held that the standard of care of a physician is essentially the same as was enunciated in the mid-19th century decisions.

---

4.   *Richie v. West,* 23 Ill. 329 (1860).

The vast majority of malpractice lawsuits in the United States filed during the second half of the 19th century and first part of the 20th century were related to orthopedic treatment of fractures, dislocations, and amputations (Rosenbaum 2003). While state courts were adding to and modifying the common law, state legislatures were developing statutory law with enactment of state licensing of physicians. Texas in 1870 was the first state to pass a modern state licensing law and by 1905, 39 of the then 48 states had similar licensing laws (Rosenbaum 2003).

A new chapter in the saga of medical malpractice began with Roentgen's discovery of the X-ray in 1895. Medical historian James Mohr has written (Mohr 2000):

> Within 20 years of their introduction, radiographs had become one of the nation's most prolific sources of malpractice actions (too much radiation, failure to read the films properly, and so forth). Litigation concerning radiographs produced many of the highest damage awards (in excess of $5,000) in the decade prior to World War I and generated a whole new body of evidentiary disputes (for example, ownership of films, interpretation of faint images). Radiographic tests also opened to exposure other sorts of medical mistakes that were previously difficult to demonstrate in court.

In a 1957 article reviewing all published State and Supreme Court cases rendered in the United States between January 1946 and 1956, Sandor (1957) found that orthopedic problems headed the list of professional liability hazards. The one single incident that gave rise to most of the claims in orthopedics was the failure to take radiographs in patients with suspected fractures. There were 14 cases involving "X-ray and radium burns," but not even one case alleging failure to diagnose a neoplasm. The findings in this survey were in stark contrast to surveys of malpractice lawsuits that were to be published four decades later.

A review of malpractice litigation over a 20-year span from 1975 to 1994 in the greater Chicago area disclosed that radiology-related cases accounted for 12% of all medical malpractice cases filed against physicians (Berlin and Berlin 1995). Physical injuries sustained by patients in or being transported to or from a radiology department accounted for 5% of the total; radiation oncology complications, 8%; complications of radiologic procedures, 16%; failure to order radiologic studies, 22%; and radiographic misses, 42%. Miscellaneous causes accounted for the remaining 7%. Between 1975 and 1984, malpractice litigation related to missed bone abnormalities accounted for the greatest percentage of radiologic misses, but the ranking changed considerably in the period between 1985 and 1994, when cancers became the most commonly missed radiographic disease.

Data in other geographic regions have also been reported. Diagnostic mishaps accounted for 75% of all adverse events due to negligence experienced by patients admitted to New York hospitals between 1985 and 1988 (Leape et. al. 1991). A report in 1985 disclosed that missed fracture-dislocation cases represented 25% of all radiologic malpractice cases nationally and that claims of failure to diagnose cancer were a distant second in frequency at 8% ("Study Shows Causes of Claims" 1985). However, two years later a report of malpractice cases involving the federal government found that missed diagnosis of cancer had become the most common claim, accounting for 30% of all cases (Hamer et al. 1987). Yet another report found that missed cancer cases accounted for 47% of medical malpractice lawsuits lodged against radiologists between 1985 and 1987 (Dahlen and Foley 1989). By the early 1990s, surveys disclosed that missed carcinomas on chest radiographs and mammograms, become the most frequent and costly allegations of malpractice filed against radiologists (McCormick 1995).

In the two decades following World War II, the frequency of malpractice lawsuits increased gradually, as did financial recoveries (Rosenbaum 2003). It wasn't until the 1970s, however, that the number of medical malpractice lawsuits filed against all physicians, and the insurance premiums charged by malpractice carriers, began to skyrocket (Rosenbaum 2003; Berlin and Berlin 1995). The degree to which the medical malpractice phenomenon spiraled dramatically upward is illustrated by the following statistics. As of 1957, the largest sum awarded in a medical malpractice case by any trial court in the United States was $230,000. Median damages in malpractice litigation hovered in the $200,000 range in the early 1980s, rose to $300,000 in the late 1980s, and exceeded $400,000 in the 1990s (Woolsey 1993). In Illinois, the average payment per paid claim increased from just under $129,000 in the period 1980-1984 to almost $500,000 in the period 1995–1999 (*Addressing the New Health Care Crisis* 2003). Texas has experienced a 500% increase in the size of judgments awarded just in the last 10 years. Settlement payments have also steadily risen over the last two decades. The average settlement payment per paid claim increased from approximately $110,000 in 1987 to $250,000 in 1999 (*Addressing the New Health Care Crisis* 2003). As of 2002, the median jury award in malpractice cases exceeded $1 million, while the average was nearly $4 million (Saxton 2003).

The annual cost of an average physician's malpractice insurance in 1957 in metropolitan New York was $106, in upstate New York $64, and in California between $300 and $400 ("The Malpractice Insurance Crisis" 2003). In 1975 the cost of all premiums paid for medical malpractice liability insurance in the United States was $2 billion and its percentage of the gross national product was 0.02%. By 2001 the total premiums paid for malpractice insurance jumped to $21 billion and its percentage of gross national product grew to 0.25%. In 2002 obstetricians in Miami paid up to $210,000 for liability insurance, while general surgeons were charged up to $174,000 ("The Malpractice Insurance Crisis" 2003).

In 2002 physician-lawyer-historian Fillmore Buckner (1999) addressed the question of how long the present medical malpractice conundrum in the United States will continue. Here is a portion of his answer:

> The only reasonable answer appears to be, "for the foreseeable future." The reasons for this answer should be obvious given the history that has gone before. We are still in an extremely innovative stage of medical research and development, an appreciable amount of which is in the realm of high technology, high-risk nature. Such periods

of massive innovation are almost always a stimulus for a new wave of malpractice cases. . . . A period of increased depersonalization of medical care with third party health plans and fourth party auditors increases career dissatisfaction among physicians and frustration on the part of patients. . . . In the depersonalized atmosphere of the future, there is little hope communication will improve; poor communication with patients will inevitably lead to increased malpractice suits.

When we speak of innovation and new technology, radiology steps to the forefront. The introduction into the medical community of new radiologic technology is inevitably followed, with varying latent periods, by medical malpractice lawsuits alleging negligence in the use—or non-use—of such technology. The first medical malpractice lawsuit in the nation alleging negligence in the use of diagnostic sonography was filed in 1982, more than a decade after its introduction (Berlin and Berlin 1995). The first medical malpractice lawsuit in Chicago alleging negligence in interpreting CT was filed in 1982, eight years after its introduction in Chicago. The first malpractice lawsuit alleging misuse of MR imaging was filed in 1983, four years after the modality was introduced. In the past several years, PET scanning, computed-assisted detection, digital radiology, highly sophisticated CT and MR techniques, and picture and archival communication systems have been introduced to and adopted by a rapidly increasing number of members of the radiologic community. While there may be only few, if any, lawsuits filed thus far in the nation alleging negligence in the use or non-use of these modalities, assuredly such lawsuits will occur.

Ever since the Institute of Medicine released its report on errors in medicine in 2000 (Kohn et al. 1999), there has been much discussion in the news media and scientific literature about the frequency and severity of errors in medical practice. It should therefore not be surprising that a recent survey disclosed that 70% of lay-public respondents believed that physicians responsible for errors that result in fatal consequences to patients should be sued and subjected to suspension of their medical licenses (Blendon et al. 2002). It appears that a great many physicians feel the same way, for more than half of physicians polled also believed that a physician who makes a medical mistake that results directly or indirectly in a patient's death should be sued for malpractice.

Before the managed care-capitation payment era, physicians who were sued for failure to order a diagnostic test were judged legally only by whether they breached the standard of medical care; that is, whether they possessed the same knowledge and skill as that possessed by other ordinary physicians. Today, however, a new type of accusation against physicians is emerging: the claim that the physician failed to order a diagnostic test or examination because of a financial incentive to withhold it.

Physicians should realize that the courts have historically held that medical care given to patients must never be motivated by financial considerations. More than 100 years ago, a New York court stated, "Whether the patient be a pauper or a millionaire, whether he be treated gratuitously or for reward, the physician owes him precisely a measure of duty with the same degree of skill and care."[5] A century later, a California court, ruling in a case in which economics influenced medical care, reaffirmed this philosophy.[6] A 40-year-old woman who had abdominal aorta surgery because of vascular insufficiency was discharged from the hospital prematurely because of regulations issued by her managed care payer. Although the patient's physicians opposed early discharge, they did not object to it. The patient later developed complications that required amputation of a leg. Alleging that the amputation could have avoided had she remained longer, the patient sued the physicians, claiming that they should be held liable for not preventing the early discharge. The court ruled in favor of the patient and stressed that the responsibility of medical decisions belongs solely to the physicians. "While we recognize, realistically, that cost consciousness has become a permanent feature of the health care system," said the court, "it is essential that cost limitation programs not be permitted to corrupt medical judgment. . . . A physician who complies without protest with limita-

---

5.   *Becker v. Janinski,* 15 N.Y.Supp. 675 (Common Pleas, 1891).
6.   *Wickline v. State of California,* 192 Cal. App.3d 1630 (1986).

tions imposed by a third party payer, when his medical judgment dictates otherwise, cannot avoid his ultimate responsibility of his patient's care."

The United States is one of the few countries in which a jury sits in judgment in the determination of whether a physician has committed malpractice. In Germany, the United Kingdom, and many other nations including most provinces in Canada, medical malpractice cases are adjudicated only by judges ("Malpractice" 2003). Other nations such as Sweden and New Zealand have no-fault systems of evaluating and paying malpractice claims. The American legal system, in which civil litigation is tried before juries, is not likely to change in the foreseeable future, nor is the manner in which the amount of compensation awarded is determined. Notwithstanding repeated attempts to convince the United States Congress to enact tort reform legislation, it has thus far failed to do so.

We have traced the path of malpractice that has led us to the present. The outlook for the future is rather grim in that there is nothing to suggest that either the frequency or severity of medical malpractice lawsuits will abate. In fact, most experts expect that the malpractice crisis will deepen and spread (Mello et al. 2003). A recent *Chicago Tribune* editorial appears to sum up the situation in realistic terms ("Solving the Malpractice Mess" 2003):

> This is not the first, nor will it be the last, malpractice rate crisis. It should be abundantly clear now that there's no simple, painless solution to this problem. But a solution is needed, one that caps the more outlandish jury awards *and* reduces the medical errors that produce them.

REFERENCES

Addressing the New Health Care Crisis: Reforming the Medical Litigation System to Improve the Quality of Health Care. 2003. Rockville, Md.: U.S. Department of Health and Human Services, Office of the Assistant Secretary of Planning and Evaluation (3 March).

Berlin, L., and J. Berlin. 1995. "Malpractice and Radiologists in Cook County, IL: Trends in 20 Years of Litigation." *AJR* 165:781–788.

Blendon, R. J., C. M. DesRoches, M. Brodie, J. M. Benson, A. B. Rosen, E. Schneider, D. E. Altman, K. Zapert, M. J. Herrmann, and A. E. Steffenson. 2002. "Views of Practicing Physicians and the Public on Medical Errors." *N. Engl. J. Med.* 347:1933–1940.

Buckner, F. 1999. *Overview of the History of Medical Malpractice.* West Hartford, Conn.: The Graduate Group.

Dahlen, R. T., and H. T. Foley. 1989. "Medical Malpractice Claims in Diagnostic Radiology: Update." Letter. *Radiology* 170:277.

Eisenberg, D., and M. Sieger. 2003. "The Doctor Won't See You Now." *Time* (9 June) 48–52, 55–60.

Hamer, M. M., F. Morlock, H. T. Foley, and P. R. Ros. 1987. "Medical Malpractice in Diagnostic Radiology: Claims Compensation and Patient Injury." *Radiology* 164:263–266.

Kohn, L. T., J. M. Corrigan, and M. S. Donaldson, eds. 1999. *To Err Is Human: Building a Safer Health System.* Washington, D.C.: National Academy Press.

Leape, L. L., T. A. Brennan, N. M. Laird, A. G. Lawthers, A. R. Localio, B. A. Barnes, L. Hebert, J. P. Newhouse, P. C. Weiler, and H. H. Hiatt. 1991. "The Nature of Adverse Events in Hospitalized Patients: Results from the Harvard Medical Practice Study II." *N. Engl. J. Med.* 324:377–384.

"Malpractice: Do Other Countries Hold the Key?" 2003. *Med. Econ.* 80(14):58–64.

"The Malpractice Insurance Crisis." 2003. *The New York Times* (17 January): A24.

McCormick, B. 1995. "Liability Rates: Mixed Signals." *American Medical News* (January): 23–30.

Mello, M. M., D. M. Studdert, and T. A. Brennan. 2003. "The New Medical Malpractice Crisis." *N. Engl. J. Med.* 348:2281–2284.

Mohr, J. C. 2000. "American Medical Malpractice Litigation in Historical Perspective." *JAMA* 283:1731–1737.

Rosenbaum, S. 2003. "Law and the Public's Health: Medical Errors, Medical Negligence, and Professional Medical Liability Reform." *Public Health Rep.* 118:272–274.

Sandor, A. A. 1957. "The History of Professional Liability Suits in the United States." *JAMA* 163:459–466.

Saxton, J. 2003. *Liability for Medical Malpractice: Issues and Evidence: Joint Economic Committee Study.* Washington, D.C.: Joint Economic Committee, U.S. Congress (May).

"Solving the Malpractice Mess." 2003. *The Chicago Tribune* (7 February): 20.

"Study Shows Causes of Claims." 1985. *ACR Bulletin* 41(3):8.

Woolsey, C. 1993. "ISMIE Update: Jury Awards Rise." *Illinois Medicine* (June): 9–10.

27

Counterclaims as a Strategy to Combat Frivolous Medical Malpractice Suits

Jeffrey J. Segal, M.D.

Frivolous medical malpractice claims are expensive and time-consuming. There are available mechanisms that may deter such suits. Countersuit for malicious prosecution or abuse of process is one such avenue. Seeking redress against expert witnesses who deliver false or exaggerated testimony is another. Some options are emerging which are designed to decrease legal costs associated with using such deterrents.

Exposure to medical malpractice litigation is part and parcel of medical practice in the 21st century. Physicians generally protect themselves against claims of malpractice by carrying insurance which pays the expenses for a legal defense and judgment up to defined limits. Insurance works by pooling premiums from many to provide for the needs of a few. Insurance typically only pays claims and does not prevent claims. (To the contrary, having insurance prompts some claims.) In Florida, where statistics are public record, the likelihood of a physician being sued in any given year is 10–20%. Hence the saying "There are only two types of physicians—those who have been sued and those who will be sued."

Medical malpractice carriers have raised rates for premiums across the country. According to *Medical Liability Monitor* ("Trends in 2001 Rates" 2001), the reasons are:

- Increased payout of individual judgments

- Increased frequency of claims

- Higher costs of defending claims

- More generous pro-plaintiff juries

Rates vary from state to state but are rising everywhere. Tort reform has provided some relief. Effective tort reform measures include a cap on payouts designated for pain and suffering; affidavit requirements by an expert medical witness before case can be filed; and medical review panels which judge the merits of a case.

No matter how effective in reducing claims or judgments in those states which have enacted them, these measures do not prevent substantial numbers of cases from being filed. Even if physicians win a malpractice case, they are dragged through a process which can consume them for years. The emotions that are experienced are similar to surviving an IRS audit. Furthermore, many physicians perceive a high number of cases to be without merit. In survey of 1800 MD's, over 80% of MD's interviewed stated that cases filed against them had no merit (*Medical Economics* 1999). Not infrequently, unscrupulous attorneys will file marginal cases hoping for a quick nuisance settlement from the carrier. It is rare for a seasoned medical malpractice attorney to employ such tactics, but even some of this caliber who trust their powers of persuasion may continue to bring cases in plaintiff-oriented jurisdictions. It is said that some attorneys with very established reputations for high jury verdicts can simply lend their names to cases in order to scare insurers into quick settlement.

What constitutes a frivolous suit and how can they be avoided? There are no formal, legal definitions of a frivolous suit. However, there are some recurring situations which strongly suggest frivolity:

- Naming every physician whose name appears in the chart- including those who were mistakenly called and the "white knights" who bailed their colleagues out of trouble

- Use of expert witnesses who have not taken care of any patient in decades, or whose practice consists of disability determinations or independent medical exams, and who are out of touch with modern standards of care or are willing to bend the truth for financial gain

- Cases where there are no damages or there was no physician-patient relationship

- Claims which are preposterous on their face, e.g., loss of fertility or consortium in the presence of pregnancy

The difficulty of formally defining a frivolous suit has analogy in other issues. Justice Potter Stewart remarked in a 1964 case that "I shall not today attempt further to define [obscenity] . . . and perhaps I never could succeed in intelligibly doing so. *But I know it when I see it.*"[1]

A relevant question is what is the actual incidence of frivolous cases, when viewed through objective lenses. Prompted by the malpractice crisis of the mid-1980s, a research team at Harvard University embarked on a review of medical records from over 30,000 hospital discharges and 3,500 malpractice claims in New York (*Patients, Doctors, and Lawyers* 1990). The reviewers found rates of adverse events and negligent adverse events (3.7 % and 1.0%, respectively) that were remarkably close to those in California (Weiler et al. 1993). Extrapolations from these rates produced alarming estimates of the burden of medical injury, including projections that negligent care caused approximately 20,000 disabling injuries and 7000 deaths in New York hospitals in 1984. Overall, there were 7.6 times as many negligent injuries as there were claims. But it was the matching of specific claims to specific injuries in New York that threw the troubling relationship between malpractice claims and injuries into sharp relief. *Only*

---

1. *Jacobellis v. Ohio* (1964).

2% of negligent injuries resulted in claims, and only 17% of claims appeared to involve a negligent injury (Localio et al. 1991). Weiler et al. (1993) have suggested the analogy of a traffic cop who regularly gives out more tickets to drivers who go through green lights than to those who run red lights. In a third study, conducted in Utah and Colorado in the late 1990s, the injury rates detected were similar to those in New York (Thomas et al. 2000), and the disconnections observed between injury and litigation were virtually identical (Studdert et al. 2000), suggesting that the core problems were neither regionally nor temporally idiosyncratic (Weiler et al. 1993).

There are a host of remedies available to those who believe they were treated unfairly by the legal system. A physician who wins his case might have grounds to countersue any proponent of that suit, including the plaintiff attorney, expert witness, or patient. The two remedies are malicious prosecution and abuse of process, and these torts are universally recognized. The essence of these torts rests on the notion that the plaintiff (in this case, the physician) was improperly subjected to the legal process.

The elements of malicious prosecution are:

- Defendant initiated a cause of action against plaintiff.

- Defendant acted with malice—malice may be inferred by failure to make a reasonable inquiry—or action was brought without a credible basis to believe that malpractice occurred or could be proven.

- Cause of action was terminated in plaintiff's favor (such as winning malpractice case in court).

- Plaintiff was damaged by defendant's action.

An abuse of process is the misuse of a regularly issued process for any purpose other than that for which it was designed. The required elements to prove abuse of process are:

- The plaintiff or attorney made improper or unauthorized use of the legal process;

- The plaintiff had an ulterior motive in bringing the suit; and

- The physician incurred damage as a result of the action.

- In an abuse of process countersuit, it is not necessary to prove that the original proceeding lacked probable cause or terminated in the plaintiff physician's favor.

Elements of compensation vary from state to state. Typically, the following may be considered in awarding damages: costs of the underlying action, loss of reputation, and punitive/exemplary damages. Countersuits have been employed by a handful of physicians across the country. *Medical Economics* reported on a neurosurgeon in Louisville, who countersued an attorney who sued him for frivolous reasons—"not for revenge, but to send a message to plaintiff's lawyers" (Rice 2001). Dr. Guarnaschelli prevailed and was awarded a judgment of $72,000. The plaintiff's attorney told the *Louisville Courier-Journal* that as a result of the trial and verdict, he would never take another medical malpractice case unless they leave the scalpel in the chest and it's showing through the skin" ("Doctor Strikes Back" 2000).

Countersuits for malicious prosecution or abuse of process have been few and far between. The reasons are both legal and practical. Malice, if required, is very difficult to prove. An attorney is understood to be an advocate for his client, and as such, is expected to be aggressive. If an attorney is accused of filing a frivolous claim, his response is that he is not a physician and that the expert physician is the one who guided him on how to proceed. Furthermore, these suits can be expensive to litigate. Even if the physician plaintiff wins, the judgment may be merely symbolic (such as $1). Proving damages related to loss of reputation is difficult, particularly if the physician is still quite busy and his accounts receivable is not much changed. So, historically, finding lawyers to take these cases on a contingency basis to sue their fellow lawyers has been a challenge. This has not been because attorneys are reluctant to take on their colleagues. The reason has generally been economic. Without obvious potential for damages in which they could share a portion, attorneys correctly argue that victory would be Pyrrhic, at best.

The most recent professional liability crisis that began in the late '90s and early '00s gave new fuel to legal arguments related to countersuits. Physicians were routinely being told by their malpractice carriers that their premiums were rising primarily because of their malpractice claims record. Physicians learned that if they are named in cases, the carrier can and will use that information to change the doctor's risk profile and increase his rates. Furthermore, some physicians learned their coverage was being cancelled *solely* because they were named in suits (whether they won or lost). Armed with this documentation, a physician now has ammunition to demonstrate that actions of attorneys are the proximate cause of specific damages (substantial rate increases or inability to practice given inability to obtain insurance). Given that medical malpractice premiums are significant, particularly for high-risk specialties, it will not be surprising to see many new countersuits being pursued using vastly increased liability premiums as the primary basis for damages. In view of this, it is also likely that attorneys will be more inclined to take on these cases.

Other legal strategies can be employed to maximize the likelihood of success in countersuit. Physicians can include a clause in their patient intake form asking the patient to agree not to bring any *nonmeritorious* claims against the physician, and if they should do so despite the agreement, to reimburse the physician for all costs associated with such action. Note that this is quite different from language tried in the past stating that the patient agrees not to sue the physician. Courts routinely strike such clauses arguing that patients cannot knowingly enter into a contract where they give up *all* of their rights without "consideration." However, to the extent it is not expressly prohibited by law, it is more likely that the contractual language "preventing a patient from suing for *frivolous* reasons" would be upheld. Arbitration has been supported in a number of court challenges. By its very nature, arbitration asks that the patient give up his or her constitutional right to trial by jury. If arbitration agreements can be uphold by courts, there is reason to believe that contracts preventing nonmeritorious claims would have teeth.

A second strategy addresses the problem of unethical expert witnesses. Many experts take time away from their busy practices, doing their duty, to expose the truth in legal proceedings by serving as expert witnesses. However, a significant number of experts do nothing but testify for the plaintiff. They feel that their job is to make a case for the attorney. Not infrequently, these cases have no merit, but proceed forward based on the word of the "expert." Experts can perform well in court only if they are perceived as credible. Credibility is buttressed by the respect of their colleagues and membership in a host of professional organizations. Various specialty societies and state/county medical societies recognize that their reputations are on the line when some of their members deliver hyperbolic or fraudulent testimony. The American Association of Neurological Surgeons (AANS) took the lead on this issue by disciplining, and, in some cases, expelling a small number of its members for delivering unsupportable testimony. As an example, in November, 1997, the AANS through its Professional Conduct Program temporarily suspended a Connecticut neurosurgeon's membership because of "unprofessional conduct." That conduct included giving testimony regarding aneurysm surgery despite the fact that he had not handled such cases himself for 15 years. The AANS agreed that the neurosurgeon's trial testimony demonstrated "inappropriate advocacy, marginal subject matter, and a lack of objective research" (*AANS Bulletin* 1998).

A court challenge to the AANS program occurred in 1997 (Pelton 2002). The Professional Conduct Committee had found that Dr. Austin provided inappropriate and unprofessional testimony as a plaintiff's expert in a medical malpractice case, and the committee had recommended suspension of his membership for six months. Dr. Austin had testified in the underlying litigation that permanent damage to the recurrent laryngeal nerve of a patient during the course of an anterior cervical fusion procedure could only have occurred as a result of negligence on the part of the surgeon, and that "the majority of neurosurgeons" would concur with his opinion. The committee concluded that Dr. Austin was wrong in both respects. The AANS Board of Directors agreed, and suspended Dr. Austin's membership in the AANS. His appeal to the general membership was unsuccessful. Dr. Austin attempted to resign during the pendency of his case before the committee, but the board refused to accept his resignation until the case was completed, in accordance with AANS bylaws. When Dr. Austin's suspension became final, his resignation was accepted.

Dr. Austin then filed a suit in U.S. District Court in Chicago alleging that he was deprived of due process (a charge he later dropped), and he also alleged that the AANS program violated public policy by discouraging physicians from testifying for plaintiffs in medical malpractice cases. He further alleged that AANS's actions had sullied his reputation and had resulted in a substantial drop in his expert witness income. The District Court granted the AANS Summary Judgment, which was affirmed on appeal by the 7th U.S. Circuit Court of Appeals. On appeal, the AANS was supported by an amicus brief filed on behalf of the American Medical Association, the American College of Surgeons and the Illinois State Medical Society. In writing the Court's opinion, Judge Posner praised the AANS professional conduct program as a public service, saying that "this kind of professional self-regulation furthers, rather than impedes, the cause of justice." He went on to state:

> By becoming a member of the prestigious American Association of Neurological Surgeons, a fact he did not neglect to mention in his testimony in the malpractice suit against Ditmore, Austin boosted his credibility as an expert witness. The association had an interest—the community at large had an interest—in Austin's not being able to use his membership to dazzle judges and juries and deflect the close and skeptical scrutiny that shoddy testimony deserves. It is no answer that judges can be trusted to keep out such testimony. Judges are not experts in any field except law. . . . Judges need the help of professional associations in screening experts. The American Association of Neurological Surgeons knows a great deal more about anterior cervical fusion than any judge, and if the association finds in a proceeding that

comports with the basic requirements of due process of law that a member of the association gave irresponsible expert testimony, that is a datum that judges, jurors, and lawyers are entitled to weigh heavily.[2]

In January 2002, the U.S. Supreme Court refused to hear a further appeal by Dr. Austin's counsel. The *Austin* decision stands today as the definitive court opinion supporting the right, and arguably the duty, of professional associations to discipline their members who engage in unprofessional conduct while testifying as expert witnesses in litigation.

Due process is afforded these members, and they are given every chance to defend themselves. But the trend is that professional societies will not tolerate those who make their living by bending the truth. Recently, the American College of Obstetricians and Gynecologists approved bylaws for disciplining fellows who deliver testimony "believed to be unethical." Many other professional organizations are following suit. Except in certain defined circumstances, malpractice cases cannot proceed unless the case is supported by an expert witness. Post-hoc remedy against these expert witnesses in the professional societies will not prevent a case from proceeding, but it will deter that witness (and possibly others who are so tempted) from continuing to testify unethically in the future.

In summary, there are available remedies to address the medical malpractice crisis. These remedies do not need to wait for additional tort reform and can be employed immediately. Countersuit in legal venue for proponents of a frivolous case can deter attorneys who are looking to obtain nuisance settlements from insurance carriers. Furthermore, alerting professional societies to members who deliver hyperbolic or fraudulent testimony will help to clear its ranks of abusive expert witnesses. Without the backing of these organizations, many of these witnesses have limited credibility and will not be effective in supporting weak cases.

---

2. *Austin v. American Association of Neurological Surgeons,* 253 F.3d 967, 972–973 (7th Cir. 2001).

REFERENCES

AANS Bulletin. 1998. 7(2):9.

"Doctor Strikes Back at Lawyer Who Sued Him." http://www.courierjournal.com/localnews/2000/0006/07/000607doc.html.

Localio, A. R., A. G. Lawthers, T. A. Brennan, N. M. Laird, L. E. Hebert, L. M. Peterson, J. P. Newhouse, P. C. Weiler, and H. H. Hiatt. 1991. "Relation between Malpractice Claims and Adverse Events Due to Negligence: Results of the Harvard Medical Practice Study III." *N. Engl. J. Med.* 325:245–251.

Medical Economics. 1999. (26 July.)

Patients, Doctors, and Lawyers: Medical Injury, Malpractice Litigation, and Patient Compensation in New York. 1990. Report of the Harvard Medical Practice Study to the State of New York. Cambridge, Mass.: President and Fellows of Harvard College.

Pelton, R. "Professing Professional Conduct: The AANS Raises the Bar for Expert Testimony." *AANS Bulletin* (Spring): 11–12.

Rice, B. 2001. "Message to Plaintiffs' Lawyers: Sue Me at Your Own Risk." *Medical Economics* (9 December): 30–39.

Studdert, D. M., M. M. Mello, and T. A. Brennan. 2004. "Medical Malpractice." *N. Engl. J. Med.* 350:283–292.

Studdert, D. M., E. J. Thomas, H. R. Burstin, B. I. Zbar, E. J. Orav, and T. A. Brennan. 2000. "Negligent Care and Malpractice Claiming Behavior in Utah and Colorado." *Med. Care* 38:250–260.

Thomas, E. J., D. M. Studdert, H. R. Burstin, E. J. Orav, T. Zeena, E. J. Williams, K. M. Howard, P. C. Weiler, and T. K. Brennan. 2000. "Incidence and Types of Adverse Events and Negligent Care in Utah and Colorado." *Med. Care* 38:261–271.

"Trends in 2001 Rates for Physicians' Medical Professional Liability Insurance." 2001. *Medical Liability Monitor* 10:9.

Weiler, P. C., H. H. Hiatt, J. P. Newhouse, W. G. Johnson, T. Brennan, and L. L. Leape. 1993. *A Measure of Malpractice: Medical Injury, Malpractice Litigation, and Patient Compensation.* Cambridge, Mass.: Harvard University Press.

28

Lessons Learned the Hard Way

Donald P. Wolfram, M.D.

In our neighborhood, the only person who comes to the door at noon is the mailman, and then only if he has a delivery. My heart sank as soon as the doorbell rang. I signed for registered mail from IDOI, the Indiana Department of Insurance. "Eye-doy," the mailman pronounced it, with a laugh. I felt no cause for levity. I was being sued.

I had been named the defendant in a case from two years prior, and the statute of limitations had expired by two weeks already. I had called my insurance agent a week before, and was assured that no such filing had occurred at State. I'd been a nervous wreck nonetheless. At least the wait was finally over.

What had gone wrong? What had I done, or not done, to bring about this whole mess? How would I know? What would I do? I couldn't have known at the time that being sued would be among the greatest blessings in my career.

I remember the patient only vaguely: a teenage girl complaining of upper abdominal pain, with equivocal exam and labs. It was routine. I diagnosed gastroenteritis and gave my usual instructions about worsening symptoms. Suspicious about gallstones, I ordered an outpatient ultrasound and asked the mom to bring her back to the ER if she didn't improve. I went on to the next patient without a second thought.

The next week I heard from the mom, via the ER medical director. The girl had gotten her ultrasound, had had persistent pain and vomiting, but hadn't returned to the ER. They registered a complaint, stating that her daughter had suffered an appendicitis; that she had taken her to another hospital for surgery; and that there were $16,000 in bills.

The ER medical director reviewed the chart and sent a report to the parents describing the salient features of acute appendicitis, none of which the girl had exhibited on my exam.. I thought that would be the end of it. Any thinking person would see the logic in the reply.

Soon the hospital medical records department notified me that the chart had been copied for a lawyer. Shortly after that came notification from my insurance agent of a "Claim for Damages," three pages of allegations, and a copy of records as evidence against me. Most damaging was an expert opinion in favor of the plaintiff.

It is difficult for me to describe what I felt as page after sordid page unfolded in front of my disbelieving eyes. Surely the plaintiff wasn't serious and this would all go away.

Not at all sure what to do next, I began digesting all the information, which had grown at an alarming rate. My career, my ego, and even my marriage all seemed in danger of unraveling as I forced myself to the task.

Life had been good until then, or so I had thought. Two years out of residency, I was working "only" 60 hours a week in the ER. That's where I gained my identity, and I still enjoyed patient contact, always looking for the next exciting case to appear. Sure, I knew that I made mistakes, but had always rolled with the punches and come back fighting for more. When cases went bad, I practiced by a "first-strike" mentality—that is, I acted on the problem or complication quickly and proactively.

This lawsuit changed me. I had fits of explosive anger. Severe anxiety attacks were almost crippling as I saw every patient as an enemy and potentially litigious. My sleep was disturbed, and I jumped every time the phone rang, expecting bad news or complaints. I began making stupid mistakes.

Fortunately, I had married the most wonderful woman in the world. She and I had many lengthy discussions about the suit, taking it apart from every angle. My wife is gifted with wisdom exceeded only by her beauty, and she wouldn't let me take the easy route. We struggled for objectivity, but weren't sure how to find it. We needed help.

That help came in two persons: first, my friend and counselor Mike; second, a great lawyer appointed by the insurance company to defend me.

I called Mike to make an appointment. He'd known me from years before, when he had helped salvage my career and my marriage on separate occasions. I trusted him with my life. He knows that I won't call until things are bad, so he had me come in right away.

We sat in the familiar comfort of his office, and I poured out the story. I related how I was privately in tears, fought with my wife over little things, and angered the nurses and patients I saw on a daily basis. My complaint rate was rising.

The hardest thing to admit was that I hated medicine and regretted the career choices I had made. I was suffering extreme burnout. Something had to change, or I'd probably quit or be fired. I wanted out!

Mike helped me gain perspective on the problems. He assured me that all my feelings were common for this type of situation. A lawsuit is about money, but the route to the money is through the defendant's heart, soul, and spirit. Nobody survives litigation without scars. Unfortunately, some doctors go so far as to commit suicide.

Talking it through made a huge difference. The weight of the world was lifted a little, and perspective returned to my life. Best of all, medicine fell in my priorities, subordinated to God, family, and other things like birthday parties and watching my children grow.

Mike helped me see, too, that anxiety is a plague in our profession. I resisted medication, but we finally settled on an SSRI, and within two weeks life was getting better. I started to feel alive again.

Meanwhile, my attorney had been assigned and we made an appointment. I had already sent her a lengthy letter describing my side of the story and where lay my strengths and weaknesses.

Here were the issues:

- The patient: female; young; uninsured; $16K in debt, with a hostile parent.

- The plaintiff's attorney: from the county where the surgery took place; he had a similar case already, giving him confidence.

- Surgery and pathological findings: ruptured and abscessed appendicitis, requiring a lengthy hospital stay. Ultimate outcome uncontestable.

- My documentation: overall thorough, although no rectal or pelvic exams performed. All the usual high points addressed; follow-up instructions were to return to the ER for further problems, but I did not give a *specific* time frame (e.g., 12 hours), nor did I explain my differential diagnosis with pertinent positives and negatives.

- Further testing: normal gallbladder ultrasound; no CT done.

Taking all of these together, I thought that I could justify my position. With a reasonable onus of responsibility on the patient to return as instructed, I should have a strong case.

There was one sticking point: "expert" witness against me. The operating surgeon, at the request of the plaintiff, reviewed my ER chart, and summarized that the "diagnosis of appendicitis should have been entertained" and the patient referred to a surgeon.

The letter was a killer. The plaintiff's case was plausible with it, and dead without it, making my job much more challenging. The approach to my defense seemed clear: I'd have to refute the expert.

I went over all of the documents again. I made sure that my dictation was clear; where it wasn't, I found ample tangential evidence for support. I looked again at the expert opinion, dissecting each bit of evidence given. I held it next to my dictation. The two didn't match!

I checked the letter again and compared it with all the ER documents, seeking to know the source of information. Finally I realized that the expert's information was gleaned *entirely from the nurse's notes!* My history and exam were quite different from those of the nurse. Not one line of my dictation was reflected in the opinion.

For the first time, I had a feeling of hope, but this raised a new issue. In order for me to refute the expert, I'd have to attack his integrity, proving that he was not thorough in his review and therefore came to faulty conclusions. I was on staff at the expert's hospital, and I respected his skills. To refute him would be to effectively burn my bridge down to the waterline.

Already my insurance agent had hinted at settling for the convenience alone. We probably could have negotiated for less than $16,000. Why not? It would be easy, relatively inexpensive, and save the agony of a trial.

There were a few good reasons not to settle. First, the National Practitioner Data Bank would have me on file as having settled the case. Second, I'd carry the extra insurance premium burden if such legislation ever passed through. Finally, and most important, I didn't know if it was the *right* thing to do. I knew that I was morally obligated to make an honest decision. If I had committed malpractice, then I would settle.

I was in no position to make an objective decision. I needed my colleagues' opinion, so I went and did a dumb thing—I told a friend about the case. I was meeting a surgeon friend in Chicago for the weekend, so I told him every detail. (Rule #1 when sued: Don't talk to anyone who can be deposed!)

Unfortunately, what he told me was not what I wanted to hear: "The defense is going to ask you, 'Doctor, do you think that the patient presented with an appendicitis when you saw her in the ER?' You'll have to say 'yes.' Settle the case."

That hurt! I took this revelation back to my attorney. She was disappointed but not unduly perturbed that I had been dumb; she saw it as simply another obstacle. If I wasn't asked, I wouldn't tell. She still thought that we had a strong case and encouraged me to take the next step, to the required Medical Review Panel.

The deposition date was set. That date was cancelled, as was the second. Finally my attorney told me that we would go to Panel without being deposed. I was happy about that, and very encouraged. All along the plaintiff's attorney had been dragging his feet, allowing required deadlines to lapse, and waiting until the last minute to do everything. My agent had said early on that some plaintiffs' lawyers do that in hopes that the defendants will settle (i.e., cut and run). I sensed lack of confidence in the plaintiff.

Time was on my side. I could wait it out unless better evidence surfaced making my position untenable. I tried to draw my attorney out on the subject, seeking justification for my hopes of dismissal. Appropriately, she wouldn't go so far as to guess the motives of the opposing lawyer.

The day came months later when submissions to the Panel were due; we still had no word from the plaintiff's attorney. Finally a letter arrived requesting a 30-day extension. The plaintiff had married and moved away, leaving no forwarding address.

The 30 days went by without incident. My attorney filed for dismissal, and a court date was set. On that day, the plaintiff's attorney agreed to sign a Stipulation of Dismissal. Now *that's* the stuff of dreams!

Does this mean that it's all over? Yes and no. The litigation is over, but the effects still linger. I think about the case every day, lest I should forget the lessons I learned the hard way.

My practice has changed dramatically. I once wanted to be the staid, battle-worn veteran who could convince people of the right actions to take. What I've discovered is that experience and common sense seem to make no difference to many ER patients. I try to make good decisions, and encourage my patients to partner with me to improve their health. Often I simply placate, and that is not very satisfying.

Another result of the lawsuit is that I have greatly increased my testing; had I done a CT on the plaintiff, I'd have either had a correct diagnosis and sent her to surgery, or I could have left the attorney without a case, had the test been normal. In the four years since the lawsuit was filed, I've ordered scores, perhaps hundreds, of very expensive tests, and I can think of no surprises along the way. My clinical suspicions are still the best indicators I have for testing. I do the tests to confirm my deductions and allay patients' concerns.

There is no doubt that I will ultimately spend hundreds of thousands, maybe millions, of dollars over the course of my career, to relieve myself of the very real threat of another lawsuit. All that is because of a near miss at a $16,000 settlement. Multiply that by the tens of thousands of other doctors and it becomes obvious where much of our health care dollars are going.

There is a huge list of lessons I've learned from this experience. Here are some of those lessons, which I frequently share with my colleagues:

- *Prevention is the best defense against litigation.* Be thorough; sit and talk with patients; cover the differential diagnoses in plain talk. Offer diagnostic and treatment options, and try to engage the patient as a partner in decisions.

- *Document thoroughly!* Include your differential diagnoses which show that you thought through the case. Set parameters for follow-up care; give a specific time limit for return, thereby making the patients responsible for their part of the treatment.

- *Notify your insurance carrier* as soon as you suspect you have a potential case. If you have information that you consider privileged regarding the case discuss it with your attorney.

- If you receive official notice of filing: **Don't panic!** The plaintiff may want you to settle pretrial; your insurance carrier may agree. Resist the urge to cut and run. Time is probably on your side, because you are not the one waiting for money. Allow yourself the opportunity to work through the process. Grieve; throw fits, voice objections—at home. Seek counseling, and be open to your own faults and shortcomings. Bite your tongue around your colleagues, as they may not be sympathetic to your cause and you may unwittingly coerce them into the plaintiff's camp.

It is imperative that you have a great defense attorney. Insist on it! I asked my excellent attorney to comment on the best and worst things physicians can do:

The best things that a physician can do are to cooperate with the lawyer retained to represent him or her and to provide that lawyer with whatever information the physician feels may be helpful to the further defense of the case, such as articles or models, and to cooperate in meeting with the lawyer as necessary. It is also important for the physician to be able to look at his own work with a critical eye, in order to aid in a realistic evaluation of the case, but also to be ready to defend his or her care.

The worst things a physician can do are to fail to cooperate or to provide information or to take an unrealistic stand as to whether the case can be defended. However, it is also detrimental for a physician to get too caught up in second-guessing his treatment, as it is important to remember that hindsight always makes it easier to evaluate treatment decisions, rather than simply looking at the information available at the time.

Strangely, I'm glad I was sued. It was a painful, heartbreaking experience. I would neither trade it nor wish it on another. It allowed me to identify paths I could no longer walk. Medicine tumbled from its lofty position, and it is tolerable and even fun again. Most importantly, I realigned my priorities in faith, family, and profession. My life has been renewed and enriched.

29

Asset-Protection Techniques

Michael J. Searcy, ChFC, CFP®

A good definition of asset protection is positioning, titling, or holding your savings, investments, business, and personal property in a way that shields you not only from malpractice lawsuits but also from business risks and claims from potential creditors of all types. In today's litigious climate, there are a multitude of potential liabilities that could have a devastating effect on your financial well-being. Although this book is focused on protection from the medical malpractice claimant, other potential creditors against your assets could include the IRS, your ex-spouse, or your daughter's ex-spouse seeking "family" assets. The claims could result from professional liability, acts by your children, accidents, general business operations, sexual harassment or environmental incidents related to real estate ownership. The major theme of asset protection planning is to discourage lawsuits against you and/or to negotiate less expensive settlements. This is done by showing creditors (mostly plaintiff attorneys) that your assets are positioned in such a way that it will be difficult for them to actually get them if they prevail in any legal action against you. In essence, most of the strategies are "deterrent" techniques.

Michael J. Searcy, ChFC, CFP® Comprehensive Financial and Strategic Planning, Searcy Financial Services, Inc, Overland Park, KS http://www.searcy financial.com/

Some are considered bulletproof, depending upon your state of residence and whether your state's laws protect the assets. On the other hand, some are not so bulletproof but rather create significant barriers that have to be hurdled before the assets can be attached by a creditor. Proper asset protection is not about secrecy or hiding assets. It is about showing potential creditors that the assets will be difficult or impossible to get to even if they win a claim against you. Therefore, be sure you plan everything using qualified experts and base every strategy utilized upon sound legal principles.

Let's say that a potential plaintiff wants to sue you. First, they consult with their attorney. The attorney has to evaluate the merits of their case. Do they think they can win a verdict or negotiate a settlement? Next, they have to look at the economics. In essence, how deep is your pocketbook? Do they think they can get enough out of you if they win, or will more money be spent on the actual lawsuit than they can reasonably expect to collect from you if they prevail? Finally, they have to determine how difficult it will be to collect the judgment. Keep in mind that the better the case and the larger the potential judgment, the more they may be interested in pursuing the case. Producing evidence that there is little available money for creditors, or that it will be inordinately difficult to collect, can reduce your risk of being sued, or improve your chance of negotiating a better settlement.

If you are already facing a lawsuit, you may elect not to read this chapter since it is too late for asset protection. This is because you cannot do anything with the intent to defraud creditors. Anything you do in this regard at this point will be considered suspect and any assets conveyed may be reallocated right back to you with access by your malpractice creditor. This concept is based upon laws against fraudulent conveyances. The rule is that you cannot make any transfers of ownership (to a spouse, a trust, family partnership, etc.) *after* the initiation of a claim.

If there is a potential claim of which you are aware (but which has not been brought), some would suggest that you consult a qualified financial planning professional to help you develop a plan that may include a variety of asset-protection strategies. The intent and presentation of these financial plans is that they be viewed as normal estate or financial planning strategies, and not as vehicles for potential asset-protection benefit. Obviously, the objective is to substantiate other legitimate reasons for setting up the structures which will also confer benafits. Such anticipatory planning may or may not actually work for you, but it may be worth a try, depending upon the specific circumstances of the potential problem.

If you have no claims pending, then some preventative ideas are worthy of your consideration. Most of this chapter deals with individual strategies, but it is worth noting that there are some defense strategies you can employ so that you are not brought into a suit by something done by a partner or an employee, unless you are responsible for supervising him or her. The easiest and simplest planning is for you to structure your business as a corporate or limited liability company (LLC). This strategy, of course, will not protect you from malpractice, but it should clearly separate you personally from claims brought against your partners or your employees, unless you are required to personally supervise them. If you own the corporation or LLC, it could be lost to a malpractice creditor. If your business mostly consists of accounts receivables and some equipment, there may or may not be too much to lose. However, in some practices this could represent a significant loss. Therefore, each type of practice has to make a determination of the risks of potential and real losses.

Sometimes we talk with doctors who mistakenly think that because they work for a corporation, it will insulate them personally from malpractice liability. This is not the case. A professional corporation will not protect you from your own malpractice, nor from the malpractice of people you supervise.

If you are a doctor who owns his or her own medical building or surgical center, it is generally best to own the real estate separately from the operational practice entity. This way, if the practice is wiped out by a serious malpractice claim, there may be some strategies employed that can save the real estate.

The same strategy may also be used for other nonprotected assets. Using this strategy, the exposure would be similar to the exposure of the other assets based upon the complexity of the planning you employed for their protection. It is important to remember that these strategies must be employed before an event occurs that may result in a liability issue. Using a reverse scenario example, in the event that something occurred within the medical building which created a liability problem, you would not want your operational medical practice brought into the suit. This is another reason to separate the real estate ownership from the operational practice, as it will insulate the actual practice if the creditor claim arose from something associated with the building. For example: if someone slipped and fell on the property and your property/casualty insurance was insufficient to handle the claim, then you would not want the incident to adversely affect the operational practice.

If you maintain substantial equipment in your practice, then it may be subject to the claims of creditors if the corporate entity is exposed (and most likely it will be). Therefore, you might want to create a separate entity that owns the equipment and then enter into a lease-back arrangement with that entity, just as you might structure the arrangement with the entity that owns the real estate. Of course, if you own the other entity, then you did not remove it from your potential creditors. Therefore, the actual ownership of the separate entities that hold the building and equipment should not be yours.

Once you get past the business-related ownership structures and strategies, then you need to explore your personal opportunities for protection. One of the first steps is to figure out the bankruptcy protection rules of the state in which you reside. Specific state laws allow some assets to be protected from creditors. The laws are different for the different states, so make sure you understand and follow your state's rules.

The following is not an all-inclusive list but should serve as a guideline. Many states protect your home, usually one automobile, the cash value in your life insurance policies, your pension/profit sharing/401(k) plan, perhaps your IRA, and possibly an annuity policy. These are some of the major exemptions, so take advantage of them to plan accordingly.

With respect to using your life insurance cash values as an asset-protection technique, consider your desire and ability to accept risk and your time horizon for accomplishing your ultimate retirement funding goal. If you have a temperament for the risks associated with the stock market and have adequate time to accumulate sufficient funds, thereby putting the time value of money concept to work, then you might want to consider using a variable universal life policy. The trick is to fund the contract up to the maximum allowable by law without creating a modified endowment contract (MEC). This strategy minimizes the death benefit and maximizes the premium deposit. The objective is to make after-tax deposits into the contract, allow it to accumulate in concert with the overall performance of the stock market for 20 to 30 years, and then the trick is to fund the contract up to the maximum allowable by law without creating a modified endowment contract (MEC). Because it is defined as life insurance, you can extract the amount you have deposited in premiums without paying tax. The balance of the extractions for supplemental retirement income is accomplished via a life insurance loan. You will want to leave just enough cash in the contract to keep the policy in force for life. Then, when you ultimately die, the accumulated loan is subtracted from the total death benefit and the balance is paid to your named beneficiary. Based upon current tax law, assuming you follow all the rules, your funds will accumulate tax-deferred and can then be used to supplement your retirement income essentially tax-free. Ultimately, the strategy is unwound at your death and the loan is paid off from the death proceeds. In the meantime, you maintain life insurance protection, maintain immediate access to the funds, and protect the accumulated value (generally referred to as cash value) from potential creditors, assuming that life insurance cash values are statutorily protected assets. This strategy works best if you are younger, are a nonsmoker, and have an excellent health history. This is because there is a cost for the life insurance protection needed to make the strategy work properly. As with any strategy, do your homework and be sure to deal with a qualified and experienced insurance advisor who has your best interests in mind.

With respect to using your retirement fund as a protected asset, always consider funding the maximum allowable by law into your plan. The plan could be a 401(k), a 403(b), a tax sheltered annuity (TSA), a multitude of SEP, IRA, or a defined benefit pension plan. The costs to you should be evaluated carefully in order to determine the overall effectiveness. Generally contributions for other employees are the single largest cost to be considered before making a decision as to the most appropriate plan to utilize.

Asset protection is not always the best strategy for proper estate tax planning, but most doctors are more interested in having something left while they are alive rather than protecting it for estate tax purposes. These taxes are imposed after the second death of the married couple. Most doctors prefer strategies that work well for both asset protection and estate planning but sometimes these two objectives are at odds with one another. If you plan properly, however, you can allocate the protected assets in the name (or trust) of the highest liability partner, if married. Then you put the exposed assets in the name (or trust) of the lowest liability partner.

If you are single, then you will want to maximize the assets protected from creditors of the state in which you reside. For goodness sake, be sure to remember what you did and review it again if you should take up residency in another state.

Due to the complexities associated with asset protection, it is critical that you surround yourself with experts in the field who are qualified to help you with the development of your overall plan. You also need to plan ahead before any problems surface. Involve the whole family because the most effective planning strategies will include them. Understand that you will need to make some compromised decisions because effective asset protection may run counter to your perceived need for direct control and ownership. Finally, review your plan regularly because your exposure, the laws, and your personal circumstances will change over long periods of time.

Before you get too creative developing sophisticated strategies in an attempt to protect yourself, you should figure out what your malpractice exposure really is from the perspective of a worst-case scenario. You also need to determine what is covered by malpractice insurance as well as liability insurance. Although this book talks about the medical malpractice issue, if you wreck your car and you are responsible for the deaths of a young heart surgeon driving a BMW, an orthopod driving a Mercedes, and possibly a plumber driving a Porsche, then you will be more concerned about pure asset protection than about malpractice protection. In this case, the purchase of a liability insurance policy that covers your vehicle and an umbrella policy that covers from the limits of your vehicle policy up to the maximum you purchased for the umbrella liability policy might be a good solution, assuming the claim is a covered claim and is not excluded by the policy. At this time you can probably buy an umbrella policy with several million dollars coverage. We normally recommend at least $2,000,000 as a minimum. This will cover you, your spouse, and your children so it's great protection to have. For those who are pilots, be sure to check this coverage to make sure your pilot activities are covered to the same limits. Often claims associated with piloting a private plane are excluded from coverage by the policy.

Now that you have insured the easy risks with proper underlying coverage (home, auto, recreational vehicles) and an umbrella policy for the rest, take a close look at your real exposure from a malpractice perspective. Check the limits in your state. Some jurisdictions still allow for whatever a jury will award, but some are starting to limit the maximum claims. If so, check your malpractice policy limits. Maybe you will find that the limits are generous and you really don't have much real exposure. However, more often than not, you have some chance of "the big one." If so, start positioning assets where they are least likely to be accessible by malpractice creditors.

For those of you who are married to another doctor and are both income earners, you need to determine who is at the lowest risk for a malpractice claim. If one of you is working for an academic, military, or government institution, that person might be a lower risk than, for example, an OB/Gyn who is in a small group practice. It is recommended that you position the non-state protected assets in the name of the person less likely to be sued or in their trust account. Keep in mind that this will not work if you are in one of the few community property states. In those cases, it is assumed that half of all assets, regardless of whose name they are in, are one-half each partner's. However, this could be a preliminary strategy if you have a spouse with relatively low liability exposure. Although simple, this strategy may not really work. There have been several court cases where the assets of a spouse were seized in order to pay the offending spouse's creditors. Therefore, the effectiveness of this strategy depends upon the laws of the state in which you reside and what the judge does as it relates to the seizure of the community assets, regardless of whose name is on the title. In some states, the malpractice claimant cannot get the assets of your spouse, just yours. This discourages the use of joint tenancy with rights of survivorship (JTWROS) on all the accounts. A much better and cleaner way from both an asset-protection standpoint and an estate-planning standpoint is to place the exposed assets in your spouse's name.

Putting the nonprotected assets in the least liability-prone spouse's name may not work in some states. In many states there is no protection for these assets because some judges ask questions like: Does the doctor control these assets? Did the doctor make all the money to accumulate these assets? Does the doctor use these assets for his or her personal benefit?

A few states allow for titling of assets as tenants by the entirety (TBE). This is when two people own the asset together in the form of an undivided interest. In these states there are specific procedures for establishing ownership in this fashion. In so doing, you can get some protection because it is assumed that you and your spouse own an undivided interest in the property and, since it assumed that your spouse is not subject to the malpractice creditor, the assets could be protected.

After you have positioned the state protected assets in the name of the exposed person, placed the nonprotected exposed assets in the name of the low-exposure spouse, and purchased proper insurance protection, then you could employ some other vehicles commonly used for asset protection. An excellent strategy is to set up a family limited liability company (FLLC) or a family limited partnership (FLP). Generally, the person with higher liability will be the general partner of the management company that runs the FLLC or FLP. The concept here is to put the assets outside the reach of your creditors so that they are protected. You do this by positioning the assets within a separate entity of which you have little or no ownership, but of which you still maintain control through the management company.

The FLLC and FLP are separate legal entities. Although they are different and one or the other may be better in certain situations and certain states, they are often used synomonously when explaining the general concept. There are two levels of ownership. One is the active managing owner, referred to as the general partner of the FLP and the managing member of the FLLC. The other level of ownership is the passive owners, referred to as limited partners of the FLP and members of the FLLC. A general partner has personal liability for the FLP, but the managing member does not for the FLLC. Therefore, many asset-protection specialists often prefer using FLLCs.

The advantage of using a FLLC or FLP to hold assets is that outstanding creditors cannot invade the entity to satisfy a judgment. They can be issued a "charging order" by the courts. This entitles them to the asset only when the entity is dissolved. They cannot get to the assets prior to ultimate liquidation, which may never take place. The theory is that the general partner or managing member can elect not to make any distributions from the FLLP or FLLC. In most states, at least in theory, any income generated within the entity is taxed to the person with the rights to it. Therefore, when income is earned within the entity, the responsibility for paying the taxes rests upon the creditor holding the charging order, but they have no cash distributed from the entity with which to pay the tax. This is thought to be an effective way to protect assets from creditors because the creditor cannot seize the assets themselves and generally would not want to pay taxes on income without the cash with which to pay them. The creditor has no voting rights and cannot force distributions, so having a charging order is generally not desirable to a creditor.

If you really want to get creative and have substantial assets to protect, you may want to consider going offshore with them. Keep in mind that some people mistakenly think that going offshore saves taxes. This is not the case for U.S. taxpayers. U.S. citizens must pay taxes on assets owned by them regardless of where the assets are held. Therefore, if you take assets offshore through the use of creditor-protection trusts, make sure you plan to report the income on your taxes annually.

Another misconception about offshore trusts is that some people believe that because they are offshore, there is an element of secrecy involved. Although the offshore trustee, bankers, and investment professionals will most likely not disclose any information about your accounts to anyone else, it could be perjury for you (subject to potential jail time) not to disclose the information yourself. Therefore, do not rely upon secrecy to protect the assets.

Although foreign asset protection trusts (FAPTs), more commonly referred to as offshore trusts, may provide a higher level of asset protection, they are not bulletproof. The general concept and real effectiveness of using an offshore trust is to put up so many barriers for the creditor that they will either give up or negotiate a reasonable settlement with you. The larger the claim, the more a creditor will do to penetrate whatever strategy you implemented, regardless of how sophisticated. However, for most claimants, going after offshore assets held in offshore trusts and in offshore jurisdictions is quite complicated and expensive. As is often the case, the claimant's lawyer is doing the work on a contingent basis. When they look at the work involved and the likelihood of being successful pursuing offshore assets, they will not take the case or they will require the client to pay the expenses (which may be substantial) upfront. Although not impenetrable, offshore trusts are a great deterrent to negotiating a better settlement.

Another strategy to help protect assets might be to set up a domestic asset protection trust (APT) in the states that have begun to actively market them. Three states that have been in the forefront of the APT business are Alaska, Delaware, and Nevada. These trusts have come to light because state statutes provide some asset protection for self-settled trusts and because many people are reluctant to transact business offshore. Alaska set the stage for these new trusts in 1997 when it enacted a statute that provided asset protection for self-settled trusts. Delaware and Nevada followed. The jury is still out on the effectiveness of these trusts. Therefore, before pursuing the use of such a trust, it makes good sense to seek competent legal counsel. There may be a greater likelihood of these trusts working effectively for asset protection if the settlor (the person who creates and funds the trust) resides in the state and uses the associated state trust.

Although the enumerated strategies may help you protect your assets, there are control, tax, and estate-planning issues that must be carefully considered. Not only do these strategies need to be established correctly, they also require ongoing maintenance. This involves continuing tax, legal, and perhaps trustee services. Therefore, it absolutely critical that you employ the assistance you need from qualified, experienced lawyers, accountants and, asset-protection financial planning specialists.

30

Medical Professional Liability Insurance

Theodore L. Passineau, J.D., H.R.M., R.P.L.U.

INTRODUCTION

In this chapter, we will discuss medical professional liability insurance. Specifically, we will talk about what medical malpractice insurance is, what you need from it, how to select the policy which is right for you, and what to do if a claim ever arises.

WHAT IS A MEDICAL PROFESSIONAL LIABILITY INSURANCE POLICY?

In legal parlance, medical malpractice insurance is an indemnification contract. An indemnification contract is an agreement whereby one party (the indemnitor) agrees to pay up to a specified amount on behalf of the other party (the indemnitee) to satisfy all or part of the liability the indemnitee has to a third party. In plain language, indemnification involves the insurer stepping into the shoes of the insured to satisfy a medical malpractice settlement or judgment. It is important to understand that agreeing to indemnify a party is not the same thing as assuming the liability of that party. If for any reason the professional liability carrier cannot or will not indemnify the insured physician, that physician remains fully personally liable to the injured party and will have to satisfy that liability by some other means. Unfortunately, more than one physician has found him- or herself insured by a company which was unable to cover the claims against its insured physicians and ended up personally obligated to satisfy the malpractice judgment. Choose your malpractice carrier carefully (we'll discuss what to look for later in this chapter).

The medical malpractice insurance contract has two main components. The first of these is the policy form, and the second is the declarations page. The policy form is usually a standardized boilerplate document which will be exactly the same for all of a given class of insureds (for instance, all physicians insured under a claims-made policy). Frequently, this policy form has been written by an insurance company trade group known as the Insurance Services Office (ISO) and is substantially similar among many companies. In other cases, the company may have crafted its own the policy form. In either case, if the carrier is what is known as an admitted carrier, the policy form has been approved by the state insurance commissioner (I'll discuss the significance of being an admitted carrier later).

The policy form has five basic elements, which specify the general terms of the insurance contract. The first of these elements is the Definitions section. In this section, terms which are used in the insurance contract will be precisely defined. Several important points will be covered in the Definitions section, including such terms as "You" (meaning the insured), "Medical Acts," and other similar terms. It is only by being familiar with the Definitions that the insured will know what is covered and what isn't.

The second element is the insuring agreement. The insuring agreement specifies that the insurer will pay money on behalf of the insured, up to the limits of liability, for medical acts which have resulted in liability against the insured.

The third element of the policy form is the Conditions. This section specifies the responsibilities of the insurer and the insured pursuant to the contract. Provisions which are commonly included in the Conditions section are things such as a "Consent to Settle Clause" (we will discuss these later) and specifications regarding where coverage is effective (such as within the United States, or worldwide). The Conditions section will also include the duties of the insured to the insurer, including such things as reporting claims or potential claims promptly, cooperating in the defense of the case, not attempting to settle the case independent of the insurance company, and the like.

The fourth element of the policy form is the Exclusions section. Under certain circumstances, even though there is an indemnification contract in existence, the insurer reserves the right not to pay anything toward indemnification of the claim. Reasons for not paying the claim (which are specified in the Exclusions section) typically include such things as the physician practicing while not currently licensed to practice, practicing under the influence of controlled substances, committing an illegal act, or engaging in any sort of sexual contact with the patient. Most exclusions are logical and pretty much obvious, but some exclusions may be surprising (such as use of a drug or device not approved by the FDA, or liability for any sort of activity in violation of state or federal antitrust laws).

The final element of the policy form is the Miscellaneous Provisions. This section will include things such as how any disputes regarding coverage under the contract will be handled (it is common that there is a provision that they will be arbitrated according to the rules of the American Arbitration Association), the law of which state will control interpretation of the insurance contract, and an integration clause (meaning that the policy form and declaration sheet comprise the entire contract between the parties). Sit down and read your professional liability policy sometime. It will be educational and may provide you with one or two surprises.

The other component of the medical malpractice insurance contract is the Declarations Sheet (sometimes known as a "Dec. page"). This is the document which is particular to the individual insured, and which specifies the exact provisions of the insured's professional liability coverage. Several important things will be specified in this Declarations Sheet. The first thing to look at is the "Named Insured." Be sure that everyone you desire to have coverage under your policy is specified as a Named Insured. Second is the policy period. You need to be aware of your policy period, especially if you think you may be changing companies; otherwise the potential for a gap in coverage exists. The next thing to look for in your Declarations Sheet is the type of coverage you have. The two most common types of coverage are occurrence coverage and claims-made coverage (I will discuss these two types of coverage in detail in a few moments). Another thing you will find in your Declarations Sheet is your individual rating information. This will include such things as your specialty, your rating territory, whether you are full- or part-time, whether you have a deductible or not, and finally, your premium amount.

The final item contained on the Declarations Sheet is the limits of liability. This is the amount the insurance company agrees to pay in indemnification of any covered liability you may acquire. The limits of liability will typically be stated as two numbers, the second of which is normally an amount three times larger than the first number. The first number is the maximum amount the insurer will pay in indemnification of any single claim. For instance, $1 million is a common per-incident limit. This means that the insurer will pay up to $1 million to satisfy your liability from a single claim. The second number, the aggregate limit, is the amount the insurer will pay in total to satisfy all of the liability you may acquire during the policy period. For example, if the per-incident limit is $1 million, the aggregate limit will probably be $3 million. This means that the insurer will indemnify any number of claims (up to $1 million each) occurring during that policy period, until the total indemnification paid reaches $3 million (for example, if the insured had four judgments against him or her in a policy period, two for $1million and two for $500,000, the insurer would fully indemnify all four of these claims but would not pay for any other liability incurred during that policy period). As you can see, the company's policy form and Declarations Sheet combine to specify the precise rights and responsibilities of the insured and the insurer.

TYPES OF COVERAGE

Generally, there are two types of coverage in the medical malpractice insurance industry today: *occurrence* and *claims made.* We will talk about the advantages and disadvantages of each, but let's start with a discussion of how they work. The principal difference between the occurrence and claims made forms is what triggers coverage under the policy.

With the occurrence format, coverage under the policy is triggered by the event which ultimately results in potential liability (what we in the insurance industry call "the loss"). Obviously, this event is normally the treatment of the patient, which eventually leads to a demand for some sort of compensation. As long as the loss occurs on a date falling within the policy period, the claim will be covered by the insurer. With the occurrence form, coverage of the claim is not directly dependent on when the claim is reported; if the claim is not excluded from coverage for some reason, the carrier will honor it whenever it is reported.

Claims-made coverage is a bit trickier. With claims-made coverage, two dates have to be identified as being within certain policy periods for there to be coverage of the claim. All claims-made policies have a date stated on the Declarations sheet which is known as the retroactive date. Normally, the retroactive date is the first date of coverage of the insured by this carrier (so that if a claims-made policy is issued and then renewed several times, the retroactive date will remain as the date the policy was originally issued). If the loss occurs after the retroactive date, that requirement as satisfied. The second date to be concerned with is the date the claim is reported to the company. The report of the claim must also occur during the policy period or the claim will be denied by the carrier.

Let's say a claims-made policy is purchased and simply allowed to renew each year. There will not be any problem with coverage of claims. However, a problem can arise if the insured chooses to discontinue the claims-made policy or move to a new company. Medical malpractice is a type of coverage known as "long-tail." This means that there is often a significant lag time between when the loss occurs (when the patient is treated) and when the demand for compensation occurs (either in the form of a notice of intent to sue, a demand letter, or formal service of process). It is common for this lag to run from several months to as long as two years or more; it will probably be at least partially dependent on your state's statute of limitations. Suppose, for instance, the insured treats a patient during the first year of coverage with company A (so that the loss occurs after company A's retroactive date), but the insured decides to discontinue her coverage with company A after year one, and she goes to company B. She is then sued regarding this patient in year 3 (she is now insured with company B). Company A will correctly deny her claim because it was not reported during their policy period. At the same time, company B will also deny the claim because the treatment occurred prior to their retroactive date. The insured has a gap in coverage and a real problem on her hands.

When the claims-made form was developed, a provision to deal with this scenario was made part of its design. If the insured is going to discontinue her claims-made coverage, she has two options. First, and most commonly, she can purchase what is called an extended reporting period endorsement, or "tail coverage," from the original insuror An alternative is to request that her new carrier back date their retroactive date to the retroactive date of the policy she is replacing (there will then not be a problem with the loss date). This second approach is called prior acts coverage, or "nose coverage." It is important to understand that when one buys tail coverage, one is not extending one's policy period; one is simply purchasing the legal right to report claims which otherwise would not be covered because of the change in carriers. What is being extended is the reporting period, not the policy.

The critical point to remember is that if the insured wishes to discontinue his or her coverage under the claims-made form, he or she can't simply cancel their policy and walk away. *It is absolutely essential that the insured acquire either tail coverage from their present carrier or nose coverage from their new carrier, otherwise a gap in coverage will occur.*

In today's malpractice insurance market, occurrence coverage for physicians is quickly becoming a dinosaur. This is for sound actuarial reasons, which I won't bore you with. If you currently have occurrence coverage, enjoy it while it lasts, because it probably won't be long. Occurrence coverage does have some advantages, probably the greatest of which is that it is simple. However, it also has some downsides. First, it is almost always more expensive than claims-made coverage. A second disadvantage to occurrence coverage is subtle but can be significant. Under an occurrence form, the limits of liability which are available to cover a claim are those limits which were in place at the time coverage was triggered (remember, that is the loss date, the date the patient was treated). In most cases, the loss date is close enough to the time suit is brought that the amount of available limits will not be an issue. However, there are exceptions.

A problem arises when the physician was insured under an occurrence policy and a claim does not arise until many years later (this might occur in the case of a retained foreign object after surgery, or very late-developing indications of birth trauma). I was involved in one case where a physician was not brought into litigation until about 20 years after he had delivered the baby in question. We were trying to negotiate his release from the case, but we only had $20,000 in limits to work with (these were the doctor's limits at the time of the delivery, and they were appropriate then). You can see what a problem this can cause. Fortunately, it is a rare problem.

Probably the biggest downside to the claims-made form is the fact that it can be confusing. Secondly, it is difficult to move from carrier to carrier when you are insured under a claims-made form because you have to purchase tail coverage, which is expensive (unless you can get your new carrier to provide you with nose coverage). Nevertheless, the claims-made form does have its advantages, not the least of which is that for individual insureds, and for insurance purchasers generally. First, claims-made coverage is usually cheaper than occurrence coverage.

In your first year of claims-made coverage, you'll probably pay a premium in the range of 45–50% of what you would have to pay if you were purchasing occurrence coverage. Over the next four years, that percentage will increase in steps from about 75% to about 95%, but it will never equal the cost of an comparable occurrence policy. The second advantage to claims-made coverage is that the limits which apply to a claim are the limits which are in effect when the claim is reported (again, under claims-made coverage, this is when coverage is triggered), as opposed to when the patient was treated (the occurrence trigger). It would be rare for limits to be lower at the time the claim is reported than the limits at the time of loss. A third advantage to claims-made coverage for insureds in general is that (again, for actuarial reasons) annual rate adjustments under the claims-made form tend to be smaller than the double digit adjustments which can be common with occurrence coverage.

Remember how I explained that during the first years of your claims-made coverage your premium will be considerably less than it would be for an occurrence policy? Put that money aside because you will need it to pay for your extended reporting period endorsement (tail coverage) at the time you terminate your current policy. However, if you do it right, you may not have to pay for your tail coverage. Some malpractice carriers have a provision in their policies that states that if you are insured with them under a claims-made form for five continuous years, are 55 years or older, and fully discontinue your practice of medicine, the carrier will provide you with a free extended reporting period endorsement. If that is the case, then the money you saved from your early years of low premiums will not be needed to purchase an extended reporting period endorsement, and you may use it as you wish.

One other point should be made regarding the extended reporting period endorsement. The best extended reporting period endorsement has three separate coverage periods contained within it. The first period would be year 1 of the extended reporting period, and this year would have its own set of limits. The next period would be year 2, which, again, has its own separate set of limits. The final portion of this reporting period would be years 3 and beyond (into infinity), which would have a third set of limits. This is the "Cadillac" form of extended reporting period endorsements. Depanding on your specialty and state statute of limitations, you can tailor your tail coverage according to your specific need.

The other thing you'll have to consider when you are purchasing (or receiving a free) extended reporting period endorsement is what the limits of liability will be during the extended reporting period. Sometimes carriers simply make the limits for the extended reporting period endorsement the same as the limits which are in place at the time the underlying policy expires. In other cases, the limits of the extended reporting period endorsement may be the limits which were in place the most during the five years prior to moving into the extended reporting period. This is an important point to clarify so that you can be sure you are carrying adequate limits of liability into your extended reporting period. This may be important, for example, if you are gradually limiting your practice rather than terminating it abruptly.

So which coverage is best? It really depends on your circumstances. If you are a year or two from retirement, or if you think you are going to want to change carriers, stay with your occurrence coverage. In most other cases, claims-made is probably the better choice, simply because it is cheaper. As long as you use your claims-made coverage the way it is intended to be used, it should be very adequate for your needs. An insurance professional can be invaluable in helping you be sure your claims-made coverage is structured properly, so that there is no risk of a gap in coverage.

HOW MUCH COVERAGE SHOULD YOU HAVE?

Let's say you were going camping in the Alaskan outback. If you were wise, you would take a gun along in case you ran into a bear. After carrying the gun for a while, your conclusion would probably be that you didn't need to bring such a big gun. Then you turn a corner and there is a bear. At that moment, you would probably conclude that you should have brought a bigger gun.

The same is true with any form of insurance, including medical malpractice insurance. It's always too much when you don't need it, and oftentimes not enough when you do. The trick is to find the right balance point for you, based on your individual circumstances. The general industry standard is $1 million/$3 million, but there is significant variation across the country. Let's look at some of the considerations which should go into your decision about how much coverage to carry.

One line of thought is to carry as little coverage as possible, because carrying higher limits "just gives the greedy plaintiffs lawyers more to go after." I suggest this is not a good way to look at it. You are not buying insurance to potentially enrich some one else, you are buying it for two reasons. First, you want to be able to provide appropriate compensation to your patient if she or he is injured by some mistake you made. Secondly, you want to protect your personal assets. Keep these objectives in mind as you choose your coverage.

First, are there minimum limits you must carry to maintain hospital privileges or participation on any payer panels? Next, consider the characteristics of your practice. A neurosurgeon practicing in Philadelphia probably should have higher limits than a dermatologist in rural North Dakota. Next, look at your personal financial profile. Do you have a lot of personal assets you need to protect (you might want to consider other methods of protecting them in addition to insurance)? Finally, can you afford a deductible?

Malpractice insurance should be one of three techniques you use to protect your personal assets. The first line of defense of your assets should be a comprehensive risk management program. A safe, well-run practice is far less likely to result in a patient injury, and if an injury does occur, it is much harder to prove the physician was negligent when everything that is reasonable was being done to provide an environment of patient safety. I don't see enough emphasis on risk management in many physician offices.

The second line of defense is malpractice insurance. Despite your best efforts at risk management, injuries to patients can occur. That's when your malpractice policy kicks in to provide compensation to the injured patient and protection to you. The third component of your asset-protection plan is financial planning. There are a variety of techniques you can use to protect your assets. That's covered in a separate chapter of this text.

Now, back to how much coverage you should buy. First, understand that the more coverage you purchase, the cheaper the higher layers of coverage become. That's because the higher layers are rarely penetrated. To illustrate, if $100,000 in coverage cost $10,000 in premium, $1 million might only cost $20–25,000, or even less. Get prices for different coverage amounts, you might be surprised at how far your dollar goes. Because the higher limits are so much cheaper, it is usually better just to buy higher primary limits than to opt for a personal umbrella or some other type of supplemental coverage. In any case, as with all of your other insurances, you should insure to adequately cover the worst possible reasonable scenario.

I'm an advocate of high limits, not because I want to sell you more insurance, but because higher limits give you much more flexibility. Allow me to illustrate. You are involved in a case with high volatility (i.e., a case where it is very unlikely, but not impossible, that you will be found liable, but the case has very high damages potential). You have low limits of liability (say, $250,000). Plaintiff's counsel will let you out for your limits. If you take their offer you will be out of the case, but you will log a Data Bank entry (the implications of which I will discuss later) and possibly a Medical Board investigation. On the other hand, if you refuse the offer and the case is tried, you run the risk of a large over-limits judgment. This is a very difficult position to be in (I have seen it), and it is because you don't have enough limits behind you.

If, on the other hand, you are insured for $2 million, you can run the risk of trying the case. If you win (as you most likely will), end of story. If you lose, even if the award is greater than $2 million, the plaintiff will almost always take the $2 million in a post-verdict settlement, rather than running the risk of an appeal and then having to go after your personal assets. They don't like to do that; they like to just have a check handed over from the insurance company. With adequate limits, you have more and better options.

You should verify one more aspect of your coverage. Most physician policies have defense costs "outside of limits." This means that however much it costs to defend your case, you still have your full limits of liability available to indemnify you. However, occasionally, you see a policy with defense costs "within the limits." This means that all costs of defense (attorney fees, expert witness fees, court costs, etc.) are taken from your limits of liability, thereby draining down your available limits of liability. These policies are usually seen with the less common coverage arrangements (such as being endorsed onto a hospital policy, coverage by a captive or risk retention group, etc.).

If your policy has defense costs within the limits, be sure your limits are adequate to cover these additional costs, otherwise you might end up in a situation where, in a protracted litigation, your limits have been drained down to the point where you have an inadequate amount available to cover the liability fully. High defense costs are most likely to occur in a high-volatility case such as the one I described above. This is exactly the kind of case where, if things go badly, you may need the full amount of your limits to take care of the matter.

One coverage arrangement I have recommended to some physicians in the past is the sliding scale approach. It is based on certain assumptions, which may or may not be true in your case, so it may or may not be a good idea for you. I find that many physicians, when they first enter practice, have a negative net worth (i.e., lots of school debt and few, if any, assets). As they progress through their career, they pay off that debt and begin to accumulate assets. In the later stages of their career, hopefully they have few debts and considerable net worth. If these assumptions are true, it suggests a policy which has limits of liability which grow over time. Obviously, such a policy becomes more expensive. The way we control premium costs is by the use of a deductible, which starts small and also grows over time. Allow me to illustrate.

As the physician begins his career, he has basically no assets to protect. All he needs professional liability insurance for is to provide some protection of his patient in the case of an iatrogenic injury, and possibly to satisfy a hospital or payer's insurance requirements. This physician might do well with fairly low limits (say, $250,000) and no deductible. As the physician gets up to about 15 years of practice, his world has changed. Now he has paid off that loan debt and has started to accumulate some assets.

Because he now has an established cash flow, he is more tolerant of a small deductible. This might be a good time to increase limits to $500,000, and carry a $10,000 deductible to largely offset the increase in premium resulting from the higher limits.

As the physician enters the later stages of his career (say, 30 years), he hopefully has considerable net worth and a good cash flow. Now we might go up to $1–2 million in coverage and carry a $25–50,000 deductible. This approach to limits structuring can, in many cases, provide coverage appropriate to the stage of the physician's career, while keeping premium costs under control.

ACQUIRING COVERAGE

So, after all we have discussed, you are now ready to purchase your professional liability coverage. Which source of professional liability coverage is right for you?

Let's talk about some different options, and the advantages and disadvantages of each. We'll start with traditional insuring arrangements through an insurance company. There are two types of carriers: admitted and nonadmitted carriers. Admitted carriers are carriers which have submitted their policy forms and their rate proposals to the insurance department of the particular state in which they wish to write coverage. The insurance department reviews the policy forms to see if the forms meet with their approval, and will also pass on what rates are appropriate for the carrier to charge. In effect, the carrier voluntarily puts itself under the regulation and control of the state insurance department. The physician enjoys the confidence of knowing that his or her carrier has been, and continues to be, monitored by the insurance department.

Admitted carriers also enjoy the benefits of the state guarantee fund. This fund is a pool of money paid into by all admitted carriers in the state, which provides a safety net for the insureds of carriers who, for financial reasons, cannot provide coverage of the claims they have agreed to indemnify. While the state guarantee fund typically has a limitation on how much indemnification they will provide, it is nevertheless a big help in the case of a failed insurance carrier.

Nonadmitted carriers do not subject themselves to the authority and supervision of the state insurance department. They use their own policy forms and set a rate which they feel is appropriate for the environment in which they wish to provide coverage. Because of this, neither their policy forms nor their rates are reviewed or monitored by any regulatory agency, and these nonadmitted carriers do not enjoy the safety net of the state guarantee fund. The main disadvantage to a nonadmitted carrier is that a physician does not have the confidence of knowing that the carrier's business practices are being scrutinized by someone with a great deal of insurance expertise. The main advantage of a nonadmitted carrier is that in some cases these carriers will provide coverage under circumstances where admitted carriers are not comfortable. Which carrier is right for you will be at least partially dependent on your particular circumstances, your confidence in a particular nonadmitted carrier, and the environment in which you practice.

The second factor to look at is whether you prefer to be insured by a commercial carrier or one of the many PIAA (doctor-owned) carriers. Commercial carriers have been providing medical malpractice insurance since the beginning of the 20th century, while doctor-owned companies generally made their appearance in the 1970s. The differences in the companies are in, more than anything else, their philosophy of business. Commercial carriers tend to view medical malpractice as simply another line of insurance. The company has no particular loyalty to the insured physician, and decisions (particularly, underwriting decisions) are made on a strictly objective business basis.

Doctor-owned companies, on the other hand, usually only provide medical malpractice insurance and tend to view their business mission as the facilitation of the practice of medicine through the provision of medical malpractice insurance. There tends to be a bit more of a loyalty factor on the part of doctor-owned companies toward their insured. However, that factor is not as strong as it may have been at one time. As a general rule, doctor-owned companies' policy forms tend to be more inclusive and protective of the physician. Accordingly, coverage from doctor-owned companies has some tendency to be more expensive than similar coverage from a commercial insurer.

Whether you go the route of a commercial carrier or a doctor-owned company, be sure to investigate what their "Best rating" is. A.M. Best is a national insurance rating service which evaluates insurance companies of all types and rates them by giving them a letter rating (A–F). This rating is based on the company's economic stability (and, therefore, its ability to cover claims) and is widely accepted as the gold standard for evaluating company stability. A company with a rating anywhere in the "A" range is a safe bet.

If a company is not in the "A" range, it doesn't necessarily mean that it is a bad choice. However, I would do two things before purchasing coverage from a "B" company (don't even consider a company not rated at least in the "B" range). First, I would check to see what the company's rating history is (that is, was it previously rated in the "A" range and has since been downgraded into the "B's," or is it working its way in a particular direction through the "B" range?). If a company is stable at, for instance, a B+, it may be perfectly adequate to meet your needs. However, if 18 months ago it was rated "A" and is now a B+, I would scrutinize that company very carefully.

The second thing I would check before purchasing coverage from a "B"-rated company is whether coverage by this company will be acceptable to your hospital credentials committee. Especially since the failure of P.I.E. in Ohio several years ago, some hospitals have instituted requirements that physicians practicing at their facilities must be insured by a company rated in the "A" range.

The other factor you need to consider is whether you wish to purchase your policy directly from the company (which is possible with some companies), or whether you'll go through an agent or broker. I do not see any advantage to the individual insured in purchasing the policy directly, as generally the price is not going to be any better. However, an insurance professional (such as an agent or broker) can bring considerable expert advice to the table, helping you to choose the coverage which will be best for you in the long term. Professional liability insurance is complicated stuff, and this advice can be invaluable; you don't want to get into the situation of having a claim and then find out that there is some problem with your coverage. Buying your own insurance is like treating yourself: it is rarely a good idea.

Finally, many new insurance mechanisms are making their way into the marketplace these days. Two types which you are likely to encounter are risk retention groups (RRGs) and captive insurance companies. Risk retention groups came into being following the passage out of the federal Risk Retention Act in the late 1980s. Risk retention groups are basically an association of persons who come together to finance their own coverage, outside of the typical insurance company approach (somewhat like a nonadmitted carrier, but less formal in its organization). Risk retention groups are typically professionally managed and can be quite suitable sources of coverage for physicians. However, be careful when dealing with risk retention groups, as the insurance departments of most of the states in which the risk retention group is writing have no regulatory control over the risk retention group. There is always the danger is that the group is not well managed, resulting in its failure. This would leave the physician uncovered for claims which have or may arise in the future.

A second type of alternative risk-financing mechanism is a captive insurance company. This is a company which is formed and managed by a single client, such as a large medical group, a health system, or the like. This captive insurance company is a form of self-funding of claims, which can be a cheaper (or, in some cases, the only available) means of providing coverage of claims. Sometimes physicians affiliated with the medical group, or members of a health system's medical staff will be given the opportunity to participate in the captive. These captives can provide a stable and affordable means of coverage for physicians. However, physicians should realize that when they purchase coverage from a captive, they may have limited control over the circumstances of their coverage. Depending on the particular arrangement, their degree of control over, for instance, how their claim is managed may be very limited.

Two final points. Risk retention groups and captives are typically not rated by A.M. Best (making it harder to know how financially solid they are), and they, like a nonadmitted carrier, do not enjoy the protection of the state guarantee fund.

So which is right for you? Again, it will depend in your particular circumstances and preferences. However, as in any other aspect of financial planning, getting some expert advice is a very good idea.

CLAIMS ISSUES

Let's talk about how your carrier might handle claims issues. First, it's important to understand when you should and when you don't need to contact your carrier. You can provide your carrier (and, ultimately, yourself) with a tremendous advantage by contacting them early, when the storm clouds of litigation first appear on the horizon.

Unfortunately, in some cases you have no indication of a problem until the process server is sitting in your waiting room. In such cases, it is absolutely critical that you contact your carrier immediately. Legal complaints have a fixed amount of time in which they must be answered (this varies by the jurisdiction and form of service), and the attorney who will be assigned to your case will need time to prepare an answer. I have seen cases where the physician was served and took the suit papers and put them in a desk drawer until he or she had cooled down or felt he or she had time to deal with the matter. In the meantime, the answer period was running, and in some cases had expired, before the carrier was even made aware of the matter. This is bad for you in at least two ways.

First, by not answering the complaint (through your attorney), you have agreed that everything stated in the complaint is true. It's called a default judgment. Default judgments can be vacated, but it's a fairly complicated, expensive process, with no guarantee that it will be successful. If it is not successful, there will still be a trial, but it will be limited to deciding how much you will pay to the plaintiff. Second, failing to report your lawsuit to the carrier in a timely manner may be a violation of your duties under the insurance contract. If that is the case, the carrier may deny the claim, leaving you with personal exposure for the full amount.

In other cases, you know right away that there is a high likelihood that there is going to be trouble. This might be because of a catastrophic, unexpected result from treatment, or actions or statements by the patient or family which indicate that they are unhappy and contemplating legal action. In such cases, contact your carrier right away. They will take the necessary information to open a claims file (thereby locking in coverage under a claims-made policy), and will advise you regarding what to say and do, and what not to. Your carrier is expert at handling these matters; getting them involved early is the smartest thing you can do.

Sometimes an indication that there might be trouble on the horizon is an attorney's request for medical records of one of your current or former patients. Such a request may come to your attention through the medical records department of your hospital, or may come to your office directly. Whether you need to contact your carrier is a matter of judgment. If you are confident the legal matter the records are being requested for has nothing to do with the care you rendered (such as a workers' compensation case, an auto accident claim, or the like), there is no need to contact your carrier. However, in those cases where you think the patient might be unhappy with something you have done, or when you don't know why records are being requested, it is best to call your carrier and seek their guidance. My rule of thumb is "When in doubt, call."

Let's assume you have been served with a complaint and summons—you are being sued. What do you do first? Start with a deep breath. This may be a new experience for you, but thousands of doctors are sued for malpractice every year. Life must go on during this time, and it will go on after this process is completed. Probably in excess of 90% of cases never make it to trial (typically more than 50% are dropped, and another 40% are settled prior to trial), let alone result in a verdict for the plaintiff (generally, only about 25% of trials result in verdicts for the plaintiff).

If this is your first time being sued, you may think the plaintiff's lawyer is just trying to get to the bottom of the matter, and if you can just sit down and explain what happened, the whole thing will go away. You can just forget all about that. If the matter has progressed to the point of a complaint and summons against you, the plaintiff's lawyer obviously thinks either he or she has a case against you which is likely to result in a payment by your carrier, or there is some other strategic reason the lawyer wants you in the case. Absolutely do not have any contact with the plaintiff's lawyer, and you should probably check with your carrier before you have any contact with the patient and/or their family. It may be necessary to terminate your relationship with the patient (if you still have one), and possibly his or her family members as well (again, seek guidance from your carrier).

Sometimes a complaint includes allegations of things which are covered under your professional liability policy (such as negligent failure to diagnose), and also acts which, if true, would not be covered under your professional liability policy (such as having sexual relations with the patient under the guise of treatment). In this case, the carrier will defend you on all charges but will probably send you a reservation of rights letter. This letter means that the carrier will fully defend you in the matter, but if it the evidence shows that the only allegations which were true are acts not covered under your policy, the carrier will seek reimbursement from you for all monies they paid out in your defense. If you receive a reservation of rights letter (which is standard procedure when both covered and uncovered acts are alleged), you should probably seek personal legal counsel to be sure you are adequately protected in your dealings with your carrier. The company will not cover these fees, but it is, nevertheless, money well spent.

One of the first things that will happen is that the carrier will appoint you defense counsel. It is important to understand the relationships among the insured physician, defense counsel, and the insurance company. While the insurance company has hired and is paying defense counsel to act on your behalf in this matter, the legal ethics rules are very clear that it is the insured physician who is the client. Both the defense attorney and the insurance company understand this very well, and they will go to considerable lengths to preserve the attorney-client privilege which exists between you and your counsel. You need to understand that the defense counsel's absolute ethical duty is to preserve your confidences. Therefore, it is very important that you share all information you have regarding this case with your defense attorney. Even if facts exist which would cause the claim not to be covered (or would otherwise affect your relationship with the insurance company), you can be assured that your defense attorney will not disclose this information to the company, and that the company would not ask them to. Tell your attorney everything.

A very bad situation occurs when the physician is aware of facts which are likely to affect the defensibility of the case (either positively or negatively), and, for whatever reason, the physician fails to disclose this information to defense counsel. Probably the most common scenario where this occurs is when the physician has altered his or her medical record in an attempt to "improve" the defensibility of the case. Needless to say, any change to the medical record (even a good-faith attempt to clarify what occurred) should never be made once you have any indication that this record may become evidence in any sort of medico-legal case. However, if an alteration to the record has already occurred, you should do two things. First, sequester the original record so that there is no chance that there will be any further changes. Second, disclose this information to your defense counsel immediately. He or she will know how to handle the situation, and the earlier it is acted on, the better. Remember, your attorney has one client she or he is responsible to, and that is you. You can and should trust him or her completely.

Let's suppose your case is well into the discovery process, and a settlement is being proposed by the insurance company. This raises several issues which you should be aware of. First, depending on an important provision of your insurance contract, you may or may not be able to control whether the case is settled or not. The better professional liability insurance contracts contain a "consent to settle" clause. This clause states that the company may not settle any case on your behalf without your consent. In my opinion, a consent to settle clause is extremely important in a professional liability policy, and well worth the additional premium you may have to pay in order to have that provision.

Some consent to settle clauses are absolute; this means that the decision is strictly yours, and there will be no consequences of your decision, whatever it is. Other consent to settle clauses are accompanied by what is known as a "hammer clause," a provision which says that if the insured physician withholds their consent and the matter continues on to and litigation, resulting in a jury award greater than what the case could have been settled for, the insured physician is responsible for the difference. While any consent to settle clause is better than none, the presence of a hammer clause certainly makes the consent clause less desirable. Nevertheless, if you have any type of consent to settle clause in your contract, it will be important for you to think carefully about whether you want to accept the company's recommendation and settle the case, or proceed toward trial.

At this point in the process, a lot of strategy will be involved. One of the things you need to consider as you deliberate whether to allow the case to be settled or not is the National Practitioner Data Bank. As you may know, the National Practitioner Data Bank was created by the United States Congress as part of the Healthcare Quality Improvement Act (the same act which provides immunity for peer review activities). The National Practitioner Data Bank requires that any payment made on behalf of a physician in settlement of a medical malpractice claim or suit must be reported to the Data Bank. This payment will become a permanent part of the physician's Data Bank record. The effects of a Data Bank record on the ability to get to hospital privileges, payer contracts, and the like are somewhat variable (and for that matter, debatable); however, most would agree that any Data Bank entry is not a desirable thing. In a malpractice case where settlement is the desirable resolution of the matter, a Data Bank entry can be a complicating factor.

A technique sometimes used to protect the physician from a catastrophic judgment is what is known as a high-low agreement, an arrangement between the attorneys whereby they agree that if the jury returns a verdict against the physician which is in excess of the high amount (the high amount is typically the maximum amount the physician is insured for, possibly with an additional amount being paid privately by the physician), the plaintiff's attorney agrees to accept the high amount in full satisfaction of the judgment. In exchange, it is agreed that if the jury returns a verdict in favor of the insured physician, the physician (through his carrier) will pay the low amount to the plaintiff and their attorney. This guarantee of the low amount is sometimes appealing to the plaintiff's attorney because it assures that at least the costs of litigation will be covered. While this arrangement works very well to protect the underinsured physician from a large, over-limits judgment, it also guarantees that a payment will be made and that a Data Bank entry will occur on behalf of the physician. Dilemmas such as these are the reason I am such an advocate of insuring for high limits.

One final point should be discussed before we leave claims issues. Anecdotal reports and empirical research have shown that being sued for malpractice (especially for the first time) can be one of the most emotionally debilitating experiences you will ever have. Almost all physicians sued for malpractice will suffer negative effects (either mentally/emotionally, physically, or both), although few acknowledge that they are suffering. Not only is this a difficult time for you (and everyone who must deal with you), it can affect your quality of clinical care. There are people and programs available to help physicians who are suffering litigation stress. Your carrier or defense attorney should be able to put you in touch with someone who can help you through this most difficult of times.

CONCLUSION

Medical professional liability insurance is an expensive, complicated aspect of modern medical practice. Professional help in choosing the coverage and carrier which is right for you, and the knowledge that skilled professionals will take care of you if you ever are sued for malpractice, should allow you to enjoy the most important benefit any insurance policy can give you: a good night's sleep.

Index

Doctor/patient relationship, 15

E

Economics, 4-5
Educational materials, 15
Egregious conduct, 240-241
Elective procedures, 17
Emotional instabilities, 17
Etiology, 41
Exclusionary hearings, 237
Exhibits, 199-200
Exit interviews, 16
Experts, 112-113
Expert-Reviews, 106-107
  -roles, 171-173

F

Family limited liability company
  (FLLC), 308-309
Family limited partnership (FLP),
  309
Federal laws
  -privacy for patient data, 7-8
Foreign asset protection trust
  (FAPT), 310

G

Guidelines
  -standard of care, 33-40

H

Health insurance portability and
  accountability act (HIPPA),
  22, 51-60
Health licensing boards, 57-58
High-risk litigious personalities, 17
  -emotional instabilities, 17
High-risk treatment modalities, 17
HIPPA (Health insurance portability
  and accountability act), 22,
  51-60
  -criminal investigation agencies,
    56-57
  -health licensing boards, 57-58

-psychological tests, 56
-release form, 99

I

Inaccurate medical history, 10
Indemnification contract, 313
Identify
  -high-risk patients, 13-20
Informed consent, 29-30
Instabilities
  -spinal or joint, 7
Insurance
  -captive insurance companies,
    328-329
  -carriers, 113-114
  -risk retention groups, 328
Insurance companies
  -duty, of, 126-128
  -lawyer, 127-128
Insurance company lawyer vs.
  personal counsel, 130-133
Insurance services office (ISO), 314
Ivory tower mentality, 9-10

J

JCAHO, 21, 27
Joint tendency with rights of
  survivorship (JTWROS), 308
Judges, 115-116
Juries, 114-115, 192-194

L

Lawsuit
  -anatomy, of, 89-99
  -start, of, 91-93
Lawyer
  -insurance company, 127-128
Lessons learned, 293-300
Licensing, 218-220
  -medical board, 217-229
Litigious personalities, 17
  -characteristics, 61-70
  -emotional instabilities, 17